Economics

Pippa Riley

Viva Books

New Delhi | Mumbai | Chennai | Kolkata | Bengaluru | Hyderabad | Kochi | Guwahati

First Indian Edition 2011
Reprinted 2014, 2016, 2018

VIVA BOOKS PRIVATE LIMITED

- 4737/23 Ansari Road, Daryaganj, New Delhi 110 002
  E-mail: vivadelhi@vivagroupindia.net, Tel. 42242200
- 76, Service Industries, Shirvane, Sector 1, Nerul, Navi Mumbai 400 706
  E-mail: vivamumbai@vivagroupindia.net, Tel. 27721273, 27721274
- Megh Towers, Old No. 307, New No. 165, Poonamallee High Road, Maduravoyal
  Chennai - 600 095 E-mail: vivachennai@vivagroupindia.net, Tel. 23780991, 23780992
- B-103, Jindal Towers, 21/1A/3 Darga Road, Kolkata 700 017
  E-mail: vivakolkata@vivagroupindia.net, Tel. 22836381, 22816713
- 194, First Floor, Subramma Chetty Road, Basavanagudi, Bengaluru 560 004
  E-mail: vivabangalore@vivagroupindia.net, Tel. 26607409, 26607410
- 101-102 Mughal Marc Apartments, 3-4-637 to 641, Narayanguda, Hyderabad 500 029
  E-mail: vivahyderabad@vivagroupindia.net, Tel. 27564481, 27564482
- Beevi Towers, First Floor, SRM Road, Kaloor, Kochi 682 018, Kerala
  E-mail: vivakochi@vivagroupindia.net, Tel: 0484-2403055, 2403056
- 232, GNB Road, Beside UCO Bank, Silpukhuri, Guwahati 781 003
  E-mail: vivaguwahati@vivagroupindia.net, Tel: 0361-2666386

www.vivagroupindia.com

Published by arrangement with
BPP Learning Media Ltd.
BPP House, Aldine Place
LondonW12 8AA

ISBN : 978-81-309-1757-3

Published by Vinod Vasishtha for Viva Books Private Limited, 4737/23, Ansari Road, Daryaganj, New Delhi - 110 002.

Printed and bound by Raj Press, R-3, Inderpuri, New Delhi - 110 012.

Contents

Introduction

Viva-BPP Learning Media's Business Essentials range is the ideal learning solution for students studying for business-related qualifications and degrees. The range provides concise and comprehensive coverage of the key areas that are essential to the business student.

Qualifications in business are traditionally very demanding. Students therefore need learning resources which go straight to the core of the topics involved, and which build upon students' pre-existing knowledge and experience. The BPP Learning Media Business Essentials range has been designed to meet exactly that need.

Features include:

- In-depth coverage of essential topics within business-related subjects
- Plenty of activities, quizzes and topics for discussion to help retain the interest of students and ensure progress
- Up-to-date practical illustrations and case studies that really bring the material to life
- A full index, with key terms highlighted in bold

Each chapter contains:

- An introduction and a list of specific study objectives
- Summary diagrams and signposts to guide you through the chapter
- A chapter roundup, quick quiz with answers and answers to activities

Titles in the Series

- Accounts
- Business Decision Making
- Business Environment
- Business Maths
- Business Strategy
- Economics
- Finance: Management Accounting and Financial Reporting
- Human Resource Development and Employee Relations
- Human Resource Management
- Management: Communications and Achieving Results
- Management: Leading People and Professional Development
- Managing Finance
- Marketing and Promotion
- Marketing and Sales Strategy
- Marketing Principles
- Organisations and Behaviour
- Research Project

Study Guide

This Course Book includes features designed specifically to make learning effective and efficient.

- Each chapter begins with a summary diagram which maps out the areas covered by the chapter. There are detailed summary diagrams at the start of each main section of the chapter. You can use the diagrams during revision as a basis for your notes.
- After the main summary diagram there is an introduction, which sets the chapter in context. This is followed by learning objectives, which show you what you will learn as you work through the chapter.
- Throughout the Course Book, there are special aids to learning. These are indicated by symbols in the margin:

Signposts guide you through the book, showing how each section connects with the next.

Definitions give the meanings of key terms. The *glossary* at the end of the book summarises these.

Activities help you to test how much you have learned. An indication of the time you should take on each is given. Answers are given at the end of each chapter.

Topics for discussion are for use in seminars. They give you a chance to share your views with your fellow students. They allow you to highlight holes in your knowledge and to see how others understand concepts. If you have time, try 'teaching' someone the concepts you have learned in a session. This helps you to remember key points and answering their questions will consolidate your knowledge.

Examples relate what you have learned to the outside world. Try to think up your own examples as you work through the Course Book.

Chapter roundups present the key information from the chapter in a concise format. Useful for revision.

- At the end of each chapter, there is a **chapter roundup** and a **quick quiz** with answers. Use these to revise and consolidate your knowledge. The chapter roundup summarises the chapter. The quick quiz tests what you have learned (the answers often refer you back to the chapter so you can look over subjects again).
- At the end of the book, there is an index.

Chapter 1 :

INTRODUCTION TO MICROECONOMICS

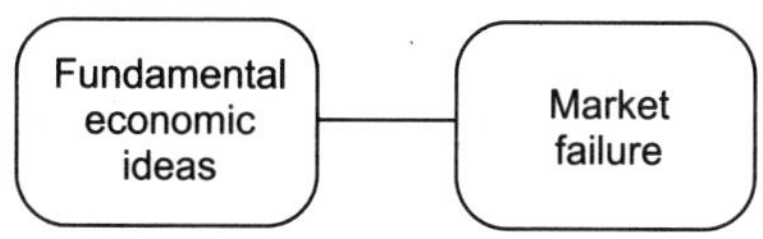

Introduction

The crux of the economics problem is unlimited wants versus limited resources. We deal first in this introductory chapter with the central problem of resource scarcity faced by all economies. Second, we introduce two key areas in economics – money and national economic output.

The second half of the chapter examines the concept of market failure. Broadly, market failure occurs when the free market, which is a market with no government intervention, produces results that are not seen as desirable. This may be that either too much or too little of a good or service is produced at a price that is either too high or too low.

Your objectives

In this chapter you will learn about:

(a) Economics as a social science

(b) Scarcity of resources

(c) Opportunity cost

(d) The nature of money

(e) Key measures of national economic output

(f) Market failures

1 FUNDAMENTAL ECONOMIC IDEAS

Fundamental economic ideas
Economics as a social science
Scarcity of resources
The production possibility curve
Opportunity cost
The nature of money
Key measures of national economic output

Market failure

Economics is concerned with how choices are made about the use of resources: what shall be produced and who shall consume it. The need to make such decisions arises because economic resources are scarce. Making decisions involves the sacrifice of benefits that could have been obtained from using resources in an alternative course of action.

1.1 Economics as a social science

Economics studies the ways in which society decides what to produce, how to produce it and who to produce it for. We are all economic agents and economic activity is what we do to make a living. Economists assume that people behave rationally at all times and always seek to improve their circumstances. This assumption leads to more specific assumptions.

- Producers will seek to maximise their profits.
- Consumers will seek to maximise the benefits (their 'utility') from their income.
- Governments will seek to maximise the welfare of their populations.

Both the basic assumption of rationality and the more detailed assumptions may be challenged. In particular, we will look again later at the assumption that businesses seek always to maximise their profits. A further complication is that concepts such as utility and welfare are not only open to interpretation, but that the interpretation will change over time.

The way in which the resource allocation choices are made, the way value is measured and the forms of ownership of economic wealth will vary according to the type of **economic system** that exists in a society.

(a) In a **centrally planned** or **command economy**, the decisions and choices about resource allocation are made by the government. Money values are attached to resources and to goods and services, but it is the government that decides what resources should be used, how much should be paid for them, what goods should be made and what their price should be. This approach is based on the theory that only the government can make fair and proper provision for all members of society.

(b) In a **market economy**, the decisions and choices about resource allocation are left to **market forces of supply and demand**, and the workings of the price mechanism. This approach is based on the observable fact that it generates more wealth in total than the command approach.

(c) In a **mixed economy** the decisions and choices are made partly by free market forces of supply and demand, and partly by government decisions. Economic wealth is divided between the private sector and the public sector. This approach attempts to combine the efficiency of the market system with the centrally planned system's approach to fair and proper distribution.

In practice, all modern national economies are mixed economies, although with differing proportions of free market and centrally planned decision-making from one country to the next. In such economies, the government influences economic activity in a variety of ways and for a variety of purposes.

(a) Direct control over macroeconomic forces can be exercised through policy on tax, spending and interest rates.

(b) Taxes, subsidies and direct controls can affect the relative prices of goods and services.

(c) Government-owned institutions such as the UK's National Health Service (NHS) can provide goods and services direct at low or nil cost.

(d) Regulation can be used to restrict or prevent the supply of goods and services.

(e) Incomes can be influenced through the tax and welfare systems.

Definitions

Microeconomics is the study of individual economic units; these are called **households** and **firms**.

Macroeconomics is the study of the aggregated effects of the decisions of economic units. It looks at a complete national economy or the international economic system as a whole.

1.2 Scarcity of resources

It is a fact of life that there are limits to available resources.

(a) For the individual **consumer** the scarcity of goods and services might seem obvious enough. Most people would like to have more: perhaps a car, or more clothes, or a house of their own. Examples of services include live theatre performances, public passenger transport and child-minding.

(b) For the world as a whole, resources available to serve human consumption are limited. For example, as we all know, the supply of non-renewable energy resources is, by definition, limited. The amount of many minerals which it is feasible to extract from the earth (for example, metals of various kinds) is also limited.

(c) Some resources are not scarce. Air to breathe is not normally scarce unless, perhaps, you are trapped underwater or underground. Ice is not scarce in Antarctica, and sand is plentiful in the Sahara desert.

In the case of producers, we can identify four types of resource, which are also called **factors of production**.

(a) **Land** is rewarded with **rent**. Although it is easy to think of land as property, the economic definition of land is not quite what you might suppose. Land consists not only of property (the land element only: buildings are capital) but also the natural resources that grow on the land or that are extracted from it, such as timber and coal.

(b) **Labour** is rewarded with **wages** (including salaries). Labour consists of both the mental and the physical resources of human beings.

(c) **Capital** is rewarded with **interest**. It is easy to think of capital as financial resources, and the rate of interest is the price mechanism in balancing the supply and demand for money. However, capital in an economic sense is not 'money in the bank'. Rather, it refers to man-made items such as plant, machinery and tools which are made and used not for their own sake, but to aid the production of other goods and services. The cost of using machinery and plant and so on is **interest**.

(d) **Enterprise**, or entrepreneurship, is a fourth of factor of production. An entrepreneur is someone who undertakes the task of organising the other three factors of production in a business enterprise, and in doing so, bears the risk of the venture. He creates new business ventures and the reward for the risk he takes is **profit**.

Definition

> **Scarcity** is the excess of human wants over what can actually be produced. A **scarce resource** is a resource for which the quantity demanded at a nil price would exceed the available supply.

Since resources for production are scarce and there are not enough goods and services to satisfy the total potential demand, choices must be made. Choice is only necessary because resources are scarce.

(a) Consumers must choose what goods and services they will have.

(b) Producers must choose how to use their available resources, and what to produce with them.

Economics studies the nature of these choices.

(a) What will be produced?
(b) What will be consumed?
(c) And who will benefit from the consumption?

Making choices about the use to be made of scarce resources is the fundamental problem of economics.

We have been introduced to economics. We are now going to look at one of the key tools of the economist – the production possibility curve.

1.3 The production possibility curve

We can approach the central questions of economics by looking first at the possibilities of production. Suppose, to take a simple example, that an imaginary society can use its available resources to produce two products, A and B. The society's resources are limited. Therefore there are restrictions on the amounts of A and B that can be made. The possible combinations of A and B can be shown by a **production possibility curve** (or frontier).

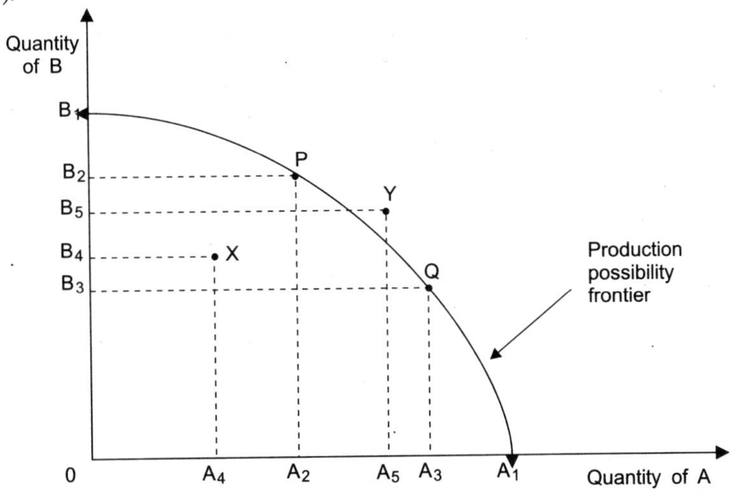

Figure 1.1: Production possibility curve

The curve from A_1 round to B_1 in Figure 1.1 shows the various combinations of A and B that a society can make, if it uses its limited resources efficiently.

(a) The society can choose to make up to:

- A_1 units of A and no B
- B_1 units of B and no A
- A_2 units of A and B_2 of B (point P on the curve)
- A_3 units of A and B_3 of B (point Q on the curve)

(b) The combination of A_4 units of A and B_4 units of B plotted at point X is within the production possibility curve. More than these quantities can be made of either or both of A and B. Point X is therefore an inefficient production point for the economy, and if the society were to make only A_4 of A and B_4 of B, it would be using its limited resources inefficiently.

(c) Note that the production possibility curve is just what it says: it defines what is achievable if **all** productive resources are fully employed. It follows that changes in the level of unemployment have no effect upon it. Similarly, changes in price levels will affect the **monetary value** of what can be produced, but not the **volume**.

The production possibility curve is an important idea in economics: it illustrates **the need to make choices** about what to produce because it is not possible to have everything. Although we have characterised the products of our hypothetical economy as A and B, we can generalise the production possibility curve to show the production possibilities for different types of good, and also for some 'good X' on one axis and 'all other goods' on the other axis.

FOR DISCUSSION

Use a production possibilities curve to investigate one of the trade-offs you make in your lives. For example, you can discuss the time you spend studying versus the time you spend socialising.

Activity 1 **(20 minutes)**

A country is capable of producing the following combinations of goods and services per period of time, assuming that it makes full use of its resources of land, labour and capital.

Goods (units)	100	80	60	40	20	0
Services (units)	0	50	90	120	140	150

(a) Draw the production possibility curve for this country.

(b) Is it possible for this country to produce the following combinations of goods and services?

(i) 80 units of goods and 50 units of services
(ii) 70 units of goods and 90 units of services
(iii) 40 units of goods and 100 units of services

(c) What is the opportunity cost (in terms of services) of producing twenty extra units of goods when this country is initially producing:

(i) 60 units of goods
(ii) 70 units of goods?

Budget lines

We can show budgets in a similar diagram to the production possibility curve. This shows how a consumer with a limited budget can allocate income on clothing and food but cannot exceed the total income available to him.

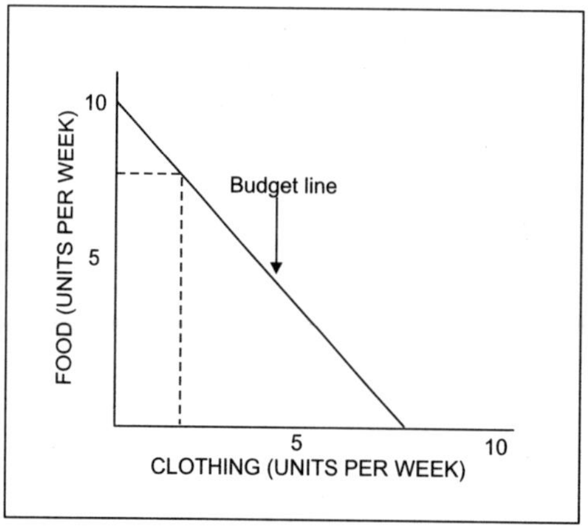

This diagram suggests the consumer could afford either seven units of clothing or ten units of food.

OR some combination of the two (say eight units of food and two units of clothing).

Figure 1.2: Budget lines

1.4 Opportunity cost: the cost of one use for resources rather than another

Choice involves sacrifice. If there is a choice between having A and having B, and a country chooses to have A, it will be giving up B to have A. The cost of having a certain amount of A can therefore be regarded as the sacrifice of not being able to have a certain amount of B. There is a sacrifice involved in the choices of consumers and firms (producers), as well as the choices of governments at the level of national economy.

Definition

> **Opportunity cost** is the cost of an item measured in terms of the alternatives forgone.

A production possibility curve illustrates opportunity costs. For example, if in Figure 1.1 it is decided to switch from making A_3 units of A and B_3 units of B (point Q) to making A_2 units of A and B_2 units of B (point P), then **the opportunity cost of making (B_2 – B_3) more units of B would be the lost production of (A_3 – A_2) units of A.**

The production possibility line is a **curve** and not a straight line because some resources are more useful for making A than for making B and *vice versa*. As a result, opportunity costs change as we move away from a situation in which production is wholly devoted to either A or B. Thus, as we move away from point A_1, and introduce an increasing level of production of B, the amount of B that we gain from losing each unit of A progressively diminishes.

At the level of the firm, the production possibility curve can be seen as showing the maximum output of different goods the firm can produce when all of its resources are fully used – for example, a firm might operate production lines capable of producing washing machines or refrigerators. Producing more washing machines bears the opportunity cost of a lower level of production of refrigerators.

If the lay person is asked what they think economics is about, most will reply that it is about money. You now know it is about scarcity and choices. However, many of the choices can be expressed in monetary terms.

1.5 The nature of money

Economic activities, whether in the private or public sector, take place within a monetary economy. Both government and businesses have financial aspects to their operations.

Money acts not merely as a measuring rod, thus making accounting possible, but also acts as a means of exchange.

The functions of money

Activity 2 **(10 minutes)**

Surely 'money' is a concept very easily understood? You will see in this chapter that it is not necessarily as simple as you might, at first, think. Before beginning on this section, try to analyse what constitutes money (for example, is a bank deposit account 'money'?) and what are the functions of money. Revise your answers in the light of what you learn while reading this section.

In modern economies, money is used as a means of paying for goods and services, and paying for labour, capital and other resources. Money is important because it provides an easy method for exchanging goods and services (ie buying and selling). It is also important because the total amount of money in a national economy may have a significant influence on economic activity and inflation.

Attempts to define money have traditionally started with identifying what money does. What are the **functions** of money? We can identify four different functions of money.

- A means of exchange
- A unit of account
- A standard of deferred payment
- A store of value

Money as a means of exchange

This is arguably the most important function of money in an economy, because without money, the only way of exchanging goods and services would be by means of **barter**, ie by a **direct exchange** of goods or services. In other words, if a shoemaker wanted to buy a horse, he would have two alternative courses open to him.

(a) To find a horse-owner prepared to exchange a horse for a sufficient quantity of shoes of equal value to the horse

(b) To find other people willing to exchange different goods such as clothes or food for shoes, and then trade these goods in exchange for a horse from the horse-owner

A monetary economy is the only alternative to a barter economy, and it is a means of encouraging economic development and growth.

(a) People are prepared to organise and work for an employer, and in return receive money wages.

(b) A business will exchange its goods or services for money in return.

(c) People will pay out money in order to obtain goods or services.

Money as a unit of account

This function of money is associated with the use of money as a means of exchange. Money should be able to measure exactly what something is worth. It should provide an agreed standard measure by which the **value** of different goods and services can be compared.

EXAMPLE: UNITS OF VALUE

Suppose that only four products are traded in a market. These are pigs, sheep, hens and corn. The relative value of these products must be agreed before exchange can take place in the market. It might be decided that:

- 1 pig has the same value as 0.75 sheep, 3 hens or 1.5 bags of corn
- 1 sheep is the same value as 1.33 pigs, 4 hens or 2 bags of corn
- 1 hen is worth 0.33 pigs, 0.25 sheep or 0.5 bags of corn
- 1 bag of corn has the same value as 0.67 pigs, 0.5 sheep or 2 hens

---

In a market with more than four products, the relative values of each product compared with others could be worked out in the same way, although there would be many more value or price ratios to calculate.

The function of money in the economy would be to establish a **common unit of value** measurement or account by which the relative exchange values or prices of goods can be established.

Activity 3 **(10 minutes)**

In the above example of a four-product market, simplify the value relationship by expressing the worth of a pig, a sheep, a hen and a bag of corn in terms of a common unit of money.

Money as a standard for deferred payments

When a person buys a good or service, he might not want to pay for it straightaway, perhaps because he has not yet got the money. Instead, he might ask for **credit**. Selling goods on credit is not an essential feature of an economy, but it certainly helps to stimulate trade. The function of money in this respect is to establish, by agreement between buyer and seller, how much **value** will be given in return at some future date for **goods** provided **now**. Similarly, when a buyer and seller agree now to make a contract for the supply of certain goods in the future, the function of money is to establish the value of the contract, that is, how much the buyer will eventually pay the seller for the goods.

In order to provide an acceptable standard for deferred payments, it is important that money should maintain its value over a period of time. Suppose, for example, that a customer buys goods for an agreed sum of money, but on three months' credit. Now if the value of money falls in the three-month credit period, the sum of money which the seller eventually receives will be worth less than it was at the time of sale. The seller will have lost value by allowing the credit.

When the value of money falls (or rises) over time, sellers (or buyers) will be reluctant to arrange credit, or to agree the price for future contracts. Money would then be failing to fulfil its function as a standard for deferred payments.

One major reason why money might lose value is because of price inflation.

(a) When inflation is high sellers will be reluctant to allow credit to buyers. For example, if a buyer asks for three months' credit, and inflation is running at 20% per annum, the 'real' value of the debt that the buyer owes will fall by about 5% over the three-month credit period.

(b) Sellers will be reluctant to agree to a fixed price for long-term contracts. For example, a house-builder might refuse to quote a price for building a house over a twelve-month period, and instead insist on asking a price which is 'index-linked' and rises in step with the general rate of inflation.

Money as a store of value

Money acts as a store of value, or wealth. So too do many other assets (eg land, buildings, art treasures, motorcars, machinery) some of which maintain or increase their money value over time, and some of which depreciate in value. This means of course that money is not the only asset which acts as a store of wealth, and we need to extend our definition of this function of money.

Money is more properly described as acting as a **liquid** store of value. This definition has two parts to it.

(a) Money is a store of value or wealth. A person can hold money for an extended period, for the purpose of exchanging it for services or goods or other assets.

(b) Money is a liquid asset.

These concepts are important again when you study demand and supply in Chapter 2.

1.6 Key measures of national economic output of national income

Definition

> **National income** is the sum of all incomes which arise as a result of economic activity, that is from the production of goods and services.

The incomes which make up national income, which include rent, employment income, interest and profit, are known as **factor incomes** because they are earned by the factors of production:

- Land earns rent
- Labour earns wages
- Capital earns interest
- Entrepreneurship earns profit

National income is also called **net national product**.

(a) The terms **income** and **product** are just two different aspects of the same circular flow of income.

(b) The term **net** means 'after deducting an amount for capital consumption or depreciation of fixed (sometimes called non-current) assets'. (We shall return to this point later.)

Gross domestic product (GDP)

Most UK national income is derived from economic activity **within the UK**. Economic activity within the UK is referred to as total **domestic income** or **domestic product**. It is measured **gross** ie before deducting an amount for capital consumption or depreciation of fixed assets and the term **gross domestic product** therefore refers in the UK to **the total value of income/production from economic activity within the UK**.

Gross national income (GNI)

'Some national income arises from overseas investments while some of the income generated within the UK is earned by non-residents. The difference between these items is **net property income from abroad**'.

Gross national income (GNI) is therefore the gross domestic product (GDP) plus the net property income from abroad – or after subtracting the net property income from abroad, if it is a negative value.

Definitions

> **Gross domestic product** is the value of the goods and services produced by an economy in a given period.
>
> **Gross national income** is GDP **plus** income accruing to domestic residents from investments abroad **less** income accruing to foreign residents from investments in the domestic economy.

The relationship between GDP, GNI and national income

The relationship between GDP, GNI and national income is therefore this.

	GDP
plus	Net property income from abroad
equals	GNI
minus	Capital consumption
equals	National income (net)

National income is technically GNI **minus** an allowance for depreciation of the nation's capital.

Just as firms calculate depreciation in arriving at accounting profits, so too do economists assess a value for depreciation of the nation's capital (referred to as **capital consumption**) to arrive at net national income.

Adjustments to GDP at market prices

The GDP, GNP and national income as defined above are expressed at market prices.

Since the prices of many goods and services are distorted by sales taxes (for example, alcohol and cigarettes) and some are distorted by subsidies (for example, many agricultural products), we often wish to view the situation without these distortions and convert GDP at market prices to **gross value added at basic prices (formerly GDP at factor cost)**.

Thus Gross value added (GVA) at basic prices = GDP at Market prices – Indirect taxes + Subsidies

Personal income

Personal income is defined as the total income received by individuals available for consumption, saving and payment of personal taxes. It is calculated as national income less corporate profits and social security taxes (since these are not paid out as income to investors), plus transfer payments, net interest and dividends (since these are paid to investors).

Disposable income

Disposable income is defined as income available to individuals after payment of personal taxes. It may be consumed or saved.

Our brief look at national income concludes the first half of this chapter. In the next section we are going to explore the causes and implications of market failure.

2 MARKET FAILURE

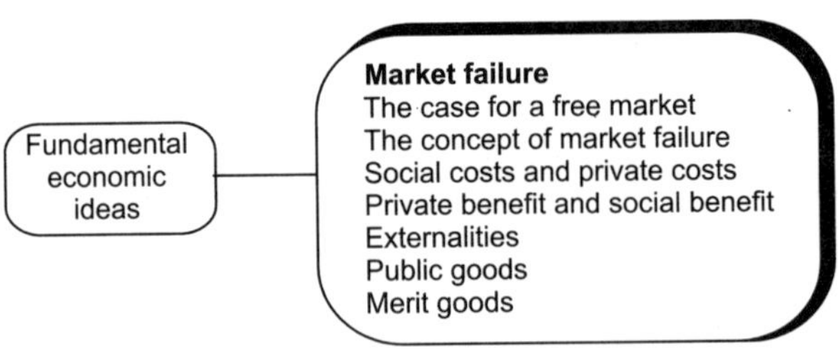

2.1 The case for a free market

What is the general case for allowing market forces to set prices? The following arguments are put forward by advocates of the free market.

(a) Free markets are **efficient**. Suppliers and consumers react fairly quickly to changes in market conditions in making their output and purchasing decisions; **resource allocation** within the economy is quick to adapt to the new conditions.

(b) The market is **impersonal**. Prices and levels of output are arrived at as a result of numerous decisions of consumers and suppliers, and not as the result of bureaucratic or political regulation.

Advocates of a free market economy argue that the market forces of supply and demand will result in an **efficient allocation of economic resources**.

(a) Consumers will want lower prices and producers will want higher prices; a balance of supply and demand is struck in the market through the price mechanism.

(b) Producers will decide what goods to produce, and in what quantities, by relating their prices to the costs of production (and the costs of the scarce resources needed to produce them).

(c) If the price of a product is too high, consumers will want to buy less of it. If the price is too low, producers will make less of it and switch their production resources into making something different.

However, the arguments in favour of a free market are based on the assumption that there is **perfect competition**. Perfect competition has a number of prerequisites.

(a) Markets each have a large number of competing firms, each producing a homogeneous product and each having only a small share of the market.

(b) Consumers and producers have perfect information about markets and prices.

(c) There is perfect mobility of factors of production, which can be switched easily from making one type of good into making another, and free entry and exit of firms into and out of the market.

In reality, these assumptions are not often completely valid. However, the markets for many goods approximate to conditions of perfect competition.

2.2 The concept of market failure

Definition

> **Market failure** occurs when a free market mechanism fails to produce the most efficient allocation of resources.

Market failure is caused by a number of factors.

- Imperfections in a market
- Divergence between private costs and social costs (externalities)
- The need to provide public goods
- The need to consider non-market goals, such as the consumption of merit goods

The following are examples of market imperfections.

(a) If a monopoly firm controls a market, it might prevent other firms from entering the market (for example, by claiming patent rights, or launching a strong marketing campaign with the intention of keeping customers away from the new firms). By restricting supply in this way, the monopolist may keep prices higher than they would be in a competitive market.

(b) Just as monopolies are firms which dominate supply to a market, monopsony buyers are large individual buyers who dominate demand in a market. Monopsonists may exert control over the market, exacting low prices or other favourable conditions from suppliers.

(c) Consumers may make bad purchasing decisions because they do not have complete and accurate information about all goods and services that are available.

(d) It takes time for the price mechanism to work. Firms cannot suddenly enter a new market or shut down operations. The slow response of the price mechanism to changes in demand creates some short-term inefficiency in resource allocation.

2.3 Social costs and private costs

In a free market, suppliers and households make their output and buying decisions for their own private benefit, and these decisions determine how the economy's scarce resources will be allocated to production and consumption. Private costs and private benefits therefore determine what goods are made and bought in a free market.

(a) **Private cost** measures the cost **to the firm** of the resources it uses to produce a good.

(b) **Social cost** measures the cost **to society as a whole** of the resources that a firm uses.

(c) **Private benefit** measures the benefit obtained directly by a supplier or by a consumer.

(d) **Social benefit** measures the total benefit to society from a transaction.

It can be argued that a free market system would result in a satisfactory allocation of resources, **provided that** private costs are the same as social costs and private benefits are the same as social benefits. In this situation, suppliers will maximise profits by supplying goods and services that benefit customers, and that customers want to buy. By producing their goods and services, suppliers are giving benefit to both themselves and the community.

However, there are other possibilities.

(a) Members of the economy (suppliers or households) may do things which give benefit to others, but no reward to themselves.

(b) Members of the economy may do things which are harmful to others, but at no cost to themselves.

When private benefit is **not** the same as social benefit, or when private cost is **not** the same as social cost, an allocation of resources which reflects private costs and benefits only **may not be socially acceptable**.

Here are some examples of situations where **private cost and social cost differ**.

(a) A firm produces a good and, during the production process, pollution is discharged into the air. The private cost to the firm is the cost of the resources needed to make the good. The social cost consists of the private cost plus the additional 'costs' incurred by other members of society, who suffer from the pollution.

(b) The private cost of transporting goods by road is the cost to the haulage firm of the resources to provide the transport. The social cost of road haulage would consist of the private cost plus the cost of repairs and maintenance of the road system (which sustains serious damage from heavy goods vehicles) plus any environmental costs, such as harm to wildlife habitats from road building.

2.4 Private benefit and social benefit

Here are some examples of situations where **private benefit and social benefit differ**.

(a) Customers at a café in a piazza benefit from the entertainment provided by professional musicians, who are hired by the café. The customers of the café are paying for the service in the prices they pay, and they obtain a private benefit from it. At the same time, other people in the piazza, who are not customers of the café, might stop and listen to the music. They will obtain a benefit, but at no cost to themselves. They are **free riders**, taking advantage of the service without contributing to its cost. The social benefit from the musicians' service is greater than the private benefit to the café's customers.

(b) Suppose that a large firm pays for the training of employees as accountants, expecting a certain proportion of these employees to leave the firm in search of a better job once they have qualified. The private benefits to the firm are the benefits of the training of those employees who continue to work for it. The total social benefit includes the enhanced economic output resulting from the training of those employees who go to work for other firms.

Activity 4 **(15 minutes)**

Think of some situations other than those mentioned above in which private costs differ from social costs and private benefits differ from social benefits.

2.5 Externalities

Definition

Externalities are effects of a transaction which extend beyond the parties to the transaction. The differences between the private and the social costs, or benefits, arising from an activity are externalities.

Less formally, an 'externality' is a cost or benefit which the market mechanism fails to take into account because the market responds to purely private signals. One activity might produce both harmful and beneficial externalities.

2.6 Public goods

Definition

> **Public goods**. Some goods, by their very nature, involve so much 'spill-over' of externalities that they are difficult to provide except as **public goods** whose production is organised by the government.

In the case of public goods, the consumption of the good by one individual or group **does not significantly reduce the amount available for others**. Furthermore, it is often difficult or impossible to **exclude** anyone from its benefits, once the good has been provided. As a result, in a free market, individuals benefiting from the good would have no economic incentive to pay for them, since they might as well be **free riders** if they can, enjoying the good while others pay for it.

EXAMPLE

National defence is perhaps the most obvious examples of a public good. It is clearly not practicable for individuals to buy their own defence systems. Policing is sometimes cited as another example of a public good, although the growth of private security firms in the private sector illustrates how some areas of policing are now becoming privatised.

2.7 Merit goods

The existence of market failure and of externalities suggests the need for intervention in markets by the government, in order to improve the allocation of resources. Another possible reason for intervention is to **increase** the consumption of **merit goods.**

Definition

> **Merit goods** are considered to be worth providing in greater volume than would be purchased in a free market, because higher consumption is in the long-term public interest.

Education is one of the chief examples of a merit good. On the other hand, many governments want to see **less** consumption of certain **demerit goods,** such as tobacco.

Apart from **providing** public goods and merit goods, a government might choose to intervene in the workings of markets by other methods.

(a) **Controlling the means of production** (for example, through state ownership of industries)

(b) **Influencing markets** through legislation and regulation (regulation of monopolies, bans on dangerous drugs, enforcement of the use of some goods such as car seat belts, laws on pollution control and so on) or by persuasion (for example, using anti-tobacco advertising)

(c) **Redistributing wealth,** perhaps by taxing relatively wealthy members of society and redistributing this tax income so as to benefit the poorer members

(d) **Influencing market supply and demand** through:

- Price legislation
- Indirect taxation
- Subsidies

(e) **Creating a demand for output that creates employment**. A free market system would match supply with demand. Demand would thus lead to **employment** because of the needs of suppliers, but the level of demand might not be high enough to ensure **full employment**. Government might therefore wish to intervene to create a demand for output in order to create more jobs.

Some externalities, particularly the problems of pollution and the environment, appear to call for co-operation between governments. The UN Conference on the Environment and Development held in Rio de Janeiro in 1992 led to a convention on climate change which included commitments about emission reduction. The Kyoto Protocol of 1997 was also directed at climate change.

Activity 5 **(15 minutes)**

An industrial company alters its production methods to reduce the amount of waste discharged from its factory into the local river. What will be the effect (increase or decrease) on:

(a) Private costs
(b) External benefits
(c) Social costs

FOR DISCUSSION

To what extent do you think governments should intervene in the markets for:

(a) Alcohol
(b) Tobacco
(c) Animal fur?

Chapter roundup

- Economics deals with the problem of scarcity. Scarcity can be represented by the production possibility curve.
- Economic activities, whether in the private or public sector, take place within a monetary economy. Both government and businesses have financial aspects to their operations.
- National income is the sum of all incomes which arise as a result of economic activity, that is from the production of goods and services.
- Free markets may not lead to an ideal allocation of resources. Market failure occurs when a free market mechanism fails to produce the most efficient allocation of resources.

Quick quiz

1 Name three economic systems for solving the economic problem of scarcity.

2 What are the four factors of production?

3 What is opportunity cost?

4 What are the four functions of money?

5 What is an externality?

6 What are the characteristics of a public good?

7 What is a merit good?

Answers to quick quiz

1 Centrally planned or command economy; market economy; and mixed economy.

2 Land, labour, capital and enterprise.

3 Opportunity cost is the cost of an item measured in terms of the alternatives forgone.

4 A means of exchange, a unit of account, a standard of deferred payment and a store of value.

5 Externalities are effects of a transaction which extends beyond the parties to the transaction.

6 (a) The consumption of the good does not significantly reduce the amount available for others.

(b) It is difficult or impossible to exclude anyone from its benefits.

7 Merit goods are goods that have positive externalities.

Answers to activities

1 (a)

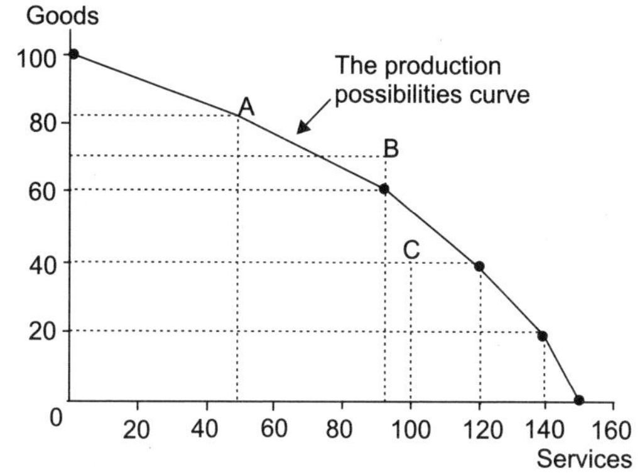

(b) (i) 80 units of goods and 50 units of services – Yes (point A)
(ii) 70 units of goods and 90 units of services – No (point B)
(iii) 40 units of goods and 100 units of services – Yes (point C)

(c) (i) Producing 60 units of goods allows 80 units of services

Producing 80 units of goods allows 50 units of services

The opportunity cost of producing an extra 20 = 40 units of services

(ii) Producing 20 units of goods allows 140 units of services

Producing 40 units of goods allows 120 units of services

The opportunity cost of producing an extra 20 = 20 units of services

2 Refer back to the chapter.

3 You might have calculated as follows.

A pig = 3 units
A sheep = 4 units
A hen = 1 unit
A bag of corn = 2 units

Other results (such as 6, 8, 2 and 4 respectively) would work just as well.

4 Your situations might include a dog fouling the pavement, a neighbour doing up a house, neighbours playing their music loudly and so on.

5 (a) Private costs of the company will presumably increase: the anti-pollution measures will have involved a financial outlay.

(b) External benefits will presumably increase: the public will benefit from a cleaner river.

(c) Social costs may stay the same: the increase in private costs may be balanced by the reduction the external costs to society.

Chapter 2 :

DEMAND AND SUPPLY

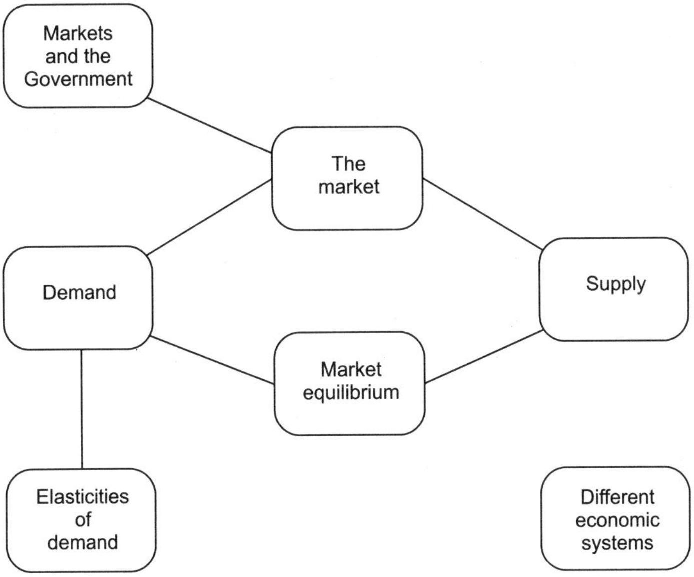

Introduction

In this chapter we look at dcmand and supply. People must both want a product and have money to buy it. How much people will buy depends on several things, not just the price. In this chapter we will look at what effects demand for goods and services.

We will look at supply and bring supply and demand together for market equilibrium.

In Chapter 1 we looked at the idea of scarcity. In this chapter we examine how society can solve the fundamental economic problem of scarcity – the market economy, the planned economy and a combination of these two – the mixed economy.

The chapter finishes with the role of the government in markets.

Your objectives

In this chapter you will learn about:

(a) The concept of a market

(b) The demand schedule

(c) Elasticities of demand

(d) Market supply

(e) Market equilibrium

(f) Different economic systems

1 THE CONCEPT OF A MARKET

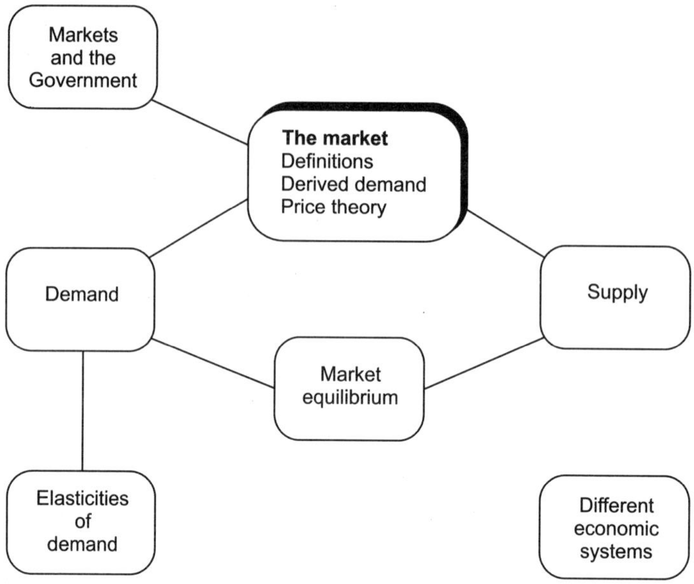

1.1 What is a market?

A market involves **the buyers and sellers of a good who influence its price**. Markets can be worldwide, as in the case of oil, wheat, cotton and copper for example. Others are more localised, such as the housing market or the market for second-hand cars.

Definition

> A **market** is a situation in which potential buyers and potential sellers (*suppliers*) of a good or service come together for the purpose of exchange.

Suppliers and potential suppliers are referred to in economics as **firms**. The potential purchasers of consumer goods are known as **households**.

1.2 Derived demand

Some markets have buyers who are other firms or government authorities. For example, a manufacturing firm buys raw materials and components to go into the products that it makes. Service industries and government departments must similarly buy in supplies in order to do their own work. The demand for goods by firms and government authorities is a **derived demand** in that it depends on the demand from households for the goods and services that they produce and provide.

Markets for different goods or commodities are often inter-related. All commodities compete for households' income so that if more is spent in one market, there will be less to spend in other markets. Further, if markets for similar goods are separated geographically, there will be some price differential at which it will be worthwhile for the consumer to buy in the lower price market and pay shipping costs, rather than buy in a geographically nearer market.

1.3 Price theory and the market

Price theory is concerned with how market prices for goods are arrived at, through the interaction of demand and supply.

A good or service has a **price** if it is **useful** as well as **scarce**. Its usefulness is shown by the fact that consumers demand it. In a world populated entirely by vegetarians, meat would not command a price, no matter how few cows or sheep there were.

2 DEMAND

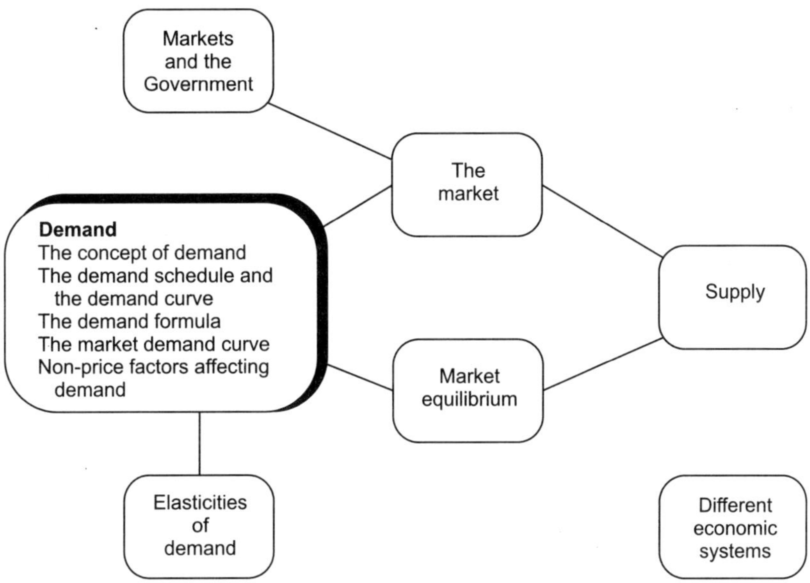

2.1 The concept of demand

Definition

> **Demand** for a good is the quantity of that good that potential purchasers would buy, or attempt to buy, if the price of the good were at a certain level.

Demand might be satisfied, and so actual quantities bought would equal demand. On the other hand, some demand might be unsatisfied, with more would-be purchasers trying to buy a good that is in insufficient supply, and so there are then not enough units of the good to go around.

Demand does not mean the quantity that potential purchasers **wish** they could buy. For example, a million households might wish that they owned a luxury yacht, but there might only be actual attempts to buy one hundred luxury yachts at a given price.

2.2 The demand schedule and the demand curve

The relationship between demand and price can be shown graphically as a **demand curve**. The demand curve of a single consumer or household is derived by estimating how much of the good the consumer or household would demand at various hypothetical market prices.

EXAMPLE

Suppose that the following **demand schedule** shows demand for biscuits by one household over a period of one month.

Price per kg	*Quantity demanded*
£	kg
1	9.75
2	8
3	6.25
4	4.5
5	2.75
6	1

Notice that in the example demand falls off as price increases. This is what normally happens with most goods. This is because purchasers have a limited amount of money to spend and must choose between goods that compete for their attention. When the price of one good rises, it is likely that other goods will seem relatively more attractive and so demand will switch away from the more expensive good.

We can show this schedule graphically, with **price on the y axis** and **quantity demanded on the x axis**. If we assume that there is complete divisibility, so that price and quantity can both change in infinitely small steps, we can draw a demand curve by joining the points represented in the schedule by a continuous line (Figure 2.1). This is the household's demand curve for biscuits in the particular market we are looking at.

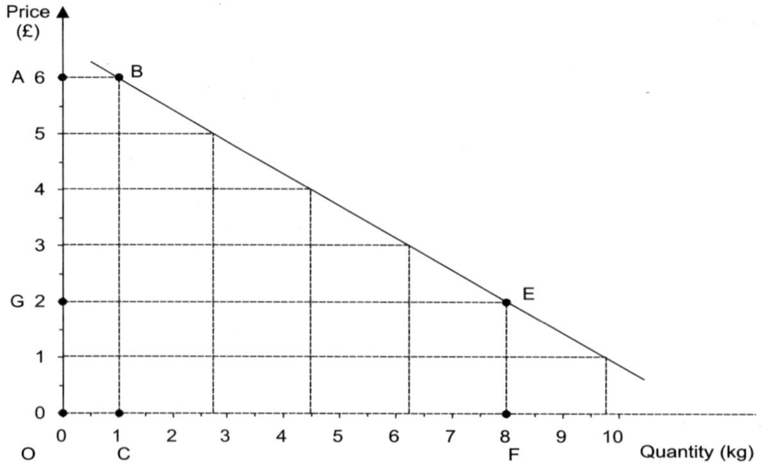

Figure 2.1: Graph of a demand schedule

The area of each rectangle in Figure 2.1 represents consumers' total money outlay at the price in question. For example, at a price of £6, demand would be 1 kilogram and total spending would be £6, represented by rectangle ABCO. Similarly, at a price of £2, demand would be 8 kilograms and the total spending of £16 is represented by rectangle GEFO.

In Figure 2.1, the demand curve happens to be a straight line. Straight line demand curves are often used as an illustration in economics because it is convenient to draw them this way. In reality, a demand curve is more likely to be a curved line convex to the origin. As you will be able to appreciate, such a demand curve means that there are progressively larger increases in quantity demanded as price falls (Figure 2.2).

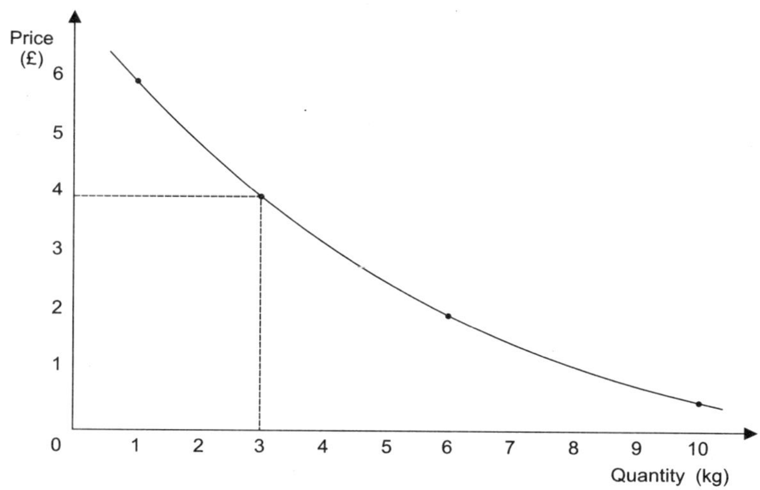

Figure 2.2: Demand curve convex to the origin

Activity 1 **(5 minutes)**

Refer to Figure 2.2. Suppose the price of the commodity is £3. What would be the (approximate) demand for the commodity? And if the price fell to £2?

Note that changes in demand caused by changes in price are represented by movements **along the demand curve,** from one point to another. The price has changed, and the quantity demanded changes, but **the demand curve itself remains the same.**

2.3 The demand formula

When demand is linear the equation for the demand curve is:

$P = a - bQ/\Delta Q$

where P = the price
Q = the quantity demanded
a = the price at which demand would be nil
b = the amount by which the price falls for each stepped change in demand
ΔQ = the stepped change in demand

The constant a is calculated as follows.

$$a = £(\text{current price}) + \left(\frac{\text{Current quantity at current price}}{\text{Change in quantity when price is changed by £b}} \times £b\right)$$

This looks rather complicated expressed in words, but it is very easy once the numbers are substituted.

EXAMPLE: DERIVING THE DEMAND CURVE

The current price of a product is £12. At this price the company sells 60 items a month. One month the company decides to raise the price to £14, but only 45 items are sold at this price. Determine the demand equation.

Solution

Step 1. Find the price at which demand would be nil.

Assuming demand is linear, each increase of £2 in the price would result in a fall in demand of 15 units. For demand to be nil, the price needs to rise from its current level by as many times as there are 15 units in 60 units (60/15 = 4) ie to £12 + (4 × £2) = £20.

Using the formula above, this can be shown as a = £12 + ((60/15) × £2) = £20

Step 2. Extract figures from the question.

The demand equation can now be determined as $P = a - bQ/\Delta Q = 20 - 2Q/15$

Step 3. Check your equation.

We can check this by substituting £12 and £14 for P.

$12 = 20 - (2 \times 60/15) = 20 - 8 = 12$
$4 = 20 - (2 \times 45/15) = 20 - 6 = 14$

Activity 2 **(10 minutes)**

The current price of a product is £30 and the producers sell 100 items a week at this price. One week the price is dropped by £3 as a special offer and the producers sell 150 items. Find an expression for the demand curve.

2.4 The market demand curve

In the example above, we have been looking at the demand schedule of a single household. A **market demand curve** is a similar curve, drawn from a demand schedule, expressing the expected total quantity of the good that would be demanded by **all consumers together,** at any given price.

Market demand is the total quantity of a product that **all** purchasers would want to buy at each price level. A market demand schedule and a market demand curve are therefore simply the sum of all the individual demand schedules and demand curves put together. Market demand curves would be similar to those in Figures 2.1 and 2.2, but with quantities demanded (total market demand) being higher at each price level.

A **demand curve generally slopes down from left to right.**

(a) As we saw earlier, the curve is downward sloping curve because progressively larger quantities are demanded as price falls.

(b) A fall in the good's price means that households with lower incomes will also be able to afford it. The overall size of the market for the good increases. The converse argument applies to an increase in prices; as a price goes up, consumers with lower incomes will no longer be able to afford the good, or will buy something else whose price is relatively cheaper, and the size of the market will shrink.

Several factors influence the total market demand for a good. One of these factors is obviously its price, but there are other factors too, and to help you to appreciate some of these other factors, you need to recognise that households buy not just one good with their money but a whole range of goods and services.

Factors determining demand for a good

- The price of the good
- The price of other goods (products and services)
- The size of households' income
- Tastes and fashion
- Expectations of future price changes
- The distribution of income among households.

A demand curve shows how the quantity demanded will change in response to a change in price **provided that all other conditions affecting demand are unchanged** – that is, provided that there is no change in the prices of other goods, tastes, expectations or the distribution of household income. This assumption is known a the *ceteris paribus* assumption.

Definition

> ***Ceteris paribus*** is the assumption that all other things remain equal.

2.5 Non-price factors affecting demand

Substitute products

Most products have alternatives. These are known as substitute goods. Some are very close, for example tea and coffee, and some are not so close, such as a new car and a luxury holiday. Goods should be treated as substitutes if an increase in demand for one of them should result in a decrease in demand for the other.

EXAMPLES: SUBSTITUTES

Examples of substitute goods and services, to a greater or lesser extent, are:

(a) Rival brands of the same commodity, for example Coca-Cola and Pepsi-Cola
(b) Lager and bitter
(c) Rail travel and car travel
(d) Films and plays

Activity 3 **(10 minutes)**

For someone who commutes from a suburban home to a city centre office each day, are rail travel and car travel close substitutes? Give reasons for your view.

The next category is complementary products. When demand for a product goes up, demand for its substitutes goes down but demand for its complementary products goes up as well.

Complementary products

These are goods that tend to be bought and used together. Thus a change in demand for one item should lead to a similar change in demand for the other related product.

EXAMPLES: COMPLEMENTS

Examples of complements are:

(a) Cups and saucers
(b) Bread and butter
(c) Motor cars and replacement exhausts

In the case of cups and saucers, the maker tends to supply both goods at the same time. With the other examples the link is less close. A supplier of replacement exhausts will have to monitor the quality of the original exhausts closely so as to forecast demand for replacements.

Activity 4 **(10 minutes)**

If the ownership of domestic deep freezers increased, would this have any effect on the demand for perishable food products?

We will now look at the effects on market demand that household income, fashion, consumer expectations and the distribution of incomes will have.

Consumer factors

Household incomes

More income will give people more to spend, and they will want to buy more goods at existing prices. However, a rise in incomes will not increase market demand for all goods and services. The effect of a rise in income on demand for an individual product will depend on its nature.

Demand and the level of income may be related in different ways.

(a) A rise in income may increase demand for a good. This is what we would normally expect, and goods like this are called **normal goods**. For instance, a rise in income may increase demand for moderately priced wine.

(b) Demand may rise with income up to a certain point but then fall as income rises further. Goods whose demand eventually falls as income rises are called **inferior goods**. An example is cheap wine. The reason for falling demand is that as incomes rise, demand switches to superior products, for example better quality wines instead of cheap 'plonk'.

Fashion and consumer expectations

As already mentioned, a change in fashion will alter the demand for a product. For example, if it becomes fashionable for middle class households in the UK to drink wine with their meals, expenditure on wine will increase. There may be passing crazes, such as rollerblades or Power Rangers, and long-term trends, such as the move away from red meat for health reasons (even before the BSE scare).

If consumers believe that prices will rise, or that shortages will occur, they may try to stock up on the product, thereby creating excess demand in the short term which will increase prices. This can then lead to panic buying. Some years ago, a rumour was spread that the Siberian salt mines were closed. This caused panic buying of salt in the UK to the extent that most shops ran out of supplies, even though salt for the UK is supplied from enormous deposits in Cheshire and not from Siberia at all!

The distribution of incomes

Market demand for products is influenced by the way in which income is shared among households.

In a country with many rich and many poor households and few middle income ones, we might expect relatively high demand for luxury cars and yachts, and also for basic necessities such as bread and potatoes. In a country with many middle-income households, we might expect high demand for TV sets and medium-sized cars.

Activity 5 **(15 minutes)**

A food supermarket chain known for its service, up-market goods and fairly high prices is looking to build a new store in the North East. They have narrowed down their choice of area to two sites and now have to make a decision. The sites are 75 miles apart and one of their criteria is distribution of income within a five mile radius of the new store. Site A has many large, new executive housing estates within the area, but also many run down older areas with high unemployment. Site B has many well established private and council housing estates within the area. Unemployment is around average in this area.

(1) Where do you think the supermarket chain might choose to build a new store and why?

(2) Can you name one factor for and against each area?

Finally in this section we look at how to show the effect of changes in demand, using the demand curve.

Changes in demand

Changes in price

If the price of a good goes up or down, given no changes in the other factors that affect demand, then there will be a change in the quantity demanded, shown as a movement along the demand curve (the demand curve itself does not move).

Shifts of the demand curve

When there is a change in other factors that affect demand, the relationship between quantity demanded and price will also change, and there will be a different demand; schedule and so a different demand curve. For example, suppose that at current levels of income, the total UK demand for cheese at a price of £4 per kg is 150,000 tonnes. This will be a point on the demand curve. If incomes increase by 10%, the total demand at £4 per kg might rise to 160,000 tonnes. This will be a point on the new demand curve, which will be further to the right on a graph than the old curve.

We refer to such a change as change in demand, so as to distinguish it from a change in the quantity demanded. A change in demand involves a new demand curve. A change in quantity demanded, resulting from a price change, simply involves a movement along the old demand curve.

Figure 2.3 depicts a rise in demand at each price level, with the demand curve shifting to the right from D_0 to D_1. For example, at price P_1, demand for the good would rise from X to Y. This shift could be caused by any of the following.

(a) A rise in household income
(b) A rise in the price of substitutes
(c) A fall in the price of complements
(d) A change in tastes towards this product
(e) An expected rise in the price of the product

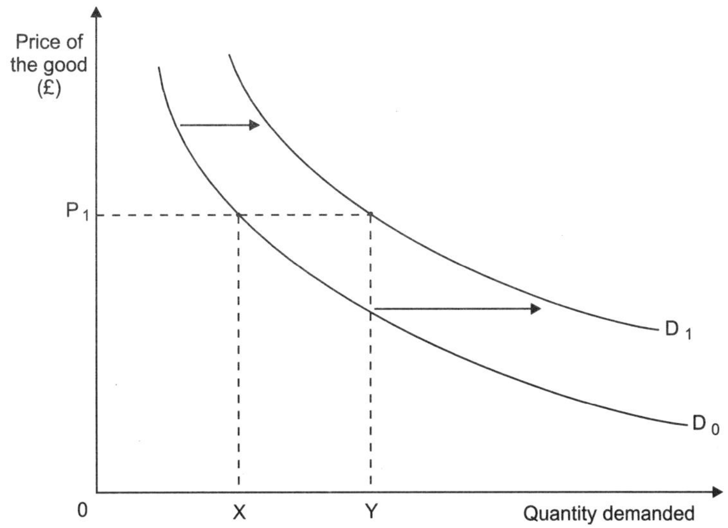

Figure 2.3: Shift of the demand curve

A fall in demand at each price level would lead to a shift of the demand curve in the opposite direction: towards the left of the graph. Such a shift could be caused by the reverse of the changes described in the previous paragraph.

Activity 6 **(5 minutes)**

Can you think of three reasons why it is important for a company to know how demand for their products will be affected by income changes?

We have looked at the factors affecting demand, but we have so far only discussed their effect in general terms. We will now see how to measure their effect.

3 ELASTICITIES OF DEMAND

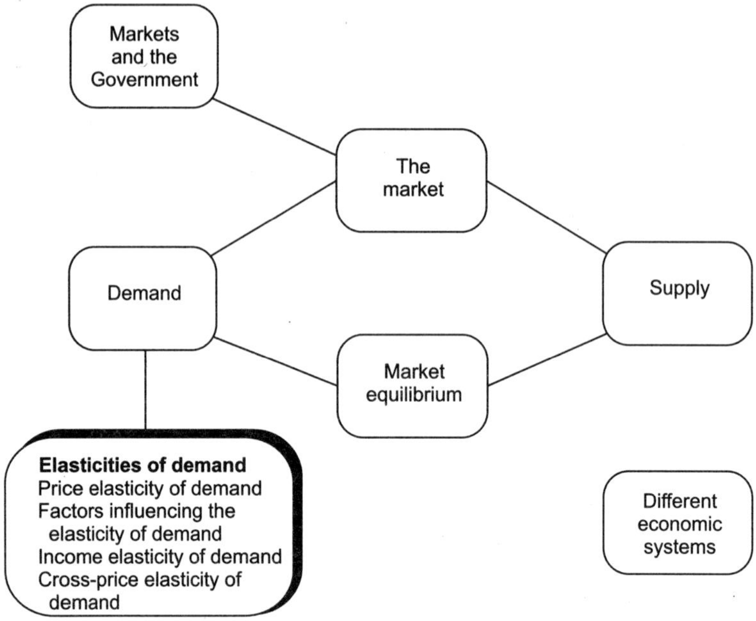

3.1 Price elasticity of demand

The price elasticity of demand measures how far the quantity demanded changes as the price changes. As explained later, the price elasticity of demand for a product is likely to be different at different prices.

The formula for the price elasticity of demand is as follows.

$$\frac{\text{Percentage change in the quantity demanded}}{\text{Percentage change in price}}$$

Because demand usually increases when the price falls and decreases when the price rises, price elasticity of demand normally has a negative value. However, it is usual to ignore the minus sign when looking at the price elasticity of demand.

Here are some examples.

(a) Price rises from £10 to £11, a 10% rise, and demand falls from 4,000 units to 3,200 units, a 20% fall: the elasticity is 20/10 = 2.

(b) Price rises from £15 to £18, a 20% rise, and demand falls from 1,000 units to 800 units, a 20% fall: the elasticity is 20/20 = 1.

Activity 7 **(5 minutes)**

Price rises from £5 to £6.25, a 25% rise, and demand falls from 8,000 units to 7,000 units, a 12.5% fall. What is the price elasticity of demand?

Note the following points.

(a) A product is said to have an elastic demand if the elasticity is greater than 1. A small change in price (up or down) leads to a large change in quantity demanded.

(b) If the elasticity equals 1, then a given percentage change in price leads to an equal percentage change in demand: this is called unit elasticity.

(c) A product is said to have an inelastic demand if the elasticity is less than 1. A large change in price (up or down) leads to only a small change in quantity demanded.

Why is price elasticity of demand important?

The price elasticity of demand is important when working out how much to charge for a product. If a company has a good idea of the price elasticity of demand for its products, that can help it to make sensible decisions on prices.

If demand is inelastic, then a company should seriously consider increasing the price, because it will not lose many sales: in fact, its total revenue will go up, even though it is selling less than before and therefore incurring lower costs. If you go back to the last example, where a price rise from £5 to £6.25 caused a fall in quantity from 8,000 units to 7,000 units, total revenue was 8,000 × £5 = £40,000 at a price of £5 and 7,000 × £6.25 = £43,750 at a price of £6.25.

Conversely, if demand is elastic, then a price rise may not be a good idea, because sales will fall fast and total revenue will fall. (Total costs will fall as well if less is being made, so a price rise might not be a disaster.) A price cut may be a good idea, because it will lead to a lot of extra sales, but of course costs will rise as well.

To find the elasticity of demand, a company may conduct market research to find out how much of a product people would buy at different prices.

Activity 8 **(20 minutes)**

The elasticity of demand generally changes as the price changes. Here is a demand schedule with the elasticity of demand worked out for the first price. Work out the elasticity of demand for the other prices and complete the table.

Price per kg	*Quantity demanded each month*	*Price elasticity of demand*
£	kg	
1	9.75	0.179
2	8.00	
3	6.25	
4	4.50	
5	2.75	
6	1.00	

We now need to analyse what factors are at play in determining how elastic demand for a product is.

3.2 Factors influencing the elasticity of demand

The elasticity of demand for any product depends mainly upon the availability of substitutes. If close substitutes are readily available then demand will be elastic: a small increase in price will cause many consumers to switch to the close substitutes, resulting in a fall in demand. If the price of canned spaghetti increases then people may switch to a close substitute – baked beans. If there are no close substitutes demand will be less elastic, because consumers will find it harder to switch to another product. If the price of milk goes up, people are likely to go on buying it in much the same quantities as before, because the closest substitutes (such as orange juice) are not really that similar.

Activity 9 **(10 minutes)**

Do you think that demand for each of the following products is price elastic or inelastic? Tick the appropriate box

	Price elastic	*Price inelastic*
Petrol	☐	☐
Commuter rail tickets	☐	☐
Holidays in Spain	☐	☐
Mars bars	☐	☐

We have looked at the price elasticity of demand, making the assumption that other factors remain unchanged. We will now see how to measure the effect on demand of a change in incomes.

3.3 Income elasticity of demand

The responsiveness of demand to changes in household incomes is known as the **income elasticity of demand**. The formula for the income elasticity of demand for any one product is as follows.

$$\frac{\text{Percentage change in the amount demanded}}{\text{Percentage change in income}}$$

The income elasticity of demand may be positive, zero or negative.

(a) Demand for a good is **income elastic** if income elasticity is greater than 1 so that quantity demanded rises by a larger percentage than the rise in income. For example, if the demand for compact discs will rise by 10% if household incomes rises by 7%, we would say that the demand for compact discs is income elastic.

(b) Demand for a good is **income inelastic** if income elasticity is between 0 and 1 and the quantity demanded rises less than the proportionate increases in income. For example, if the demand for books will rise by 6% if household income rises by 10%, we would say that the demand for books is income inelastic.

(c) If the income elasticity is negative, then as people's incomes rise, they buy less of the product. This could happen if people switch to more expensive products. For example, as incomes rise people might switch from lager to wine: the income elasticity of demand for lager would then be negative.

Goods whose demand is positively income elastic or income inelastic are said to be **normal goods**, which means that demand for them will rise when household income rises. If income elasticity is negative, the commodity is said to be an inferior good since demand for it falls as income rises.

Activity 10 **(20 minutes)**

Complete the table to show the income elasticity for each product.

	Positive elasticity	Zero elasticity	Negative elasticity
White bread	☐	☐	☐
Croissants	☐	☐	☐
Salt	☐	☐	☐
Bars of chocolate	☐	☐	☐
Boxes of Belgian chocolates	☐	☐	☐

We have seen that both prices and incomes may cause people to switch from one product to another. We will now look at the relationship between the demand for one product and the price of another.

3.4 Cross-price elasticity of demand

The way in which the price of one product affects demand for another is measured by the *cross-price elasticity of demand*. The formula is as follows.

$$\frac{\text{Percentage change in the demand for product X}}{\text{Percentage change in the price of product Y}}$$

The result may be positive, zero or negative.

(a) If it is positive, then X and Y are substitutes, like butter (X) and margarine (Y). If the price of margarine goes up, the demand for butter will rise because some people will switch from margarine to butter. A margarine maker would have to consider the sales he would lose in consequence before going ahead with a price rise.

(b) If it is zero, then the products are unrelated. For example, a change in the price of newspapers (Y) is unlikely to affect the demand for holidays (X).

(c) If it is negative, then the goods are **complements**, like tyres (X) and petrol (Y). If the price of petrol goes up, then people will drive less. This means that they will not have to replace their tyres so often, so the demand for tyres will fall.

4 SUPPLY

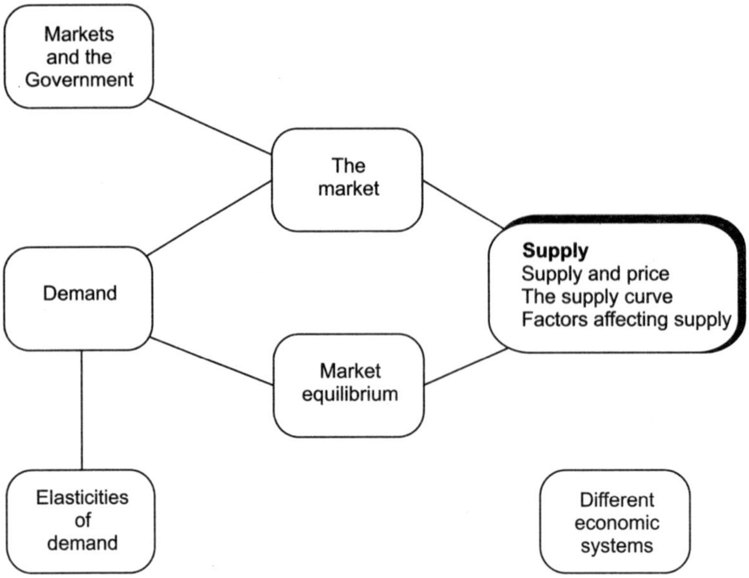

4.1 Supply and price

Definition 

> **Supply** is the quantity of a product that existing or would-be suppliers would want to produce at a given price. As with demand, supply is measured per time period – for example 17,000 kg of cheese a week, or 50,000 tonnes of coal a year.

As you would expect, supply depends largely on price. The higher the price that a product can be sold for, the more of it businesses will be willing to supply. The quantity of the product on offer may change because existing businesses choose to increase production as the selling price rises, or because new businesses are attracted into the market by the prospect of good profits. Conversely, if the price falls, some businesses will reduce their production and others will go out of business altogether (voluntarily or because they have gone bust).

Although a high price will attract producers, it will put consumers off. Thus a high price may result in over-supply, which means that more is being produced than consumers want. One possible result is a price war, with each producer cutting his price in the hope of attracting enough consumers. In the very short-term, one producer (probably the first one to reduce the price) may benefit, but other producers will follow suit in order to win back some customers. The result is that all producers will suffer. In the long-term, some producers may choose to withdraw, reducing supply and solving the problem, but before that happens some producers may run out of cash to pay their bills and be forced into liquidation. This is what happened in the package holiday business when Intasun, one of the three largest tour operators, went out of business.

Activity 11 **(20 minutes)**

The retail grocery industry suffers from some over-supply. Some major supermarkets have specifically avoided using price as a weapon to beat their competitors in the fight for customers. How have they avoided this? What would happen if they decided to compete aggressively on price?

As with demand, we must distinguish between the total market supply and the individual business' supply.

(a) The total market supply is the total quantity that all firms in the market would want to supply at a given price.

(b) An individual business's supply is the quantity which that business would want to supply to the market at a given price.

We will sometimes find a business charging prices which are higher than those charged by other businesses in the same market, that is non-market prices. There may be many reasons why this is so. Here are two.

(a) Individual businesses may be able to use marketing, and particularly brand names, to ensure that even if they charge high prices, they can still get customers. Thus for example, Marks & Spencer can charge more than the major supermarkets for many foods, because people associate the St Michael brand with high quality.

(b) Reciprocal buying may occur, in order to maintain good business links. For example a manufacturer of computer chips may buy computers from important customers even if there are cheaper alternatives available elsewhere. Reciprocal buying may also take place between members of the same group of companies.

4.2 The supply curve

We can draw up a supply schedule and supply curve:

(a) For an individual supplier, or
(b) For all suppliers together

A supply curve is constructed in the same way as a demand curve (from a schedule of quantities supplied at different prices), but it shows the quantity suppliers are willing to produce at each price. It slopes upwards from left to right, because greater quantities will be produced at higher prices.

EXAMPLE

Suppose, for example, that the supply schedule for television sets of a given type is as follows.

Price per unit	*Quantity that suppliers would supply at this price*
£	Units
100	10,000
150	20,000
300	30,000
500	40,000

The relationship between output and price is shown as a supply curve in Figure 2.4.

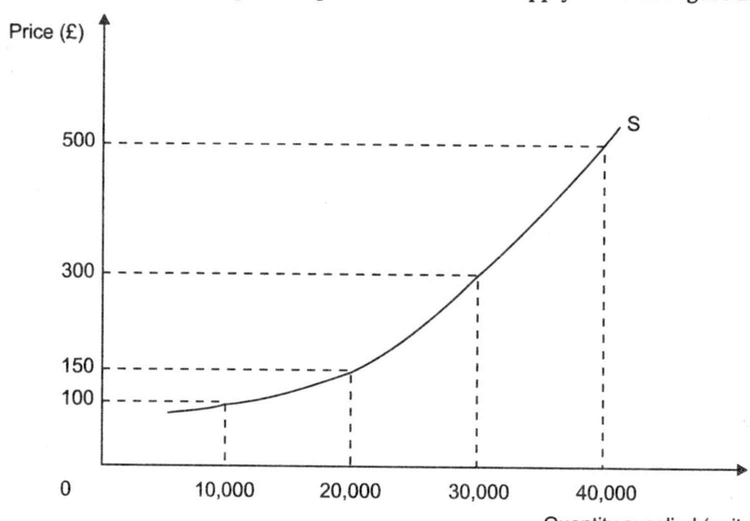

Figure 2.4: A supply curve

In the next section we look at the main factors that affect supply. Some of these are similar to those that affect demand.

4.3 Factors affecting supply

The quantity supplied of a good depends both on the market selling price and on the supplier's costs. There are five main factors as follows.

(a) The **price** obtainable for the product.

(b) The **prices of other products**. Increases in the prices of other products would make the supply of a product whose price does not rise less attractive: if other products become more profitable, suppliers will be tempted to switch to producing them, if they are able to. Of course, some products are produced as by-products of others, and a rise in the price of one will then increase the supply of the other. For example, if the price of beef rises, suppliers will decide it is worthwhile to supply beef and the supply of beef will rise. One effect of this will be an increase in the supply of leather.

(c) The **costs of making the product**, including wages, raw materials and the cost of money to run the business (the interest rate). If any of these costs rise, some producers will be put off and will go out of business, reducing the total supply. They may not go out of business entirely, of course. They may simply change to products which are not so affected by the increase in production costs. Thus the jeweller, faced with a sharp rise in the cost of gold, might decide to stop making gold jewellery and switch to silver jewellery instead. (See below on *productivity*, which affects cost.)

(d) **Changes in technology**. Technological developments which reduce costs of production will increase the quantity of a product supplied at a given price.

(e) **Other factors**, such as changes in the weather (very important for agriculture), natural disasters and strikes.

Activity 12 **(5 minutes)**

Think of specific examples of products whose supply has been affected by the following.

(a) The weather
(b) A natural disaster
(c) A strike

Productivity

Definition

Productivity is a measure of the *efficiency* with which output has been produced.

Suppose that an employee is expected to produce three units in every hour that he works. The standard rate of productivity is three units per hour, and one unit is valued at $^1/_3$ of a standard hour of output. If, during one week, the employee makes 126 units in 40 hours of work the following comments can be made.

(a) **Production** in the week is 126 units.

(b) **Productivity** is a relative measure of the hours actually taken and the hours that should have been taken to make the output.

(i)	*Either*, 126 units should take	42 hours
	But did take	40 hours
	Productivity ratio = 42/40 × 100% =	105%
(ii)	*Or alternatively*, in 40 hours, he should make (× 3)	120 units
	But did make	126 units
	Productivity ratio = 126/120 × 100% =	105%

A **productivity ratio** greater than 100% indicates that actual efficiency is better than the expected or 'standard' level of efficiency

Management will wish to **plan** and **control** both production levels and labour productivity.

(a) Production levels can be raised as follows.

  (i) Working overtime
  (ii) Hiring extra staff
  (iii) Sub-contracting some work to an outside firm
  (iv) Managing the work force so as to achieve more output.

(b) Production levels can be reduced as follows.

  (i) Cancelling overtime
  (ii) Laying off staff

(c) Productivity, if improved, will enable a company to achieve its production targets in fewer hours of work, and therefore at a lower cost.

Labour cost control is largely concerned with **productivity**. Rising wage rates have increased automation, which in turn has improved productivity and reduced costs.

The supply curve and changing supply conditions

The supply curve shows how the quantity supplied will change in response to a change in price, provided that all other conditions affecting supply remain unchanged (the *ceteris paribus* assumption which we also made in connection with demand). If supply conditions (such as the prices of other products, costs of production or changes in technology) alter, a different supply curve must be drawn. In other words, a change in price will cause a shift along the supply curve, which we call a change in the quantity supplied. A change in supply conditions will cause a shift in the supply curve itself, which we call a change in supply. We are here making the same distinction that we made in the last chapter between a change in the quantity demanded and a change in demand.

Figure 2.5 shows a shift in the supply curve from S_0 to S_1.

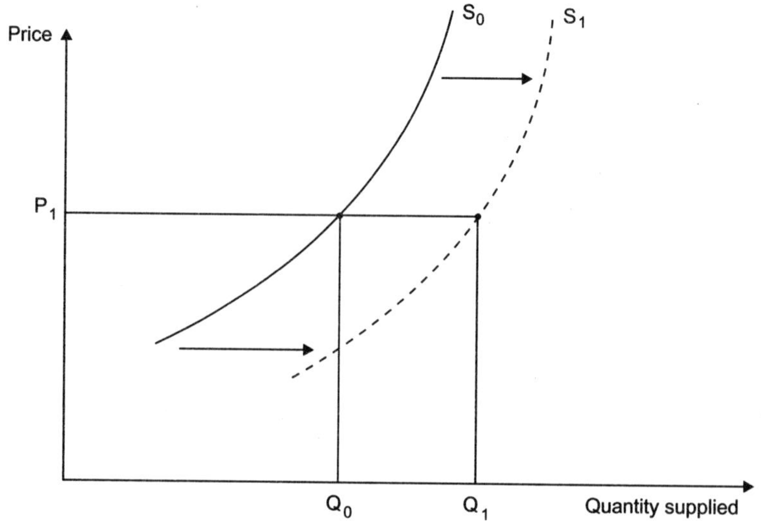

Figure 2.5: A shift in the supply curve

This diagram shows a rightward shift of the curve, representing an expansion of supply. If the market price of the product is P_1, suppliers would be willing to increase supply from Q_0 to Q_1 because of the new conditions of supply. The change in conditions might be:

(a) A fall in costs of production
(b) A fall in the prices of other products
(c) Technological progress

Suppliers need to be able react to changed conditions of supply.

5 THE MARKET EQUILIBRIUM

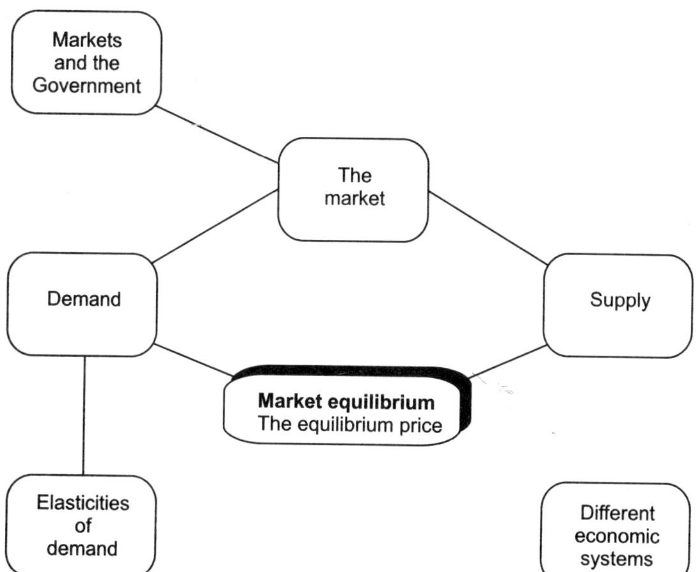

5.1 The equilibrium price

We have seen how, as price rises, more of a product is supplied but less is demanded. If supply exceeds demand, then suppliers will cut their prices in an attempt to win customers. This may lead to some suppliers going out of business, reducing the supply. It may also attract some new consumers, increasing demand. Conversely, if demand exceeds supply, some suppliers will raise their prices. This may put some customers off, reducing demand, and may also attract new suppliers into the market, increasing supply.

The end result of these changes will be that both price and quantity will settle down to equilibrium. The equilibrium is the point at which there are no longer any pressures to change the price or the quantity, because at the equilibrium price suppliers want to sell the same quantity as consumers want to buy.

We can find the equilibrium by showing the supply curve and the demand curve on the same graph: the equilibrium is the point where they cross (Figure 2.6).

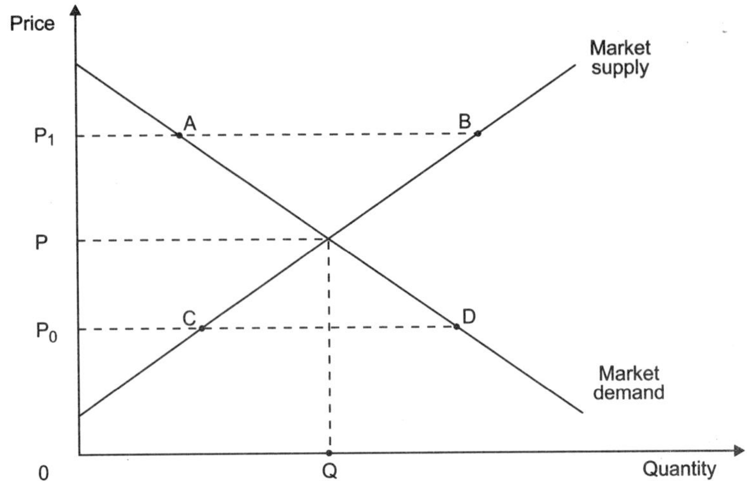

Figure 2.6: Point of equilibrium

At price P the amount that sellers are willing to supply is equal to the amount that customers are willing to buy (Q). There will be no unusual variation in stocks and, so long as nothing else changes, there will be no change in price. Customers will be willing to spend a total of £(P × Q) on buying Q units of the product. Suppliers will supply Q units and earn a revenue of £(P × Q). P is the equilibrium price.

At price P_1 sellers want to supply more than customers want to buy. The gap between supply and demand is represented by the length AB. At price P_0 customers want to buy more than sellers want to supply, and the gap between supply and demand is represented by the length CD. In either case, the market is said to be in disequilibrium. Suppliers and customers will behave as explained above, in order to get to the equilibrium price P and quantity Q.

Supply and demand can be seen working in this simple manner in commodity markets, such as the markets for gold and coffee, where prices move rapidly in response to deals done. In most markets, the mechanism may not be so obvious or efficient. For example, if car manufacturers are selling more cars than they can make, they may not increase prices straightaway because it may take them a while to realise what is happening, and because a sudden price rise may look bad. They may let waiting lists grow for a while instead.

Activity 13 **(20 minutes)**

Use the following supply and demand schedules to draw supply and demand curves on the same graph, and find the equilibrium price and quantity.

Unit price	*Monthly supply*	*Monthly demand*
£	Units	Units
15	60,000	150,000
25	90,000	120,000
35	120,000	90,000
50	150,000	60,000
75	180,000	30,000

We have seen how if a market is in disequilibrium, the price will change, leading the quantity supplied and the quantity demanded to change until they are equal. Once the market is in equilibrium, we can expect it to stay there unless either the supply curve or the demand curve shifts: a change in supply or a change in demand. Either of these could happen for any of the reasons we have already covered, for example a change in consumer tastes or a change in the weather.

Activity 14 **(10 minutes)**

Suggest three conditions which you think determine the supply and demand curves in a retail fruit and vegetable market.

Activity 15 **(15 minutes)**

Customers may be prepared to wait for some products. A sports car company has chosen to supply only a fixed quantity a month which is below the current demand level. A waiting list build up and people sell their places on the list.

How do you think the price of a place on the list is determined? How do you think that the price of a place is related to the price which the company should charge to make demand equal supply? Why does the company not simply charge that price and make more money?

6 ECONOMIC SYSTEMS

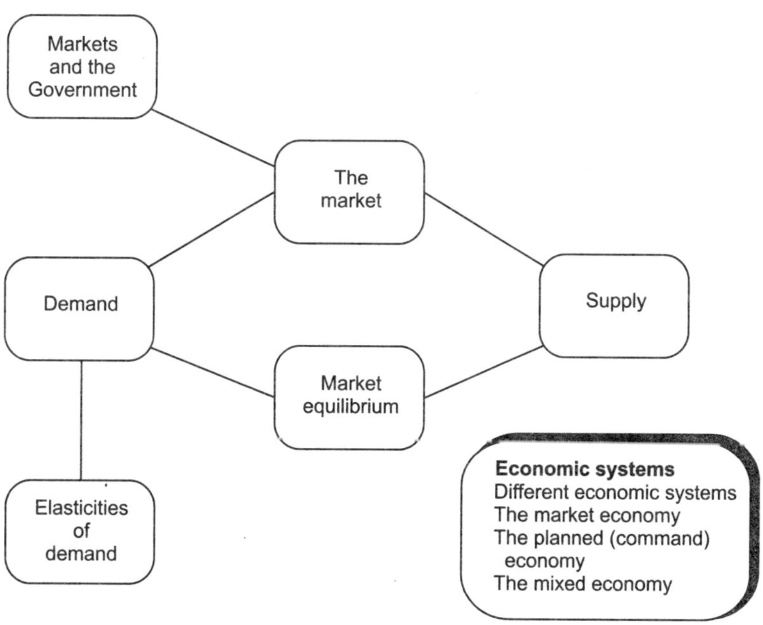

6.1 Different economic systems

In advanced economies there are various ways to deal with the question of scarcity. Different countries use different approaches or types of economic system.

Definitions

Free market economy – sometimes called capitalism. In this type of economy most decisions are taken through the operation of the market mechanism. Supply and demand and the ability to pay influence decision-making. There is very little government intervention in business decision-making.

Command economy – sometimes referred to as state controlled. In this type of economy decisions are taken collectively, usually by central planning committees. The government controls what is produced, how much is produced, the price and who the goods are available to. Decisions are intended to benefit all members of society. Citizens all contribute to the common good of the state. There is a lot of state intervention in this type of economic system.

The **mixed economy**. In this type of economy there is a balance between market forces and state intervention. The view is taken that certain activities need to be regulated by the state whilst others can be left to the influence of the market. A mixed economy usually comprises:

- A free enterprise sector, where economic decisions are based on market forces
- Public ownership and control of key central industries
- Welfare sector to provide a minimum level of medical, social and educational services for all citizens regardless of wealth

Arguments about the merits of markets and planning proceed at different levels. For example, opponents of the market system are often found really to be attacking 'capitalism'. Private ownership of the means of production leads, they claim, to an inequitable distribution of income and wealth and to the exploitation of labour by the capitalist class. That was the basic thinking of *Karl Marx* in his monumental work, *Capital,* published in 1867.

At the other end of the political spectrum there are those who are fundamentally opposed to socialism and planning on the grounds that it restricts the freedom of individuals to choose where they work and invest, what they produce and what they consume.

No country uses one system to the exclusion of the other; every society has a mixed economy and, particularly since the demise of the socialist regimes of Central and Eastern Europe, the argument focuses much more on the **extent** of government intervention in the economy.

6.2 The market economy

The market economy is based upon an ideology that assumes that consumer choice will influence market forces to ensure an optimum allocation of resources with no need for interference from government. The only role for government is to ensure that the 'invisible hand' of market forces is free to operate via the price mechanism or forces of supply and demand.

The assumptions of a free market system include the following.

(a) Firms seek to maximise profits.

(b) Consumers seek the greatest benefit for least cost.

(c) Workers seek to maximise their wage relative to the cost of working.

(d) Individuals are free to make their own decisions, eg where to work, what to buy. Firms are free to choose what to produce and to whom to sell.

(e) The 'price mechanism' decides prices in the free market. Prices rise if there are shortages of a good or service (supply) and fall if there is a surplus.

(f) Prices will also rise if consumers suddenly wish to purchase a large quantity of the good (demand) and fall if the good suddenly becomes unpopular.

(g) If there is an excess of supply then the price of the good will fall. As the price falls consumers will get more benefits for less cost and thus demand more. The price will eventually reach a point at which all the excess supply will have been bought up.

(h) Because of the interaction of supply and demand, prices will fluctuate. But they will always tend towards the 'equilibrium price' where the amount consumers wish to buy equals the amount producers wish to supply.

Using markets to allocate resources is diametrically opposed to planning. In a pure market system decisions about what is produced, how and who gets what is produced are decentralised. All these things would be the outcome of millions of separate individual decisions made by consumers, producers and owners of productive services. As such, of course, they reflect private preferences and interests.

Suppose both food and furniture were bought and sold in free and competitive markets. This means that there is no attempt by the government to influence or regulate the decisions of individual buyers and sellers and that there are large numbers of them with no one sufficiently powerful to 'corner' the market. Essentially, the two product markets will be self-regulating through the medium of prices.

EXAMPLE: INDIRECT DISCRIMINATION

Imagine that we start at point D in Figure 2.7 with production of 14,000 thousand units of food and 13,500 units of furniture. Producers of both goods are making adequate profits at the current prices and buyers too can obtain all they want at those prices. In other words, there is a matching-up of supply and demand.

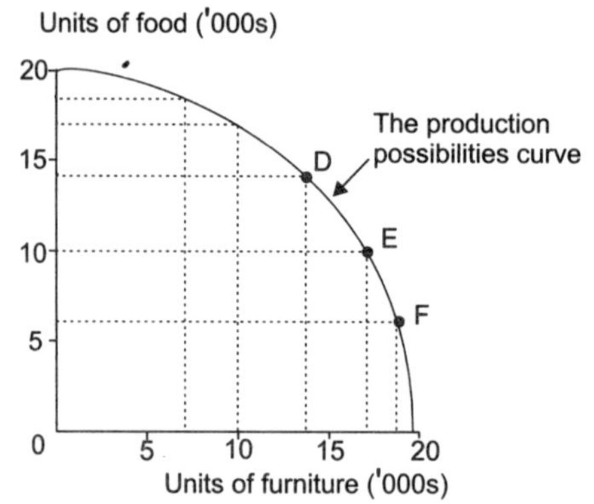

Figure 2.7: Production possibilities curve

Then, suppose more people want to buy furniture. At the current price they now want to buy, say, 18,000 units. We know that, so long as food output stays at 14,000 units, the economy cannot meet this extra demand for furniture; resources will have to be diverted out of food into furniture production along the production possibilities curve. In a market economy the increased demand for furniture will drive up the price, making furniture production more profitable than food. Firms making furniture will therefore expand their output and will attract factors of production out of the food industry by offering higher wages for labour and bigger rents for land. Equally, some food producers might be induced to move into furniture production instead.

The outcome is that the rise in furniture prices will divert resources into furniture and out of food. In the graph production will thus move away from D towards F. Also, the rise in furniture prices will choke off some of the demand to, say, 16,500 units. Point E, in fact, could be a new point of 'equilibrium' at which firms in both industries are again satisfied with their profitability and buyers can obtain precisely what they want of both goods at the new prices.

This adjustment of supply to demand takes place purely as a result of the independent decisions of producers, consumers and resource owners in response to an automatic change in the relative price of food and furniture and with no need for intervention by some external planning agency.

Problems with the market economy – reasons for market failure

According to free market theory, if consumers desire a good they are willing to pay a high price for it, and producers sensing a chance for profit, increase or start production. Thus the allocation of resources and mix of goods available is in accordance with society's wants. But can the invisible hand of supply and demand and producers' desire for profit be relied upon in all instances? Not always.

(a) **Unwillingness on the part of consumers to pay for 'merit goods' or 'public goods'.**

Goods and services provided by the government (or public sector) are called public goods and those by the market system (private sector) **private goods. Merit goods** are goods whose social benefit to the community exceeds their benefit to the individual (you first encountered these terms in Chapter 1). A good example is education. If schools charged the full rate for their services then many families would withhold their children, as they are unable or unwilling to pay. Governments on the whole believe that schooling is beneficial for its people and the economy and therefore steps in.

Public goods and merit goods are mainly provided by the government and are funded through taxation. Expenditure is therefore not at the individual's discretion and not because the objective is socially worthwhile. There may still be unwillingness to find public and merit goods among individuals.

In the price system, people demand and purchase goods and services because they personally wish to consume them. This exclusion principle applies to what are termed '**private goods**'. There is another category of goods – public goods – like defence, law and order, and street-lighting where if they are provided everyone can consume them, ie, the provider does not have the ability to exclude others from consuming them and hence is not able to charge others for their enjoyment of the goods concerned. As a result, it is unlikely that such goods would be produced in a totally free economy. If the State feels that a more substantial provision is socially desirable then it must intervene to ensure an increased supply.

(b) **Willingness on the part of consumers to pay for 'demerit goods'**

The opposite of goods that the government thinks are under-consumed are those that are over-consumed (**de-merit goods**). Governments may wish to intervene to discourage the use of resources in the production of demerit goods such as tobacco because the social costs exceed the private costs. (The private cost means the price at which such goods would be sold in a free market.)

(c) **Inequality of power in the market place**

Resources gravitate to the production of those goods with the highest profit margins that, by implication, are those in greatest demand. However, if the distribution of income and wealth is uneven, those sections of society blessed with the greatest monetary muscle are in a position to outbid others in the determination of prices and, consequently, the allocation of resources. Hence, the pattern of production may not be a reflection of what society as a whole wants produced, but of what the richest elements are able to ensure is produced.

(d) **Barriers restricting entry to the market place and the immobility of factors of production**

The working of the free market depends on an increased demand for a good causing an increase in production, with existing producers raising output levels and new producers entering the market. Given that producers aim to maximise profits they may be tempted to combine with each other to restrict the supply of goods and thus drive up prices and profits. This exploitation of the consumer can also arise when producers take over their competitors, resulting in a similar increase in monopolisation.

Also, in practice, resources do not always move quickly between uses. First, there may be insufficient information available about employment and entrepreneurial opportunities in other sectors of the economy. Second, resources currently being used in one sector may be unsuited for use elsewhere: accountants cannot become solicitors overnight, it requires years of training to qualify for either occupation. By the same token, if there is a surplus in wheat production one year but a shortage of dairy produce, it takes a full growing season for farmers to adjust their supplies. These problems are referred to as friction, or immobility of factors.

(e) **Producers may ignore 'externalities'**

When producers determine the amount they wish to supply, they weigh up the expected benefit from selling the good, ie, price, against the expected cost of production. When they consider the cost of production, they will only consider the *private* cost, ie, the money they have to lay out to produce the good, ignoring any external cost or spill over effect on society, such as increased smoke, noise or congestion. If an activity confers substantial social costs of this sort, the good concerned may be over-supplied from society's point of view. Conversely, some activities may provide net social benefits as a result of 'good' externalities and may thus be underprovided by a market economy.

6.3 The planned (command) economy

A **command economy** is one in which the fundamental economic questions; what, how, and for whom to produce, are answered by reference to state determined priorities rather than the interaction of supply and demand in the market place. It is based on an ideology, which assumes that left alone the market will create an unjust and undesirable allocation of resources; consequently the state must take over the running of the economy and dictate the use of the factors of production.

Usually we associate command economies with socialist countries but they could equally be right-wing dictatorships. At present, the only remaining socialist command economies are North Korea and Cuba.

The state plans at three levels.

(a) At the **macroeconomic** level central authorities decide between allocating resources for (a) current consumption goods that raise living standards in the present, and (b) investment goods that will help build for the future. This answers the 'what to produce' question.

(b) At a **micro** level it plans the output of each industry and firm. Once the level of output is decided calculations can be made to determine the inputs required. For example, if 200 bicycles are needed then the inputs will be 400 wheels, 200 handlebars, 200 chains etc. If 400 wheels are needed then 1,200 steel spokes are required. If 400 spokes are required then 200 metres of steel wire needs to be made. This means that there are thousands of calculations needed just to produce one bicycle. This answers the 'how to produce' question.

(c) It plans the **distribution of output between consumers**. This will depend on a government's aims. In socialist countries the basis of this decision tends to be 'for each according to their needs'. This means that the product of the economy is distributed equitably, eg a family of four would receive more than one person living alone. Goods and services may be given out directly eg flats and houses are allocated to citizens, or some degree of choice may be allowed by paying workers salaries.

In the latter case the state may influence the distribution of these goods or services by setting prices. Goods the authority wishes to encourage are priced cheaply and goods that are to be discouraged are priced more expensively. This answers the 'for whom to produce' question.

Resource allocation decisions are generally made by a central committee, which determines both the target level and composition of output in accordance with a medium-term plan, usually expressed on a five-year timescale. To meet the requirements of the plan, detailed decisions have to be made concerning the resource requirements of each industrial sector. In assessing these, the planners have to predict the impact on all other sectors , for example, a scaling-up of output in certain sectors, to identify any likely resource bottlenecks. To take a simple example, the steel industry requires input of coal equivalent to 50% of its own output. Therefore to double steel output, the coal industry must double the proportion of coal production which is required for steel making. However, the increased output in the steel industry has resource requirement implications elsewhere and a further set of secondary resource requirements can be determined.

In a complete command economy it is possible to guarantee everyone a job. Ostensibly, the elimination of unemployment is a major advantage of planning. However, the corollary of this is that the government will also have to determine the allocation of labour to different occupations. The planners will therefore need to predict the requirements for the many types of skills to fulfil their overall production targets. People will have to be educated and trained appropriately and directed or induced into particular jobs. Restrictions might have to be imposed on individual freedom of choice of jobs and places of work. Finally, the government will have to decide the distribution of income. This is often claimed as another major advantage of planning since, in principle, the national income can be shared out on an equitable basis of what people need rather than on their luck in inheriting wealth or intelligence. The reality, however, is likely to be different as those in power, including the planners, use their influence to secure privileges for themselves.

The main failings of command economies include the following.

(a) **Lack of investment**. The main stimulus to investment is competition; the threat that if you do not improve your product or your production process, your rivals will, and they will take your market share. In East Germany all organisations were state monopolies and the stimulus of competition was absent. While competition led West Germany to develop the Mercedes, the BMW and the Volkswagen, East Germany had a single car maker – Trabant – producing an antiquated and unreliable vehicle which sold for more second hand than it did new because of its enormous waiting list.

(b) **No incentive to productivity**. In free market economies it is necessary to cut costs and raise output per person in order to compete, and those who can achieve this are rewarded. In command economies success is measured not by the maximisation of production but the achievement of targets. There are no rewards for over-filling the plan, only penalties for under-filling it. Accordingly a manager's first task is always to get the target reduced, and then to meet the target whether it is sensible or not. If the plan states your factory should send ten machines a year to the state repair shop, you send ten machines, even if only eight need repair.

(c) **Wastage of resources**. Inevitably, a planned economy needs to divert resources into planning, rather than actually producing. In the USSR *Gosplan,* the state planning organisation, needed to calculate 12 million prices a year, and plan the output of 24 million products. Inefficiency was rife, waste and pollution at alarming levels, the lack of high quality information for the planners and the ability to be able to communicate the plans effectively all led to economic decline and, as the eighties drew to an end, the gap between the wealth and economic power of the West and that of the Soviet Union was rapidly widening.

(d) **Black markets**. Black markets have a way of coming into existence wherever wants are unsatisfied, and if there is a market willing to pay for a good, someone will find a way to supply it. In some parts of Eastern Europe black markets were fairly open affairs.

Activity 16 **(20 minutes)**

Describe the economic problems of planning that have led to its declining popularity as a means of allocating resources.

6.4 The mixed economy

Definition

A **mixed economy** is one which combines elements of both private enterprise, where individuals have the freedom to set up in business in their own right and personally reap the rewards of their enterprise (or suffer the penalties of their mistakes) and intervention, in varying guises, by the state.

In reality no such thing as a 100% planned or 100% free market economy exists. The Western industrialised economies are all mixed, with the governments being involved in economic activity to varying degrees. There is probably no optimum degree of mixture of an economy – it rather depends on the political persuasion of the government and how badly it wishes to correct the drawbacks of the market economy.

There are two broad strategies for governments to pursue – replacing the market or augmenting the market. The three main types of intervention are as follows.

(a) **Provision or prohibition**. Public goods are provided at zero prices to maximise consumption and increase social benefit. Alternatively the worst demerit goods, such as heroin and paedophile literature, may be judged to be so harmful, both to individuals and society, that it is banned.

(b) **Subsidy or taxation**. Merit goods are encouraged by subsidies to increase their consumption. Conversely, some demerit goods are taxed heavily, eg tax on spirits to deter excessive consumption and reduce the social costs. The government also gives public health information at zero prices because there is no incentive for the private sector to do so.

(c) **Regulation**. Price and quantity controls can be used to change production and consumption patterns. Externalities that are bad, eg river pollutants, may be taxed, illegalised or limited by quality/quantity. In contrast, good external benefits, eg home improvements may be subsidised. Regulation has been extensively used in post-war Britain to limit monopolies and cartels. Since 1979 there has been deregulation in many sectors of the British economy.

FOR DISCUSSION

History has shown that command economies always fail. Do you agree?

---

7 MARKETS AND THE GOVERNMENT

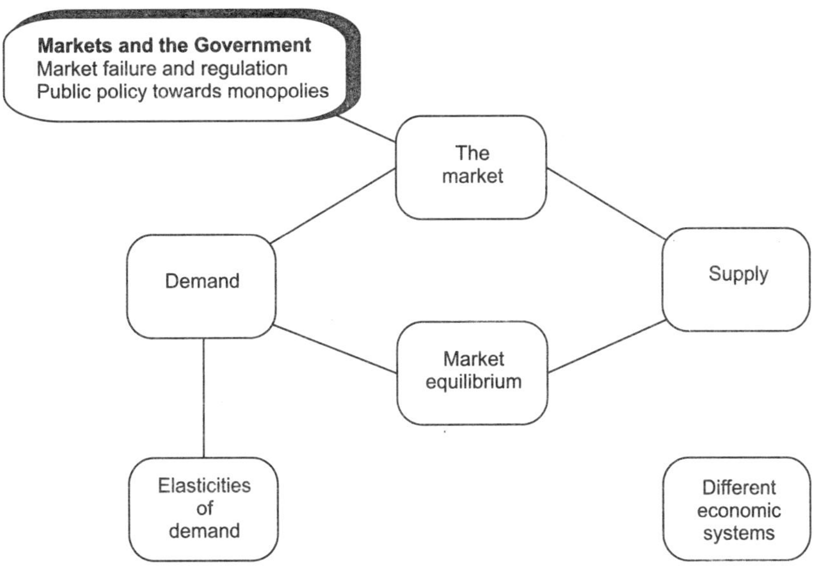

7.1 Market failure and regulation

In response to the existence of market failure, and as an alternative to taxation and public provision of production, the state often resorts to **regulation of economic activity** in a variety of ways. Of the various forms of market failure, the following are the cases where regulation of markets can often be the most appropriate policy response.

Market failure	Regulation
Imperfect competition	Where monopoly power is leading to inefficiency, the state will intervene through controls on, say, prices or profits in order to try to reduce the effects of the monopoly.
Externalities	A possible means of dealing with the problem of external costs and benefits is via some form of regulation. Regulations might include, for example, controls on emissions of pollutants, restrictions on car use in urban areas, the banning of smoking in public buildings, compulsory car insurance and compulsory education.
Imperfect information	Regulation is often the best form of government action whenever informational inadequacies are undermining the efficient operation of private markets. This is particularly so when consumer choice is being distorted. Examples here would include legally enforced product quality/safety standards, consumer protection legislation, the provision of job centres and other means of improving information flows in the labour market and so on.
Equity	The government may also resort to regulation for social reasons for example, legislation to prevent racial, sexual, age or religious discrimination in the labour market; regulation to ensure equal access to goods such as health care, education and housing; minimum wage regulations and equal pay legislation.

Types of regulation

Regulation can be defined as any form of state interference with the operation of the free market. This could involve regulating demand, supply, price, profit, quantity, quality, entry, exit, information, technology, or any other aspect of production and consumption in the market.

EXAMPLE: OLD LABOUR

The UK Labour Government of the 1970s and shadow government of the 1980s had very different objectives to those of today's Governments. 'Old' Labour (socialist) objectives involved giving significant power to workers (through the trade unions) and intervening very directly in markets.

In the 1970s there were a large number of nationalised industries (British Gas; the National Coal Board; British Telecom; British Aerospace; British Leyland and many others) which had been brought together by amalgamating many smaller companies. The Government believed that it could control key resources and create huge economies of scale while employing large numbers of people.

The reality of this policy was rather different, and the majority of countries have moved to a system where state intervention has been reduced. The main reasons for this relate to progress, efficiency and incentives. 'Privatising' a state enterprise opens it up to the 'rigours' of the market (ie it must compete to survive), will in theory lower prices to consumers (competition should encourage efficiency and drive down costs); and offer incentives to those it employs – by sharing in the success of the company, they are more committed to organisational goals.

Privatisation and denationalisation

Definition

> **Privatisation** is the transfer by government of state-owned activities to the private sector.

Privatisation as originally envisaged takes three broad forms.

(a) The **deregulation of industries**, to allow private firms to compete against state owned businesses where they were not allowed to compete before (for example, deregulation of bus and coach services; deregulation of postal services).

(b) **Contracting out** work to private firms, where the work was previously done by government employees – for example, refuse collection or hospital laundry work.

(c) **Transferring the ownership of assets** from the state to private shareholders, for example the denationalisation of British Gas, BT and many other enterprises.

The UK government, like many other governments of developed countries, has carried out a policy of denationalisation. British Gas, BT, the regional water authorities and much of the electricity industry have been among the enterprises which have been privatised. Many of the privatised firms are still subject to the scrutiny of industry regulators (such as OFWAT) to ensure that customers' interests are put before generation of profit.

The Private Finance Initiative

A fourth type of privatisation was established in the UK. The **Private Finance Initiative** (PFI) enlists private sector **capital** and **management expertise** to provide public services at reduced cost to the public sector budget. The capital aspect of the scheme has been particularly welcome to government as it allows for expansion of public services without an increase in the Public Sector Net Cash Requirement. (You will meet this term again in your later studies.)

A typical PFI contract would involve a consortium of private companies that undertakes to design, build, manage and finance a facility such as a school or hospital over a thirty-year period. The consortium accepts the **risk** of the project and takes its **returns** in the form of **periodic fees**. Because they usually involve the provision of services, PFI contracts tend to be very complex in order to ensure that performance standards are rigorously defined.

Claimed advantages of PFI

(a) Government is able to finance improved provision of goods and services for the public without increasing its borrowing.

(b) Risks are transferred to the private sector.

Criticisms of PFI

(a) Public projects will be more expensive because a private company cannot borrow as cheaply as the government.

(b) There is no real transfer of risk, as the government will be forced to support projects that suffer financial failure.

For and against privatisation generally

The following are **possible advantages of privatisation.**

(a) Privatised companies may be **more efficient.**

(b) Denationalisation provides an immediate **source of money** for the government.

(c) Privatisation **reduces bureaucratic and political meddling** in the industries concerned.

(d) Privatised companies may have a **more flexible** and **profit-oriented management culture.**

(e) There is a view that **wider share ownership** should be encouraged. Denationalisation is one method of creating wider share ownership, as the sale of BT, British Gas and some other nationalised industries have shown in the UK.

There are arguments against privatisation too.

(a) State owned industries are more likely to respond to the **public interest,** ahead of the profit motive. For example, state-owned industries are more likely to cross-subsidise unprofitable operations from profitable ones; for example, the Post Office will continue to deliver letters to the Scottish Islands even though the service might be very unprofitable.

(b) Encouraging private competition to state-run industries might be inadvisable where **significant economies of scale** can be achieved by monopoly operations.

(c) Government can **provide capital more cheaply** than the market to industries whose earning potential is low, but which are deemed to be of strategic importance, such as aircraft manufacture. Opponents of this idea suggest that the very idea of a strategic industry is spurious.

(d) State-owned industries can be run in a way that **protects employment,** as was the case in the UK coal industry, for instance. The problem with this is that the taxpayer is effectively **subsidising technical inefficiency.**

(e) Surpluses from state-run industries can be used for **public welfare** rather than private wealth. The problem here is that points (a) and (d) above tend to preclude the creation of surpluses.

7.2 Public policy towards monopolies

Public policy towards monopolies

Monopolies might be harmful or beneficial to the public interest.

(a) A beneficial monopoly is one that succeeds in achieving economies of scale in an industry where the minimum efficiency scale is at a level of production that would mean having to achieve a large share of the total market supply.

(b) A monopoly would be detrimental to the public interest if cost efficiencies are not achieved. *Oliver Williamson* suggested that monopolies might be inefficient if 'market power provides the firm with the opportunity to pursue a variety of other-than-profit objectives'. For example, managers might instead try to maximise sales, or try to maximise their own prestige.

Methods of government control

There are several different ways in which a government can attempt to control monopolies.

(a) It can stop them from developing, or it can break them up once they have been created. Preventing monopolies from being created is the reason why a government might have a public policy on mergers.

(b) It can take them over. Nationalised industries are often government-run monopolies, and central and/or local government also have virtual monopolies in the supply of other services, such as health, the police, education and social services. Government-run monopolies are potentially advantageous.

  (i) They need not have a profit-maximising objective so that the government can decide whether or not to supply a good or service to a household on grounds other than cost or profit.

  (ii) The government can regulate the quality of the good or service provided more easily than if the industry were operated by private firms.

  (iii) Key industries can be protected (for example, health, education).

(c) It can allow monopolies or oligopolies (firms with few competitors) to operate, but try to control their activities in order to protect the consumer. For example, it can try to prohibit the worst forms of restrictive practice, such as price cartels. Or it may set up regulatory 'consumer watchdog' bodies to protect consumers' interests where conditions of natural monopoly apply, as in the privatised utility industries of the UK.

Control over markets can arise by firms eliminating the opposition, either by merging with or taking over rivals or stopping other firms from entering the market. When a single firm controls a big enough share of the market it can begin to behave as a monopolist even though its market share is below 100%.

Several firms could behave as monopolists by agreeing with each other not to compete. This could be done in a variety of ways – for example, by exchanging information, by setting common prices or by splitting up the market into geographical areas and operating only within allocated boundaries.

In a perfect monopoly, there is only one firm that is the sole producer of a good that has no closely competing substitutes, so that the firm controls the supply of the good to the market. The definition of a monopoly in practice is wider than this, because governments seeking to control the growth of monopoly firms will probably choose to regard any firm that acquires a certain share of the market as a potential monopolist.

The Competition Commission in the UK

The Director General of Fair Trading may ask the Competition Commission (CC) to investigate if any firm or group of firms controls 25% or more of the market, or the Secretary of State may do the same if any proposed takeover or merger would create a firm that controlled 25% or more of the market. The CC may also investigate proposed mergers where the assets involved exceed £70 million in value. The Commission will then investigate the proposed merger or takeover and recommend whether or not it should be allowed to proceed.

The **public interest** includes the promotion of competition and the extension of consumer sovereignty, efficiency and enterprise.

The **interpretation** of the public interest leads to conflicts in many cases. For example, actions which enhance competition and consumer sovereignty may conflict with the objective of allowing firms to be large enough to take advantage of competitive conditions in the international economy.

(a) The CC may agree to a merger, but set conditions which are designed to protect consumers, or it may require that some assets be sold by the merged enterprise in order to prevent a dominant market position being established in a particular area of its operations.

(b) The CC will consider whether any **excessive profits** have been made. In the *Roche Products* case for example, a return on capital of 70% was deemed to be evidence of **excessive pricing.** In another case, *Pedigree Petfoods*, 44% was held to be **not excessive**.

(c) The CC will also see whether there is on the face of it a **high degree of interdependence** between a small number of firms. This evidence could be in the form of parallel pricing, predatory pricing or price discriminating policies, sometime prevalent in oligopolies in which there are say only four or five firms.

(d) A firm carrying out 'anti-competitive' practices will not be favoured. An example of this could be 'socially unproductive advertising', where firms in a dominant position have huge advertising spends with the objective of building a barrier over which firms unable to spend a lot on advertising cannot climb. If the merger involves any anti-competitive **distribution policies** such as single supplier agreements, it could be opposed.

(e) The CC will wish to avoid splitting up large companies, thus depriving them of economies of sale. The CC may also throw out applications if they could aggravate unemployment in an area in which unemployment is already significantly high.

(f) The CC will be mindful to protect the needs of merging firms to secure adequate returns for enterprise, risk taking, innovation, improved efficiency research and development, and the need to compete with multinational firms on a global scale. Supernormal profits will not in themselves be a reason to refer merger proposals.

The conflicts between objectives present one problem for the CC, while another problem is that governments may be motivated by other political and economic considerations in deciding whether to adopt CC recommendations.

Enterprise Act 2002

The Enterprise Act 2002 includes provisions to reform UK competition law.

Under this Act, criminal sanctions for operating a cartel are introduced with a maximum penalty of five years in prison for those found guilty of dishonestly operating deliberate agreements to fix prices, share markets, limit production and rig bids.

Chapter roundup

- A market is a situation where buyers and sellers meet.
- A demand schedule shows the quantity demanded of a product at each price level. The figures can be plotted on a graph to give a demand curve.
- There are several factors that determine demand as well as price.
- The responsiveness of the quantity of a product demanded to changes in price is measured by the price elasticity of demand.
- The effect of changes in consumers' income on demand is measured by the income elasticity of demand.
- Demand for a product is affected by changes in the prices of related products. This is measured by the cross-price elasticity of demand.
- A supply schedule shows the quantity supplied of a product at each price level.
- There are several factors that determine supply as well as price.
- Equilibrium is reached when supply is equal to demand.
- Different countries use different types of economic system.
- Governments intervene in markets because of market failure.

Quick quiz

1. What is a market?
2. What is a demand schedule?
3. What does *ceteris paribus* mean?
4. Give examples of complementary products.
5. What is the formula for price elasticity of demand?
6. If a market is in disequilibrium what will market forces do?
7. What is a mixed economy?
8. What is privatisation?

Answers to quick quiz

1. A market is a situation in which potential buyers and potential sellers of a good or service come together for the purpose of exchange.
2. The relationship between quantity demanded and price.
3. Everything else being equal.
4. Cups and saucers, bread and butter.
5. $$\frac{\text{Percentage change in the quantity demanded}}{\text{Percentage change in price}}$$
6. Market forces will move towards equilibrium.
7. A mixed economy is a type of economy where there is a balance between market forces and state intervention.
8. Privatisation is the transfer by government of state-owned activities to the private sector.

Answers to activities

1. Demand is about 4.2 kilos at a price of £3 per kilo, rising to six kilos at the reduced price of £2 per kilo.
2. a = £30 + (100/50 × £3) = £36

   P = 36 – 3Q/50 or Q = (1,800 – 50P)/3

   Check

27 = 36 – 3Q/50	150 = (1,800 – 50P)/3
3Q/50 = 9	50P = 1,800 – 450
Q = 150	P = 27

3. On the face of it the two products should be closely related. They both satisfy the same need, to get the commuter to and from work. There are, however, some big differences. Driving into a city and finding somewhere to park is difficult and stressful. On the other hand, trains only run at set times, which may not be convenient for the commuter. A commuter may not be able to afford the capital outlay for a car at all.

4 Domestic deep freezers and perishable food are complements, because people buy deep freezers to store perishable food. Perishable food may be supplied fresh or ready frozen. If more people have freezers, the demand for frozen produce will rise. The demand for fresh food may fall, but on the other hand it might keep up because people may buy fresh food and freeze it.

5 You may have chosen site A but B is equally possible. They may choose site B. At site B, people will have been in homes longer and may have more money to spend than those who have just taken out large mortgages. However, Site A has high income families but high unemployment in some parts. Site B may have middle income families but no pockets of high unemployment.

6 The company may wish to make substitutes, they know whether it is possible to put up prices without losing too many sales and they may decide to switch to other products.

7 12.5/25 = 0.5

8

Price per kg	*Quantity demanded each month*	*Price elasticity of demand*
£	kg	
1	9.75	0.179
2	8.00	0.437
3	6.25	0.848
4	4.50	1.556
5	2.75	3.182
6	1.00	10.479

9 The demand for petrol is inelastic within a modest range of prices: people will not cut back on their motoring significantly just because petrol goes up by 5p a litre. However, people do cut back when fuel costs soar significantly, and demand is then elastic.

The demand for commuter rail tickets is likely to be inelastic in a city with serious traffic congestion: people have to get to work, and they will pay quite a lot more to do so rather than switch to driving to work. Where car journeys take less time, there may be more substitution and demand for rail tickets will be more elastic.

The demand for holidays in Spain is likely to be elastic: many people go there simply for a beach holiday with reliable sunshine, and will happily switch to Greece or some other country if Spain becomes relatively more expensive.

The demand for Mars bars might be elastic, because there are many alternative chocolate bars which people could switch to. On the other hand, they might stick with Mars bars, because they have been made highly aware of the brand by advertising and because the cost of buying them is only a very small part of income.

10 White bread: negative, because as incomes rise people will switch to more expensive alternatives.

Croissants: positive, because people will only switch to them as incomes rise.

Salt: zero, because income levels are not likely to have much effect on consumption.

Bars of chocolate: as incomes rise, positive at first, because people feel able to indulge in chocolate more often; then negative, as people feel able to afford 'luxury' chocolates.

Boxes of Belgian chocolates: positive, because people will only switch to them as their incomes rise.

11 Some major groups such as Waitrose, Sainsbury and Tesco have avoided using price as a key marketing device even in the face of competitive pressures because they need high profits in order to fund their superstore programmes. Low price ranges are available, but they are not heavily promoted. Marketing strategies have been based upon quality as indicated by the range of goods and services offered to customers. If you compare the range of goods available as recently as five years ago to that available today you will see a marked change. The quality of service offered has improved to include such things as a range of different styles of shopping trolleys, more efficient checkouts, cafés and mother and baby rooms.

A price war would reduce profits. This would cause shareholders to look to invest in sectors offering a better return. They would sell their shares and the share price would fall as supply exceeded demand. A lower share price would affect the ability of companies to raise more capital to fund expansion plans. A loss of profitability could also lead to store closures, job losses and even company failures. This would lessen consumer choice.

12 Agriculture is always vulnerable to weather conditions. The supply of coffee can be disrupted by a frost in Brazil. A natural disaster may affect the availability of transport and accommodation in an affected region and prevent exports of local produce. In the UK there were broccoli shortages as a result of the floods in the South of England in 2007. Strikes can bring the supply of certain products and services to a standstill, eg rail and postal disputes in the UK.

13 Your graph should look like this.

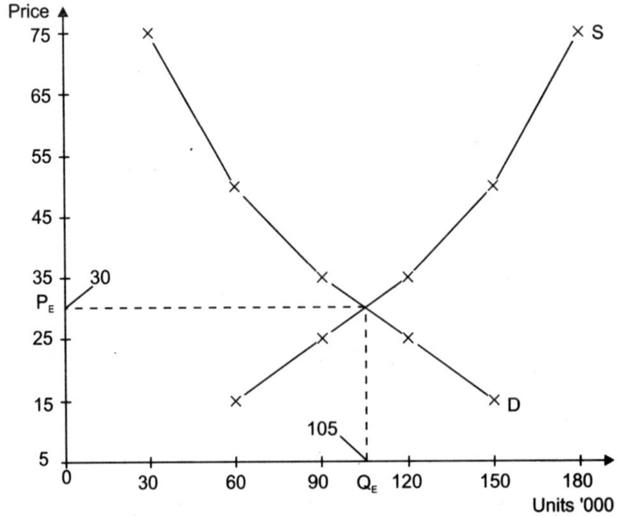

The equilibrium price, P_E is £30 and the market quantity exchanged at this price is Q_E 105,000 units.

14 A retail fruit and vegetable market will probably consist of many small traders, each with their own stall and competing directly with one another.

The conditions determining the supply curve include:

(a) Costs: the main cost to the traders will be the cost of their own wholesale supplies; although there will also be costs of renting a stall and costs of labour

(b) Availability of stalls: the prices that traders can charge will depend to some extent on the number of stalls that there are and the ease with which new traders can acquire stalls and thus enter the market

The conditions determining the demand curve include:

(a) Prices of similar goods in supermarkets

(b) Shopping habits: some people are in the habit of using markets, while others prefer supermarkets

(c) How much money shoppers have to spend

15 The price may be determined by adding a mark-up for profit on to the total costs. If the price was determined by demand it would rise until demand = supply. The company could set prices by demand and make a much higher profit which could be invested in the business. However, it may be that the company feels the cars are good value at the price they are and this is why they are so popular. By making them so desirable they are sure of sales and customers know they can obtain a good second-hand price for them. If the price were to rise, they might not appear such good value.

16 If markets can 'fail' so can central planning. Major problems with the centrally planned economies of Eastern Europe led to a decisive move away from total state control of the economy. Some of the more obvious problems includes the following.

(a) Shortages – where the price mechanism is not used to allocate goods, supply and demand cannot easily be brought into balance. Deliberate under-pricing of consumer goods (to suppress inflation) leads to shortages and queues and to black markets where goods are (illegally) sold at high but market-clearing prices.

(b) Informational problems – the information necessary for central planners to make optimal decisions is beyond the ability of any organisation to process and understand. In any case, enterprise managers have an incentive to suppress information when it is to their advantage. (For example, under-reporting plant capacity means factories are set easier targets to achieve.)

(c) Lack of appropriate incentives – there is no simple relationship between effort and economic reward in many centrally planned economies, where political status may be a more important influence on the living standards of individuals. Ordinary workers, even those with quite high incomes, have been denied access to many goods reserved for the political elite. Even where there exist economic incentives for effort, they may not be appropriate to the economy's needs. For instance, reliance on physical targets (so many shoes, so many tonnes of steel) may mean workers and managers are rewarded for quantity irrespective of quality.

(d) Inefficient use of resources – because wages and the cost of capital equipment do not reflect supply and demand considerations, and because prices of output do not reflect costs of production, managers have little incentive to use resources efficiently. This often results in overstaffing of factories, shops and service industries and the under-utilisation of valuable machinery and plant.

(e) Limitations on personal freedom – control over resource allocation implies controls over employment, and free movement between jobs and between areas is often tightly controlled.

Chapter 3 :

MARKET STRUCTURES, COSTS AND REVENUES

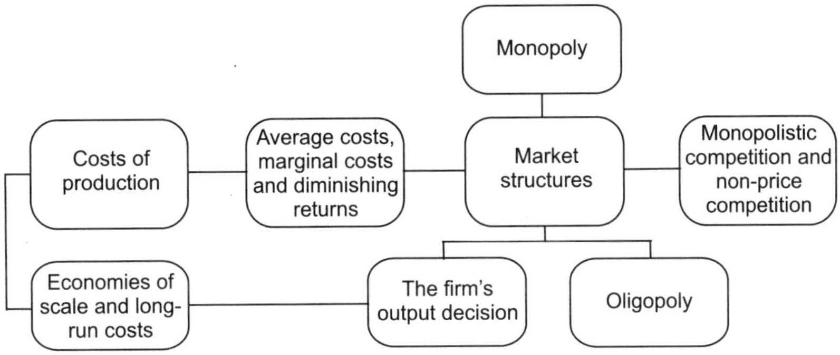

Introduction

In this chapter we shall be looking at the costs and output decisions of an *individual* firm. In other words, we shall look at what the costs of production are for a single firm, and how these are affected by both short-run and long-run factors.

We contrast the concept of *opportunity cost* with financial cost as seen from the accountant's point of view.

We also consider how much output a firm will produce at a given market price.

The aggregate amount of goods supplied by every individual firm adds up to the market supply. By studying an individual firm we are looking at the 'building blocks' of market supply.

We round the chapter off by contrasting perfect competition with models of imperfect competition – monopoly, monopolistic competition and oligopoly.

Your objectives

In this chapter you will learn about:

(a) The behaviour of costs in the short run and the long run

(b) Concepts of costs

(c) Economic profits and opportunity costs

(d) Profit maximisation

(e) Law of diminishing returns

(f) Economies and diseconomies of scale

(g) Perfect competition

(h) Monopoly

(i) Monopolistic competition

(j) Oligopoly

1 COSTS OF PRODUCTION

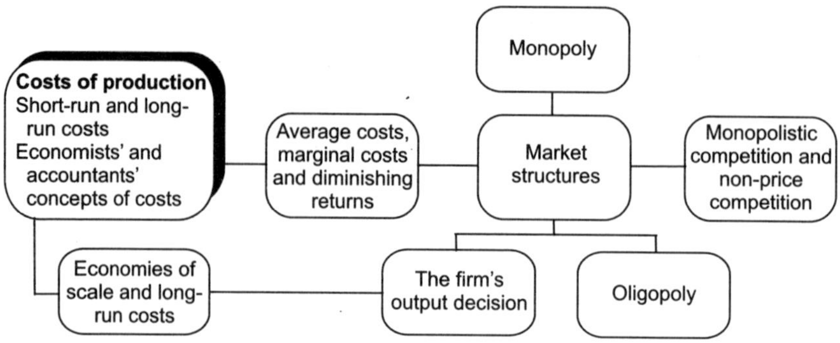

1.1 Short-run and long-run costs

Production is carried out by firms using the factors of production which must be paid or rewarded for their use. The cost of production is the cost of the factors used.

Factor of production	Its cost
Land	Rent
Labour	Wages
Capital	Interest
Enterprise	Normal profit

Notice that normal profit is viewed as a cost. This may seem odd to an accountant, who thinks of profit as the difference between revenue and cost – a point we shall return to later. Any profit earned in excess of the profit needed to reward the entrepreneur (in other words, the **opportunity cost** of keeping the entrepreneur from **going elsewhere**) is called **supernormal, abnormal or excess profit.**

The behaviour of costs is usually analysed under two sets of conditions: the short run and the long run.

Definitions

> The **short-run** is a time period in which the amount of at least one input is fixed. The **long-run** is a period sufficiently long to allow full flexibility in all the inputs used.

Fixed costs and variable costs

In the short-run, certain costs are fixed because the availability of resources is restricted. Decisions must therefore be taken for the short-run within the restriction of having some resources in fixed supply. In the longer-run, however, most costs are variable, because the supply of skilled labour, machinery, buildings and so on can be increased or decreased. Decisions in the long-run are therefore subject to fewer restrictions about resource availability.

Inputs are variable at the decision of management. For example, management might decide to buy more raw materials, hire more labour, start overtime working and so on.

(a) **Labour is usually considered to be variable** in the short run. Inputs which are treated as **fixed** in the short-run will include **capital items,** such as buildings and machinery, for which a significant lead time might be needed before their quantities are changed.

(b) All inputs are variable in the long-run. A decision to change the quantity of an input variable which is fixed in the short-run will involve a change in the **scale of production.**

Short-run costs: total costs, average costs and marginal costs

Let us now turn our attention to short-run costs: the costs of output during a time period in which only some resources of production are variable in availability and the remaining resources of production are fixed in quantity.

Figure 3.1 shows how the various elements of cost vary as output changes.

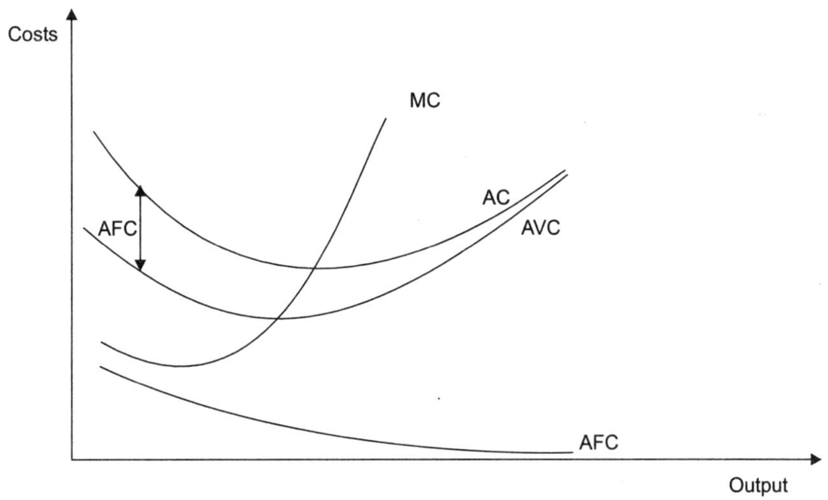

Figure 3.1: Components of a firm's short-run costs

Definitions

- **Total cost** (TC). Total cost for a given level of output comprises total fixed cost (TFC) and total variable cost (TVC).
- **Average cost** (AC). Average cost for a given level of output is simply the total cost divided by the total quantity produced.

  Average cost is made up of an average fixed cost per unit plus an average variable cost per unit.

  $$AC = \frac{TC}{N} = \frac{TFC}{N} + \frac{TVC}{N}$$

  AC = AFC + AVC

  Average fixed cost per unit (AFC) will get smaller as more units (N) are produced. This is because TFC is the same amount regardless of the volume of output, so as N gets bigger, AFC must get smaller.

  Average variable costs per unit (AVC) will change as output volume increases.
- **Marginal cost** (MC). This is the addition to total cost of producing one more unit of output. For example, the marginal cost for a firm of producing the 50th unit of output is the total cost of making the first 50 units minus the total cost of making the first 49 units.

Activity 1 **(15 minutes)**

To test your understanding of these concepts, look at the three definitions given below. Which one(s) of them, if any, correctly describes the marginal cost of producing one extra unit of output?

(a) MC = increase in total cost of production
(b) MC = increase in variable cost of production
(c) MC = increase in average cost of production

EXAMPLE: NUMERICAL ILLUSTRATION

Let us suppose that a firm employs a given amount of capital which is a fixed (invariable) input in the short run: in other words, it is not possible to obtain extra amounts of capital quickly. The firm may combine different amounts of labour with this capital, which we assume to be an input that is variable in the short term. Thus fixed capital and variable labour can be combined to produce different levels of output.

Here is an illustration of the relationship between the different definitions of the firm's costs. (The figures used are hypothetical.)

Units of output	*Total cost*	*Average cost*	*Marginal cost*	
n	*TC*	*AC*	*MC*	
	£	£	£	
1	1.10	1.10	1.10	
2	1.60	0.80	0.50	(1.60 – 1.10)
3	1.75	0.58	0.15	(1.75 – 1.60)
4	2.00	0.50	0.25	(2.00 – 1.75)
5	2.50	0.50	0.50	(2.50 – 2.00)
6	3.12	0.52	0.62	(3.12 – 2.50)
7	3.99	0.57	0.87	(3.99 – 3.12)
8	5.12	0.64	1.13	(5.12 – 3.99)
9	6.30	0.70	1.18	(6.30 – 5.12)
10	8.00	0.80	1.70	(8.00 – 6.30)

(a) *Total cost* is the sum of labour costs plus capital costs, since these are by assumption the only two inputs.

(b) *Average cost* is the cost per unit of output, ie $AC = \frac{TC}{output} = \frac{TC}{n}$

(c) *Marginal cost* is the total cost of producing n units minus the total cost of producing one less unit, ie (n – 1) units.

Note the following points on this set of figures.

(a) *Total cost.* Total costs of production carry on rising as more and more units are produced.

(b) *Average cost.* AC changes as output increases. It starts by falling, reaches a lowest level, and then starts rising again.

(c) *Marginal cost.* The MC of each extra unit of output also changes with each unit produced. It too starts by falling, fairly quickly reaches a lowest level, and then starts rising.

(d) *AC and MC compared.* At lowest levels of output, MC is less than AC. At highest levels of output, though, MC is higher than AC. There is a 'cross-over' point, where MC is exactly equal to AC. In this example, it is at five units of output.

1.2 Economists' and accountants' concepts of cost

As we have already mentioned, to an economist, cost includes an amount for normal profit which is the reward for entrepreneurship. **Normal profit is the opportunity cost of entrepreneurship**, because it is the amount of profit that an entrepreneur could earn elsewhere, and so it is the profit that he must earn to persuade him to keep on with his investment in his current enterprise.

A further feature of **cost accounting** is that costs can be divided into fixed costs and variable costs. Total fixed costs per period are a given amount, regardless of the volume of production and sales. Cost accountants usually assume that the variable cost per unit is a **constant amount,** so that the total **variable cost** of sales is directly proportional to the **volume** of sales.

Economists do not take this approach. In the short run, there are fixed costs and variable costs, but the variable cost of making an extra unit of output need not be the same for each extra unit that is made. As a result, the marginal cost of each extra unit is not constant, either.

Accounting profits consist of sales revenue minus the **explicit costs** of the business. Explicit costs are those which are clearly stated and recorded, for example:

- Materials costs – prices paid to suppliers
- Labour costs – wages paid
- Depreciation costs on fixed assets
- Other expenses, such as rates and building rental

Economic profit consists of sales revenue minus both the explicit costs and the **implicit costs** of the business. Implicit costs are benefits forgone by not using the factors of production in their next most profitable way.

It is a well established principle in accounting and economics that relevant costs for decision-making purposes are **future costs incurred as a consequence of the decision.** Past or 'sunk' costs are not relevant to our decisions now, because we cannot change them: they have already been incurred. Relevant future costs are the **opportunity costs** of the input resources to be used.

EXAMPLE: ECONOMIC PROFITS AND OPPORTUNITY COSTS

Suppose that a sole trader in 20X7 sells goods worth £200,000. He incurs materials costs of £70,000, hired labour costs of £85,000, and other expenses of £20,000. He has no fixed assets other than the building, on which depreciation is not charged. In accounting terms, his profit would be as follows.

	£	£
Sales		200,000
Materials	70,000	
Labour	85,000	
Other expenses	20,000	
		(175,000)
Profit		25,000

But suppose the buildings he uses in his business could have been put to another use to earn £15,000, and his own labour as business manager could get him a job with a salary of £20,000. The position of the business in economic terms would be as follows.

	£
Sales less explicit costs	25,000
Implicit costs	(35,000)
Loss	(10,000)

In economic terms, the business has made a loss. It would pay the trader to put his buildings and capital to their alternative uses, and employ his own labour another way, working for someone else at a salary of £20,000.

Activity 2 **(20 minutes)**

Wilbur Proffit set up his business one year ago. In that time, his firm has earned total revenue of £160,000, and incurred costs of £125,000, including his own salary of £12,000. Before, he had been a salaried employee of Dead End Ventures Ltd, earning an annual salary of £20,000.

To finance the business, Wilbur had to sell his investment of £200,000 in government securities which earned interest of 10% pa. He used £80,000 of this to buy a warehouse, whose annual commercial rental value would be £11,000 pa. The remaining £120,000 has been used to finance business operations.

Required

Calculate the following.

(a) The accounting profit earned by Wilbur in the last year
(b) The economic profit or loss earned

2 AVERAGE COSTS, MARGINAL COSTS AND DIMINISHING RETURNS

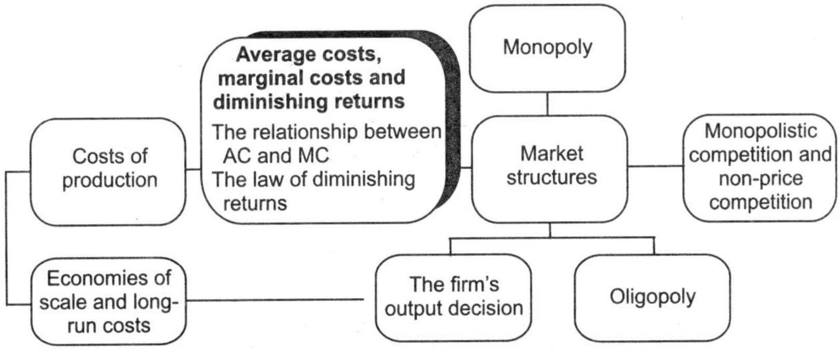

2.1 The relationship between AC and MC

The relationships between average and marginal costs are important.

(a) **When the average cost schedule is rising, the marginal cost will always be higher than the average cost.** If the cost of making one extra unit of output exceeds the average cost of making all the previous units, then making the extra unit will clearly cause an increase in the average unit cost.

(b) In our example in Section 1.1, the average cost schedule rises from six units of output onwards and MC is bigger than AC at all these levels of output (six to ten units).

(c) **When the average cost curve is falling, marginal cost lies below it.** This follows similar logic. If the cost of making an extra unit is less than the average cost of making all the previous units, the effect of making the extra unit must be a reduction in average unit cost. In our example this happens between production of one and four units.

(d) **When the average cost curve is horizontal, marginal cost is equal to it.** In our example, when there are five units of output, the average cost stays at £0.50 and the marginal cost of the fifth unit is also £0.50.

Activity 3 **(10 minutes)**

(a) It is possible for the average total cost curve to be falling while the average variable cost curve is rising. True or false?

(b) Marginal fixed costs per unit will fall as output increases. True or false?

The marginal cost curve always cuts through the average cost curve at the lowest point of the average cost curve (see Figure 3.1 earlier).

The short-run average cost curve (AC in Figure 3.1) is U-shaped. We now consider why.

Fixed costs per unit of output, ie average fixed costs, will fall as the level of output rises. Thus if fixed costs are £10,000 and we make 10,000 units, the average fixed cost (AFC) will be £1 per unit. If output increases to 12,500 units the AFC will fall to 80p (10,000 ÷ 12,500) and if output increases to 15,000 units, the AFC will fall again to 67p (10,000 ÷ 15,000), and so on. Spreading fixed costs over a larger amount of output is a major reason why (short-run) average costs per unit fall as output increases.

Variable costs are made up from the cost of the factors of production whose use can be varied in the short-run – for example, wages, fuel bills and raw material purchases. **Total variable costs therefore vary with output in the short-run as well as in the long-run.**

(a) The accountant's assumption about short-run variable costs is that **up to a certain level of output, the variable cost per unit is more or less constant** (eg wages costs and materials costs per unit of output are unchanged). If the average fixed cost per unit is falling as output rises and the average variable cost per unit is constant, it follows that the average total cost per unit will be falling too as output increases.

(b) However, there are other reasons for the initial fall in average total cost. The first are the effects of the **division of labour** and **specialisation**. Imagine a small but fully equipped factory, with a variety of machinery and equipment and a workforce of, say, ten. If each person attempts to perform all the operations on a single item, production is likely to be low.

  (i) They will be unable to develop a high level of skill at every one of the jobs.

  (ii) Time will be lost as they move from machine to machine.

  (iii) Individual variability will produce a high rate of defects, perhaps with each person tending to produce different faults.

  (iv) Individuals will work at different rates on different operations: as a result, queues will form at some machines and others will be under-utilised.

  If there is a degree of specialisation, expertise and speed will rise, machines will be run at optimum rates and output will rise. Average costs will therefore fall.

(c) **The second reason is the utilisation of indivisibilities.** If a machine has an output capacity of 100 units per day but is only used to produce 50 units per day, the machinery cost of each of those 50 units will be twice the level it would be if the machine was used to capacity. Operation of a plant below normal output is uneconomical, so there are cost savings as production is increased up to capacity level.

2.2 The law of diminishing returns

Definition

Eventually, as output increases, average costs will tend to rise. The **law of diminishing returns** says that if one or more factors of production are fixed, but the input of another is increased, **the extra output generated by each extra unit of input will eventually begin to fall**. To illustrate using a factory as an example, as more labour is engaged queues start to form at machines; it becomes more difficult to co-ordinate work; machinery starts to break down through over-use and there simply is not enough space to work efficiently.

The law of diminishing returns states that, given the present state of technology, as more units of a variable input factor are added to input factors that are fixed in supply in the short run, the resulting increments to total production will eventually and progressively decline. In other words, as more units of a variable factor (eg labour) are added to a quantity of a fixed factor (eg a hectare of land), there may be some **increasing returns** or **constant returns** as more units of the variable factor (eg labour) are added, but eventually, **diminishing returns** will set in. Putting more people to work on a hectare of land will increase the yield up to a point, but eventually it will be costing more to employ additional labour than is being earned in additional yield. Observation of agriculture is the origin of the law of diminishing returns.

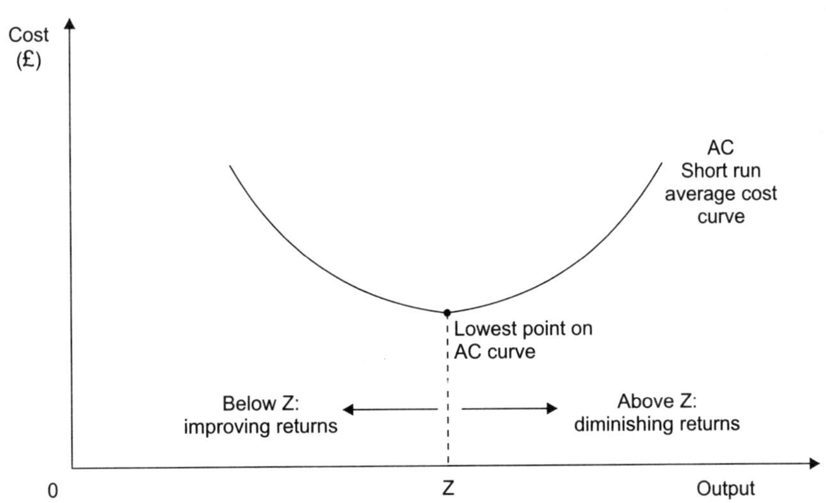

Figure 3.2: U-shaped short-run cost curve and diminishing returns

Remember that this is a short-run phenomenon; at least one factor of production is fixed.

The law of diminishing returns is expressed in production quantities, but it obviously has direct implications for short-run average and marginal **costs**. Resources cost money, and the average and marginal costs of output will depend on the quantities of resources needed to produce the given output.

Activity 4 **(10 minutes)**

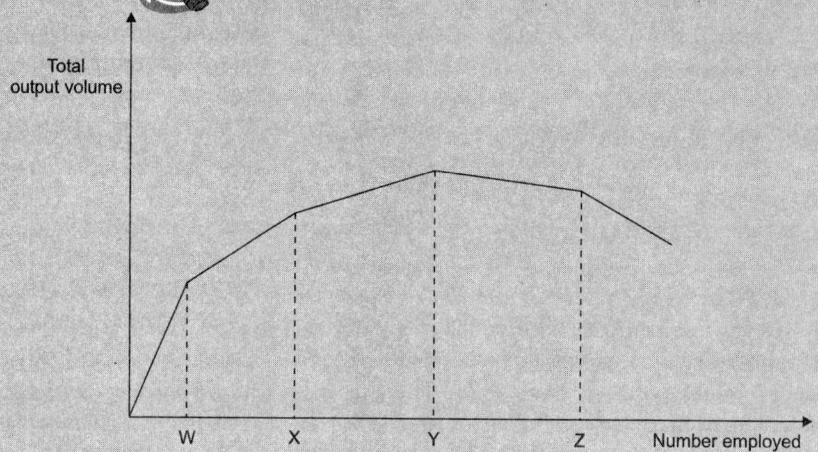

In the figure above, from what level of employment do diminishing returns start to occur?

3 THE FIRM'S OUTPUT DECISION

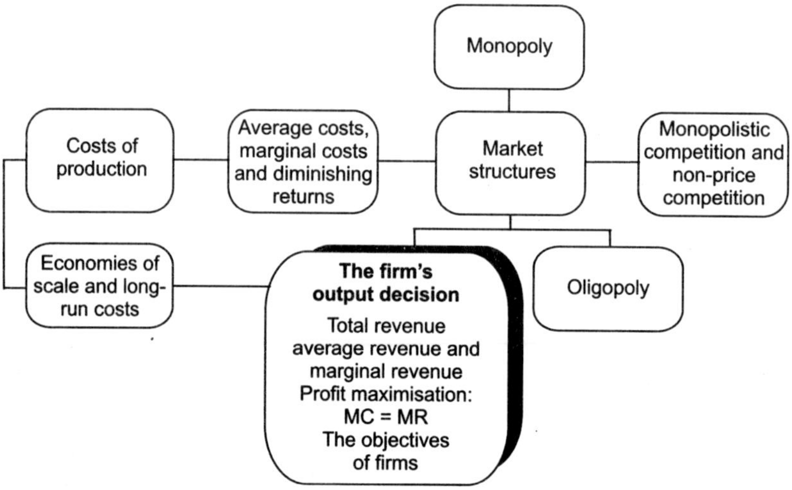

3.1 Total revenue, average revenue and marginal revenue

The assumption of **profit maximisation** provides a basis for beginning to look at the output decisions of individual firms.

Definition

> **Profit** is equal to total revenue minus total cost of any level of output.

There are three aspects of revenue to consider.

(a) **Total revenue** (TR) is the total income obtained from selling a given quantity of output. We can think of this as quantity sold multiplied by the price per unit.

(b) **Average revenue** (AR) we can think of as the price per unit sold.

(c) **Marginal revenue** (MR) is the addition to total revenue earned from the sale of one extra unit of output.

When a firm can sell all its extra output at the same price, the AR 'curve' will be a straight horizontal line on a graph. The **marginal revenue** per unit from selling extra units at a fixed price must be the same as the **average revenue** (see Figure 3.3).

If the price per unit must be cut in order to sell more units, then the marginal revenue per unit obtained from selling extra units will be less than the previous price per unit (see Figure 3.4). In other words, when the AR is falling as more units are sold, the MR must be less than the AR.

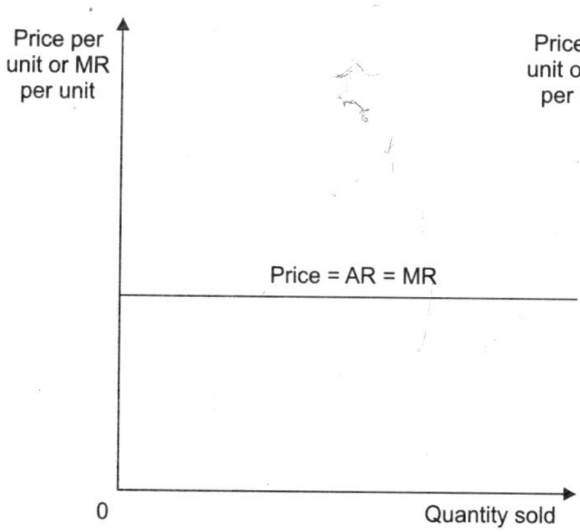

Figure 3.3

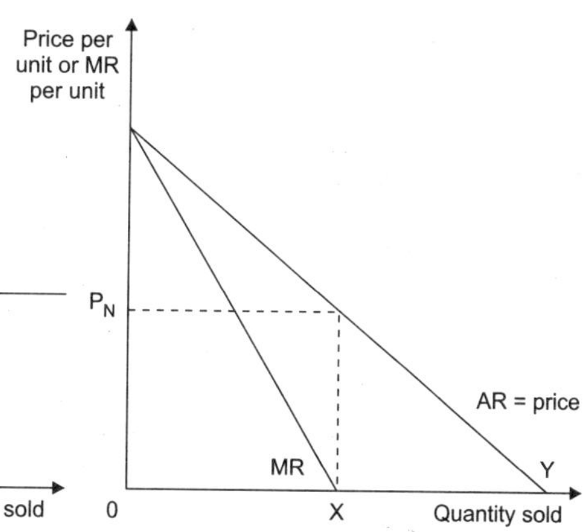

Figure 3.4

In Figure 3.4, with straight line MR and AR curves, the length OX is exactly half of the length OY.

Figure 3.4 is another important diagram and forms the basis of other more detailed illustrations.

Note that in Figure 3.4, at any given level of sales, **all units are sold at the same price**. The firm has to reduce its price to sell more, but the price must be reduced for *all* units sold, not just for the extra units. This is because we are assuming that all output is produced for a single market, where a single price will prevail.

When the price per unit has to be reduced in order to increase the firm's sales the marginal revenue can become negative. This happens in Figure 3.4 at price P_N when a reduction in price does not increase output sufficiently to earn the same total revenue as before. In this situation, demand would be price inelastic.

We have defined profit as TR minus TC.

(a) Figure 3.5 shows, in simplified form, how TR and TC vary with output. As you might expect, TC increases as output rises. The effect of increasing marginal cost (caused by diminishing returns) is that the rise in TC accelerates as output increases and so the TC curve becomes steeper.

(b) Conversely, the gradient of the TR curve reduces as output and sales increase. This is because most firms operate under the conditions illustrated in Figure 3.5. That is to say, they must reduce their prices in order to sell more. The rate of growth of TR therefore declines.

(c) Notice carefully that the vertical axis of Figure 3.6 shows total values whereas in Figures 3.4 and 3.5, it shows value per unit.

(d) Profits are at a maximum where the vertical distance AB between the TC and TR curves is greatest.

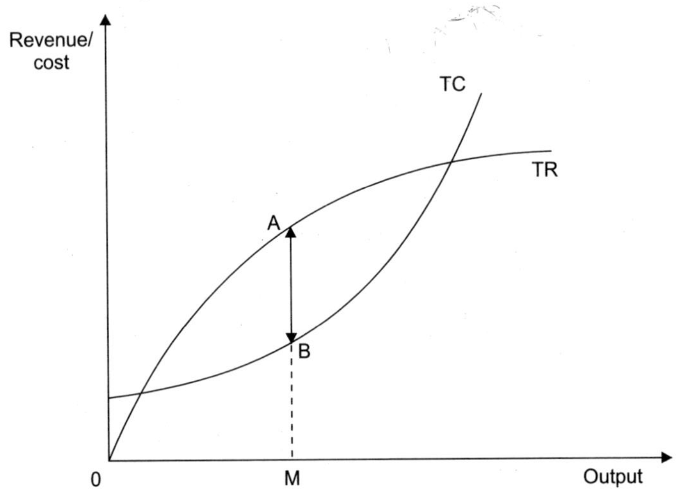

Figure 3.5: Profit maximisation

3.2 Profit maximisation: MC = MR

As a firm produces and sells more units, its total costs will increase and its total revenues will also increase (unless demand is price inelastic and MR has become negative).

(a) Provided that the extra cost of making an extra unit is **less than** the extra revenue obtained from selling it, the firm will increase its profits by making and selling the extra unit.

(b) If the extra cost of making an extra unit of output **exceeds** the extra revenue obtainable from selling it, the firm's profits would be reduced by making and selling the extra unit.

(c) If the extra cost of making an extra unit of output is **exactly equal** to the extra revenue obtainable from selling it, bearing in mind that economic cost includes an amount for normal profit, it will be worth the firm's while to make and sell the extra unit. And since the extra cost of yet another unit would be higher (the law of diminishing returns applies) whereas extra revenue per unit from selling extra units is never higher, the profit-maximising output is reached at this point where MC = MR.

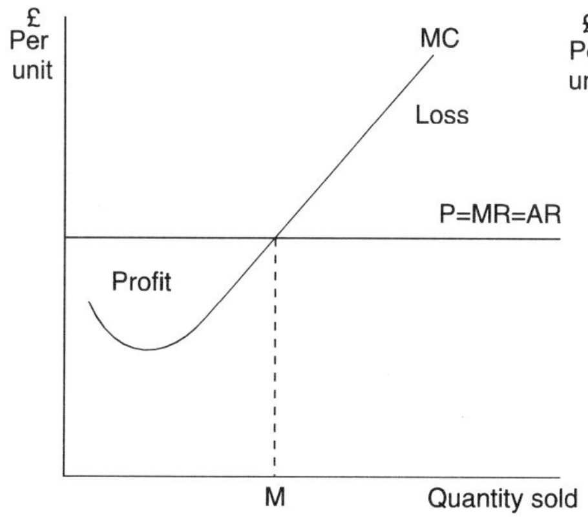

Figure 3.6

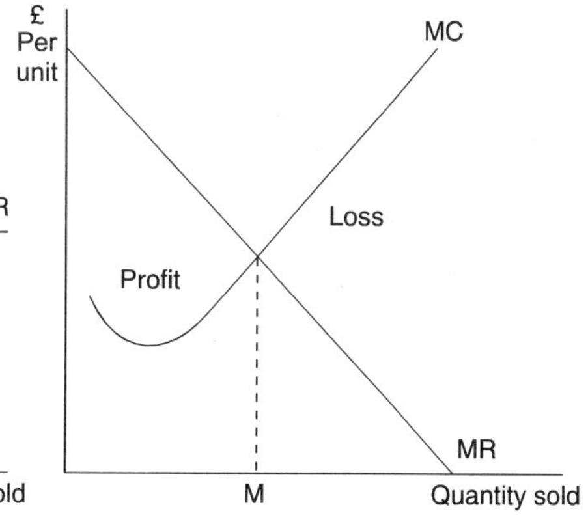

Figure 3.7

(d) Figures 3.6 and 3.7 show the profit maximising output quantity M for the two types of firm shown in Figures 3.3 and 3.4. In both cases, the marginal cost function is as discussed earlier in this chapter. The firm makes a profit on each extra item it produces, albeit a smaller one, until output M is reached. At this level of output the MC and MR curves cross. The addition to total revenue from the next unit is less than the increase in total cost which it causes. This level of output corresponds to the level M shown in Figure 3.5.

In other words, given the objective of profit maximisation there are **three possibilities**.

(a) If MC is less than MR, profits will be increased by making and selling more.

(b) If MC is greater than MR, profits will fall if more units are made and sold, and a profit-maximising firm would not make the extra output.

(c) If MC = MR, the profit-maximising output has been reached, and so this is the output quantity that a profit-maximising firm will decide to supply.

Activity 5 **(20 minutes)**

The following data refer to the revenue and costs of a firm.

Output	*Total revenue*	*Total costs*
	£	£
0	–	110
1	50	140
2	100	162
3	150	175
4	200	180
5	250	185
6	300	194
7	350	229
8	400	269
9	450	325
10	500	425

Required

(a) Calculate the marginal revenue for the firm and state which sort of market it is operating in.

(b) What level of output will the firm aim to produce and what amount of profit will it make at this level?

3.3 The objectives of firms

Although it is convenient for economists to assume that **profit maximisation** is the central objective of firms, we should not overlook the fact that in reality the motives of managers may operate to serve **alternative goals.**

Profit maximisation and other objectives

Profit maximisation is assumed to be the goal of the firm in most economic textbooks and in a great deal of economic theory. This is not universally accepted: the great management thinker *Peter Drucker* said that a business exists 'to create a customer', by which he meant that its activities were best explained in terms of marketing activity. Other writers have suggested that **survival** is the main long-term aim.

Agency theory

Where the management of a business is separated from its ownership by the employment of professional managers, the managers may be considered to be the agents of the owners. **Agency theory** is concerned to analyse the way agents may be expected to behave and how they can be motivated to promote their principals' interest.

In fact, few large businesses are managed by their owners. In the case of larger companies, the shareholders are numerous and unlikely to wish to take part in the management of the company, viewing it simply as a vehicle for investment. Even where ownership is concentrated, large companies tend to be managed mostly by professional managers who have little ownership interest, if any. This **separation of ownership from control** has arisen for several reasons.

(a) Limited liability structure does not give shareholders power to manage the company (unless they are also managers); their influence normally extends only to proposing and voting on resolutions at company meetings.

(b) It is impracticable for a large number of shareholders to exercise managerial powers jointly; to be effective, power must be concentrated.

(c) Many shareholders are not interested in being managers, and are content to employ professional managers so long as their investment prospers.

(d) Many organisations are so large or complex or deal with such advanced technology that they can only be managed effectively by well-qualified professionals

Separation of ownership from control has been a feature of business for over a century and brings with it a recurring problem: the business should be managed so as to promote the economic interest of the shareholders as a body, but the power to manage lies in the hands of people who may use it to promote their own interests. How can the managers be made to favour the interest of the owners rather than their own?

This problem is not confined to the management of companies: it is the general problem of the **agency relationship** and occurs whenever one person (the **principal**) gives another (the **agent**) power to deal with his affairs.

Resolving the agency problem

A common approach to ensuring that company managers act in the owners interest is to offer them **reward incentives** that depend on the achievement of ownership goals. Thus, it is common for Chief Executives' remuneration to depend, at least in part, on satisfactory achievement in such matters as profit and share price. At lower levels, **bonus schemes** can be based on achievement of targets that support good overall performance, such as improved sales or reduced costs. **Profit sharing schemes** that provide shares to large numbers of employees are intended to align their interests with those of the wider body of shareholders.

Unfortunately, these types of approach can be flawed in that they have to be designed – and the designers themselves are in an agency relationship with the owners. Thus executive remuneration schemes have been criticised for emphasising the wrong targets or for setting the targets too low.

Alternative managerial goals

Under the conditions of the agency relationship between owners and managers , the goal of profit maximisation might not fully explain management behaviour, because managers have interests of their own.

Managers will not necessarily make decisions that will maximise profits.

(a) They may have no **personal interests** at stake in the size of profits earned, except in so far as they are accountable to shareholders for the profits they make.

(b) There may be a **lack of competitive pressure** in the market to be efficient, minimise costs and maximise profits, for example where there are few firms in the market.

It has been suggested that price and output decisions will be taken by managers with **managerial objectives** in mind. Rather than seeking to **maximise** profits, managers may choose to achieve a **satisfactory** profit for a firm: this is called **satisficing.** Satisficing is also a common managerial response when there are multiple objectives, such as boosting share price, and achieving revenue growth. Similarly, if directors' remuneration schemes are based on criteria such as growth or corporate social responsibility, then they are unlikely to make the maximisation of profit their sole objective.

Baumol's sales maximisation model

One managerial model of the firm – *Baumol's* **sales maximisation model** – assumes that the firm acts to **maximise sales revenue** rather than profits. The management of a firm might opt for sales revenue maximisation in order to maintain or increase its market share, ensure survival, and discourage competition. Managers benefit personally because of the prestige of running a large and successful company, and also because salaries and other perks are likely to be higher in bigger companies than in smaller ones.

Williamson's management discretion model

Another managerial model – *Williamson's* **management discretion model** – assumes that managers act to further their own interests and so **maximise** their own **utility** (or satisfaction), subject to a minimum profit requirement. Utility may be thought of in terms of prestige, influence and other personal satisfactions. The profit aimed for will not be maximum profit, because of management's wish for expenditure on themselves, their staff and the perquisites of management.

A behavioural theory of the firm

Cyert and March suggested that a firm is an **organisational coalition** of shareholders, managers, employees and customers, with each group having different goals, and so there is a need for **political compromise** in establishing the goals of the firm. Each group must settle for less than it would ideally want to have. Shareholders must settle for less than maximum profits, and managers for less than maximum utility, and so on.

Business objectives and management discretion

There are differing views about the extent to which external pressures modify business objectives and form boundaries to the exercise of management discretion.

Ansoff suggested that a company has a number of **different levels of objectives**.

(a) A **primary economic objective**, aimed at optimising the efficiency and effectiveness of the firm's 'total resource-conversion process'.

(b) **Non-economic, social objectives**, which are secondary and modify management behaviour. These social objectives are the result of interaction among the individual objectives of the differing groups of stakeholders.

(c) **Responsibilities** are obligations which a company undertakes, but which do not form a part of its 'internal guidance or control mechanism'. Responsibilities would include charitable donations and contributions to the life of local communities.

(d) **Boundaries** are rules that restrict management's freedom of action, and include government legislation (on, for instance, pollution levels, health and safety at work, employment protection, redundancy and monopolies) and agreements with trade unions.

FOR DISCUSSION

The Body Shop was a successful independent retailer of cosmetics and toiletries before it was sold to cosmetic giant L'Oreal. Much has been made of its social objectives. To what extent are profit maximiation and social objectives mutually exclusive?

---

4 ECONOMIES OF SCALE AND LONG RUN COSTS

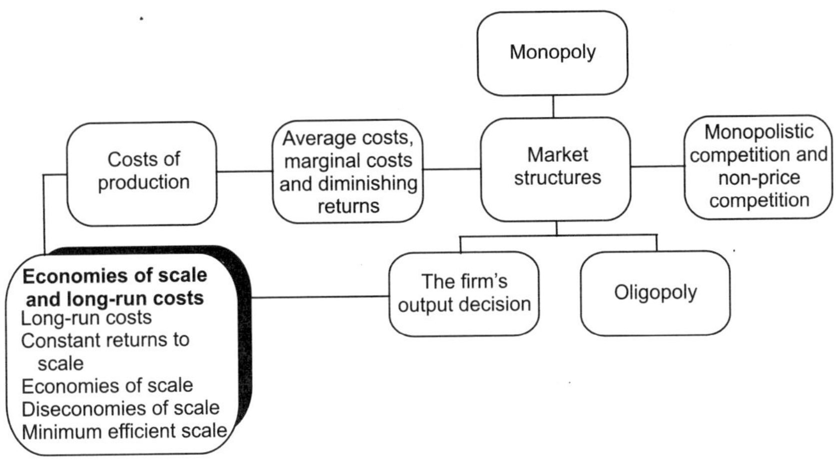

4.1 Long-run costs

We have not yet considered a firm's long-run costs of output. In the long-run, all inputs are variable, so the problems associated with the diminishing returns to variable factors do not arise; in other words, the law of diminishing returns applies only to short-run costs and not to long-run costs. Whereas short-run output decisions are concerned with diminishing returns given fixed factors of production, **long-run output decisions** are concerned with **economies of scale** when all factor inputs are variable.

Output will vary with variations in inputs, such as labour and capital.

(a) If output increases in the **same proportion** as inputs (for example, doubling all inputs doubles output) there are **constant returns to scale.**

(b) If output increases **more than in proportion** to inputs (for example, doubling all inputs trebles output) there are **economies of scale** and in the long run average costs of production will continue to fall as output volume rises.

(c) If output increases **less than in proportion** to inputs (for example, trebling all inputs only doubles output) there are **diseconomies of scale** and in the long run average costs of production will rise as output volume rises.

Returns to scale are, for example, concerned with improvements or declines in productivity **by increasing the scale of production**, for example by mass-producing instead of producing in small batch quantities.

4.2 Constant returns to scale

A feature of constant returns to scale is that **long-run** average costs and marginal costs per unit remain constant. For example:

Output	*Total cost (with constant returns)*	*Average cost per unit*	*Marginal cost per unit*
	£	£	£
1	6	6	6
2	12 (2 × 6)	6	6
3	18 (3 × 6)	6	6
4	24 (4 × 6)	6	6

In the real world, the duplication of all inputs might be impossible if one incorporates qualitative as well as quantitative characteristics in inputs. One such input is entrepreneurship. Doubling the size of the firm does not necessarily double the inputs of organisational and managerial skills, even if the firm does hire extra managers and directors. The input of entrepreneurship might be intangible and indivisible.

4.3 Economies of scale

Definition

Economies of scale: factors which cause average cost to decline in the long run as output increases.

The effect of economies of scale is to shift the whole cost structure downwards and to the right on the graph. A long-run average cost curve (LRAC) can be drawn as the 'envelope' of all the short-run average cost curves (SRAC) of firms producing on different scales of output. The LRAC is tangential to each of the SRAC curves. Figure 3.8 shows the shape of such a long-run average cost curve if there are increasing returns to scale – economies of scale – up to a certain output volume and then constant returns to scale thereafter.

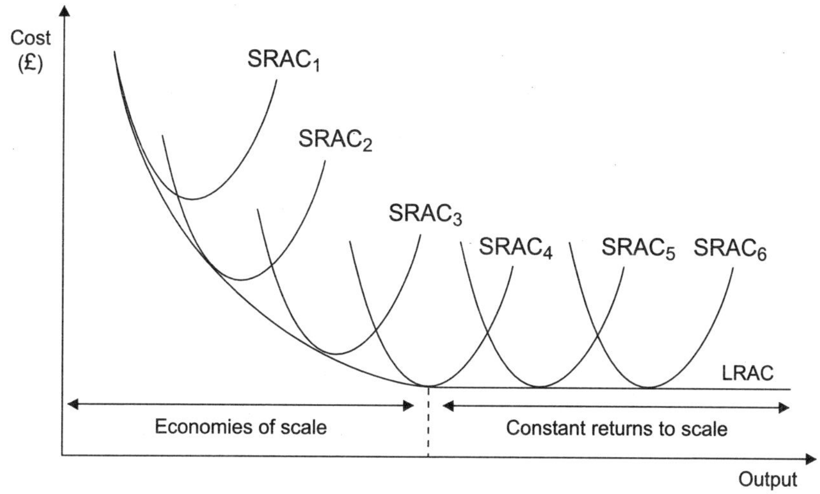

Figure 3.8: Economies of scale

4.4 Diseconomies of scale

It may be that the flat part of the LRAC curve is never reached, or it may be that diseconomies of scale are encountered. Diseconomies of scale might arise when a firm gets so large that it cannot operate efficiently or it is too large to manage efficiently, so that average costs begin to rise.

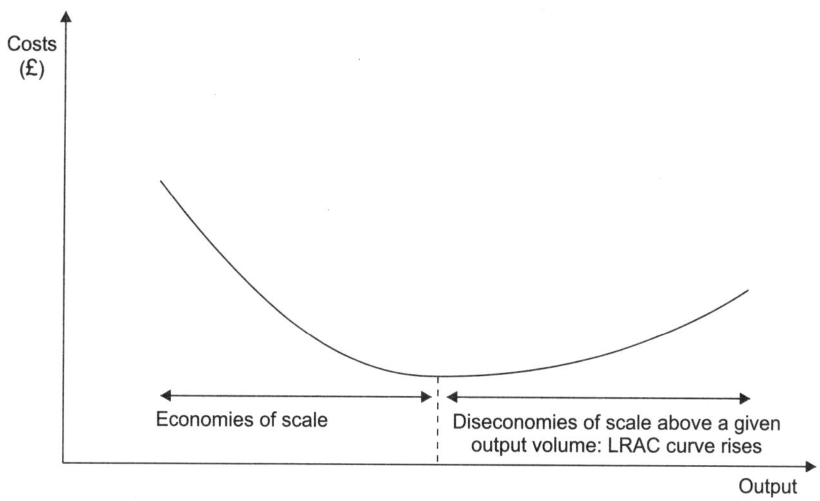

Figure 3.9: Diseconomies of scale

A firm should try to minimise its average costs in the long run, and to do this it ought to try to produce output on a scale where the LRAC curve is at its lowest point. While there are economies of scale, a firm should always be trying to grow.

Reasons for economies of scale

The economies of scale attainable from large scale production fall into two categories.

(a) **Internal economies**: economies **arising within** the firm from the organisation of production

(b) **External economies**: economies attainable by the firm because of the growth of the industry as a whole

Internal economies of scale

Technical economies

Technical economies arise in the production process. They are also called **plant economies of scale** because they depend on the size of the factory or piece of equipment.

Large undertakings can make use of **larger and more specialised machinery**. If smaller undertakings tried to use similar machinery, the costs would be excessive because the machines would become obsolete before their physical life ends (ie their economic life would be shorter than their physical life). Obsolescence is caused by falling demand for the product made on the machine, or by the development of newer and better machines.

Indivisibility of operations

(a) There are operations which must be carried out at the same cost, regardless of whether the business is small or large; these are fixed costs and **average fixed costs always decline as production increases.**

(b) Similarly, other operations' costs vary a little, but not proportionately, with size (ie having 'semi-fixed' costs).

(c) Some operations are not worth considering below a certain level of output (eg advertising campaigns).

Dimensional economies of scale arise from the relationship between the volume of output and the size of equipment (eg storage tanks) needed to hold or process the output. The cost of a container for 10,000 gallons of product will be much less than ten times the cost of a container for just 1,000 gallons.

Commercial or marketing economies

Buying economies may be available, reducing the cost of material purchases through bulk purchase discounts. Similarly, **stockholding** becomes more efficient. The most economic quantities of inventory to hold increases with the scale of operations, but at a lower proportionate rate of increase.

Organisational economies

When the firm is large, centralisation of functions such as administration, Research and Development and marketing may reduce the burden of overheads on individual operating locations.

Financial economies

Large firms may find it easier to obtain loan finance at attractive rates of interest. It is also feasible for them to sell shares to the public via a stock exchange.

Activity 6 **(15 minutes)**

List of reasons given above is not exhaustive. Can you add to it?

External economies of scale

External economies of scale occur as an **industry** grows in size. Here are two examples.

(a) **A large skilled labour force is created** and educational services can be geared towards training new entrants.

(b) **Specialised ancillary industries will develop** to provide components, transport finished goods, trade in by-products, provide special services and so on. For instance, law firms may be set up to specialise in the affairs of the industry.

The effect of size

The extent to which both internal and external economies of scale can be achieved will vary from industry to industry, depending on the conditions in that industry. In other words, big-sized firms are better suited to some industries than others.

(a) **Internal economies of scale** are potentially more significant than external economies to a supplier of a product or service for which there is a large consumer market. It may be necessary for a firm in such an industry to grow to a certain size in order to benefit fully from potential economies of scale, and thereby be cost-competitive and capable of making profits and surviving.

(b) **External economies of scale** are potentially significant to smaller firms who specialise in the ancillary services to a larger industry. For example, the development of a large world-wide industry in drilling for oil and natural gas off-shore has led to the creation of many new specialist supplier firms, making drilling rigs, and various types of equipment. Thus, a specialist firm may benefit more from the market demand created by a large customer industry than from its own internal economies of scale.

Diseconomies of scale

Economic theory predicts that there will be **diseconomies of scale** in the long-run costs of a firm, once the firm gets beyond an ideal size. The main reasons for possible diseconomies of scale are human and behavioural problems of managing a large firm. In a large firm employing many people, with many levels in the hierarchy of management, there may be a number of undesirable effects.

(a) Communicating information and instructions may become difficult.

(b) Chains of command may become excessively long.

(c) Morale and motivation amongst staff may deteriorate.

(d) Senior management may have difficulty in assimilating all the information they need in sufficient detail to make good quality decisions.

There will not usually be **technical** factors producing diseconomies of scale. The technology of higher volume equipment, on the contrary, is more likely to create further economies of scale.

The implication of diseconomies of scale is that companies should achieve a certain size to benefit fully from scale economies, but should not become too big, when cost controls might slacken and organisational inefficiency is likely to develop.

4.5 Minimum efficient scale

Given the idea of economies of scale, it is generally accepted that in any industry, there is a **minimum efficient scale** of production which is necessary for a firm to achieve the full potential economies of scale.

Just what this **minimum efficient scale** (MES) is will vary from industry to industry. In the paint manufacturing industry, for example, it might be necessary to have a 15% share of the market in order to achieve maximum scale economies, whereas in frozen food production, a 25% share of the market might be necessary, and so on. If a firm has a production capacity below the minimum economic scale, its unit costs of production will be higher than the unit costs of its bigger competitors, and so it will not compete successfully and it will make lower profits, or even losses. A profit maximising firm should be attempting to minimise its unit costs, and this means striving to achieve maximum scale economies, which in turn may mean having to grow bigger.

5 MARKET STRUCTURES

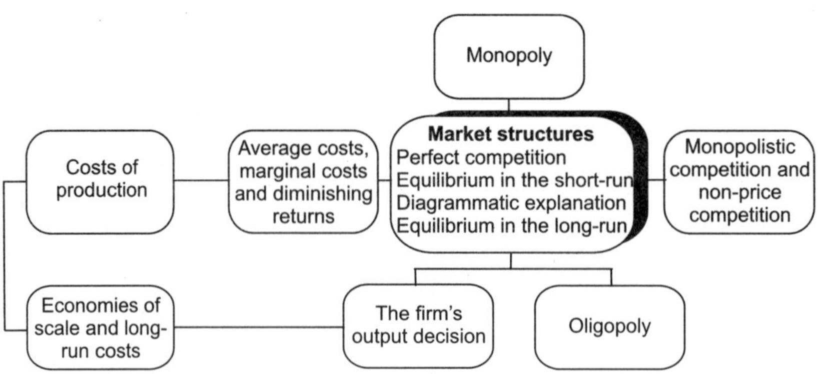

5.1 Perfect competition

Definition

> **Perfect competition** is a theoretical market structure in which no supplier has an advantage over another.

Perfect competition acts as a useful theoretical benchmark.

(a) We can use it to **judge or predict what firms might do** in markets where competition shows some or most of the characteristics of being perfect.

(b) We can also **contrast the behaviour of firms in less perfect markets**. We shall be looking in this chapter and the next at imperfect types of market structure – namely, monopoly, monopolistic competition and oligopoly.

Characteristics of perfect competition

- There are a large number of buyers and sellers in the market.
- Firms are 'price takers', unable to influence the market price individually.
- Producers and consumers act rationally and have the same information.
- The product is homogeneous: one unit of the product is the same as any other unit.
- There is free entry of firms into and free exit of firms out of the market.
- There are no transport costs or information gathering costs.

Activity 7 **(10 minutes)**

Think about the market for a particular product – say motor cars. To what extent is this market 'perfect', as defined by the six criteria above?

5.2 Equilibrium in the short-run

How are price and output determined in the case of the profit-maximising firm operating under conditions of perfect competition in the short-run?

The short-run is a period in which the number of firms in the market is **temporarily fixed.** In these circumstances it is possible for firms to make supernormal profits or losses.

5.3 Diagrammatic explanation

Figure 3.10 shows the cost and demand curves of a firm in the short run making supernormal profits. The demand curve is the horizontal line D_1 at price P_1. The curve is a horizontal line indicating that **the firm has to accept the price that the market as a whole fixes** for it. If the firm were to charge a higher price it would lose all its sales and there is no point charging a lower price as it can sell all its output at the given price. The demand curve is thus also the marginal revenue curve; every new unit sold at price P_1 increases total revenue by an amount P_1.

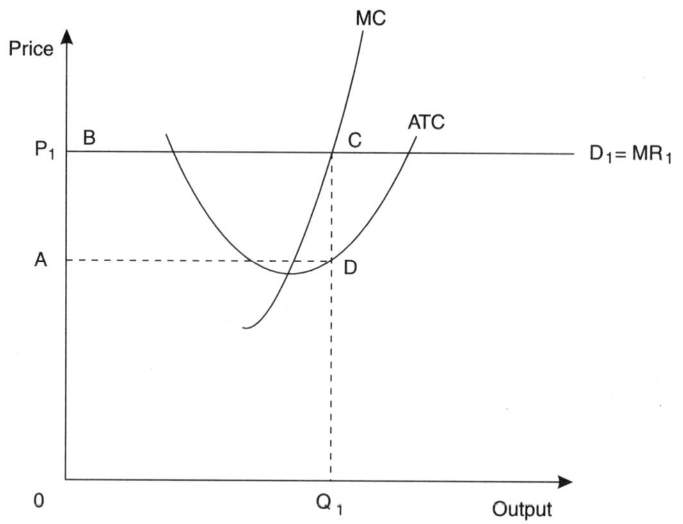

Figure 3.10: Supernormal profits in the short run

Figure 3.10 also shows the average total cost curve (ATC) and the marginal cost curve (MC), with the MC cutting the ATC at the lowest point of the ATC. Given these cost curves and the demand curve D_1, the firm will produce the output Q_1, where the MC curves cuts the MR horizontal curve at the point C. This is the **profit maximising level of output**.

At the output Q_1 the firm is making **supernormal profits** indicated by the rectangle ABCD. This will attract new firms into the industry and the price will be bid down, possibly to price P_2 as shown in Figure 3.11. Here the firm makes a loss shown by the rectangle WXYZ. Once again the firm produces where MC = MR giving an output of Q_2. A firm could choose to do this for a short period so long as revenues covered its **variable** costs, since any excess of revenue **over** variable cost will help to pay the fixed costs. In the long-term, however, revenues must cover both fixed and variable costs in full.

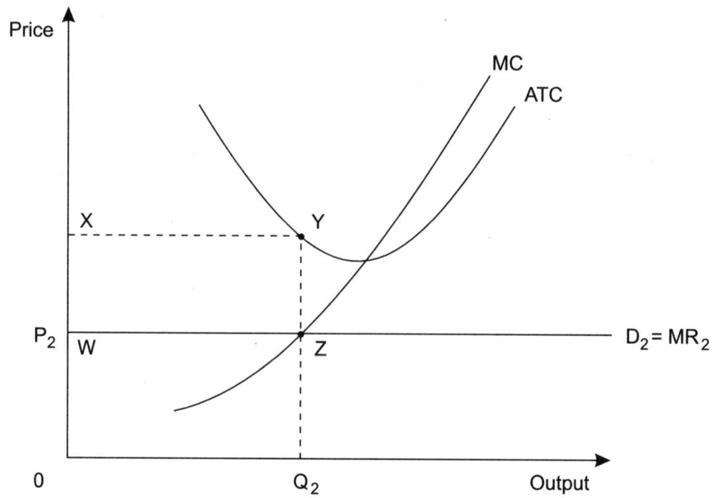

Figure 3.11: Losses in the short run

In the long-run, whenever profits are being made new firms will enter the industry and the price will fall. Similarly, when losses are made firms will leave the industry and the price will rise.

Firms may make less than normal profits in the short-term ($AR < AC$) but will continue production providing $AR > AVC$, ie that price has not fallen below its shutdown level. In the long-run market exit will reduce supply and allow price to rise to where $AC = AR$.

Activity 8 **(5 minutes)**

In conditions of perfect competition, the demand curve for a firm's product is:

(a) Identical to the firm's marginal revenue curve. True or false?
(b) Perfectly inelastic. True or false?

5.4 Equilibrium in the long-run

In a perfectly competitive market in the **long-run**, the firm **cannot influence** the market price and its average revenue curve is horizontal. The firm's average cost curve is U-shaped. The firm is in equilibrium and earns normal profits only (and so no supernormal profits) when the AC curve is at a tangent to the AR curve as shown in Figure 3.13. In other words, long-term equilibrium will exist when supernormal profits and losses are eliminated. There is no incentive for firms to enter or leave the industry and the price will remain at P with the firm making normal profits only.

Note the following points about Figure 3.12.

(a) The market price P is the price which all individual firms in the market must take.

(b) If the firm must accept a given MR (as it must in conditions of perfect competition) and it sets MR = MC, then **the MC curve is in effect the individual firm's supply curve** (Figure 3.13). The **market supply curve** in Figure 3.12 is derived by aggregating the individual supply curves of every firm in the industry.

(c) Consumer surplus is represented by the area to the left of the demand curve above P.

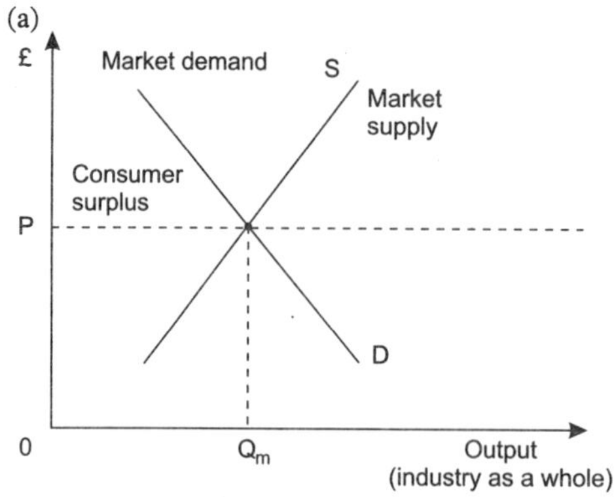

(a) *Market as a whole*

Figure 3.12

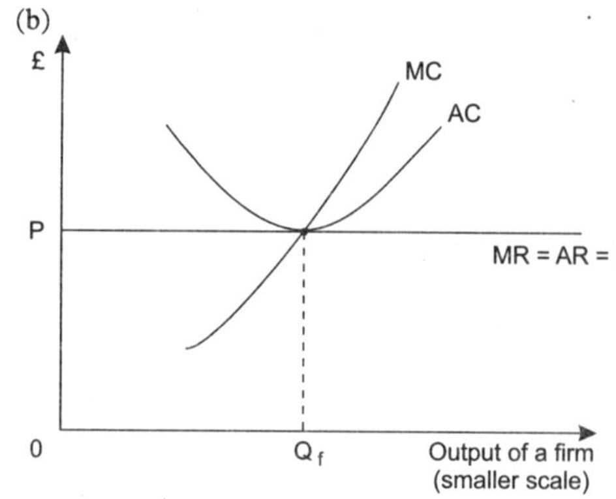

(b) *Individual firm in perfectly competitive market*

Figure 3.13

Long-run equilibrium will, then, occur in the industry when there are no more firms entering or leaving the industry because no new firm thinks it could earn higher profits by entering and no existing firm thinks it could do better by leaving. In the **long-run**, then, all firms in the industry will have MR = MC = AC = AR = price, as in Figure 3.13.

Activity 9 **(5 minutes)**

A perfectly competitive firm will be in equilibrium where price is equal to marginal cost. True or false?

Activity 10 **(10 minutes)**

A small perfectly competitive firm manufactures 200 wooden garden benches each month which it sells for £40 each. The table below shows the firm's costs.

Total variable cost	£7,200
Marginal cost	£40
Total fixed cost	£1,800

What should the firm do in the short-term?

A Increase output
B Cease production
C Lower its price
D Maintain output at its present level

6 MONOPOLY

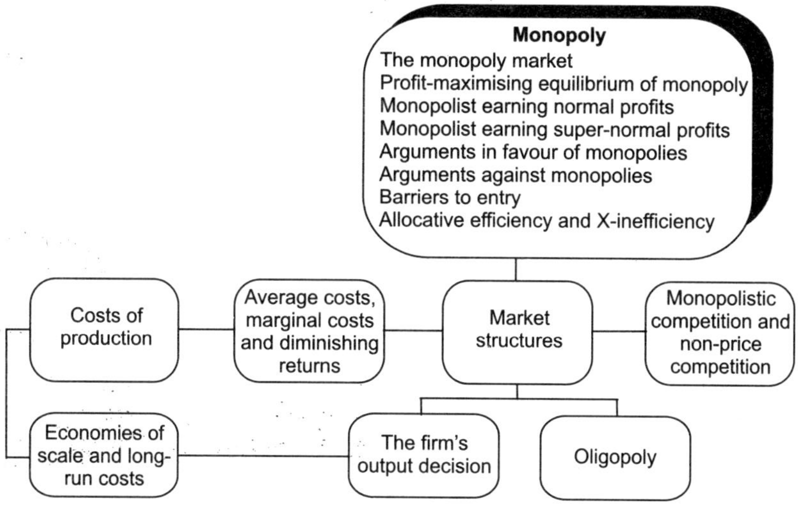

6.1 The monopoly market

Definition

> In a **monopoly**, there is only one firm, the sole producer of a good which has no closely competing substitutes.

A firm's monopolistic position may result from some natural factor which makes it too costly for another firm to enter the industry. For example, in the domestic water supply industry it will normally be too costly for a second firm to lay a second water supply system to compete for part of the business of an existing sole supplier: the sole supplier enjoys a **natural monopoly**. In other cases, a monopoly may be formed by mergers of a number of firms in an industry. However formed, **monopoly can only exist if potential competitors are kept out of the market by barriers to entry** (see below). For a monopoly, the total market supply is identical with the single firm's supply and the average revenue curve in monopoly is the same as the total market demand curve.

If price must be reduced to increase unit sales, average revenue is falling and marginal revenue will always be lower than average revenue; if the monopolist increases output by one unit the price per unit received will fall, so the **extra revenue** generated by the sale of the extra unit of the good is **less** than the **price** of that unit. The monopolist therefore faces a downward sloping AR curve with an MR curve below the AR curve (Figure 3.14).

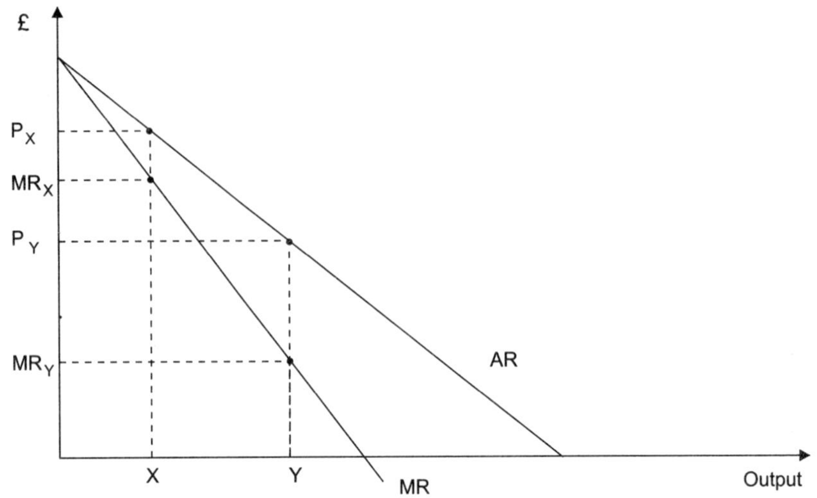

Figure 3.14: A monopolist's average revenue (AR) and marginal revenue (MR) curves

Marginal revenue can be negative. This occurs when demand is price inelastic and, although lowering the price increases sales demand, the volume increase is small and so total revenue falls.

Activity 11 **(5 minutes)**

Study the Figure 3.14 above. At what price and output level would the firm maximise its sales revenue?

It is obviously important that you should understand what the MR and AR (demand) curves are showing us in Figure 3.14.

(a) At output quantity X, the marginal revenue earned from the last unit produced and sold is MR_X, but the price at which all the X units would be sold is P_X. This is found by looking at the price level on the AR curve associated with output X.

(b) Similarly, at output quantity Y, the marginal revenue from the last unit produced and sold is MR_Y, but the price at which all Y units would be sold on the market is, from the AR curve for Y output, P_Y.

6.2 Profit-maximising equilibrium of a monopoly

The condition for profit maximisation is, as we have seen, that marginal revenue should equal marginal cost. This is true for any firm. As long as marginal revenue exceeds marginal cost, an increase in output will add more to revenues than to costs, and therefore increase profits.

6.3 Monopolist earning normal profits

Figure 3.15 shows a monopoly equilibrium where the AC curve touches the AR curve at a tangent, at exactly the same output level where MC = MR. Since AC = AR and AC includes normal profits, the monopolist will be earning normal profits but no super normal profits.

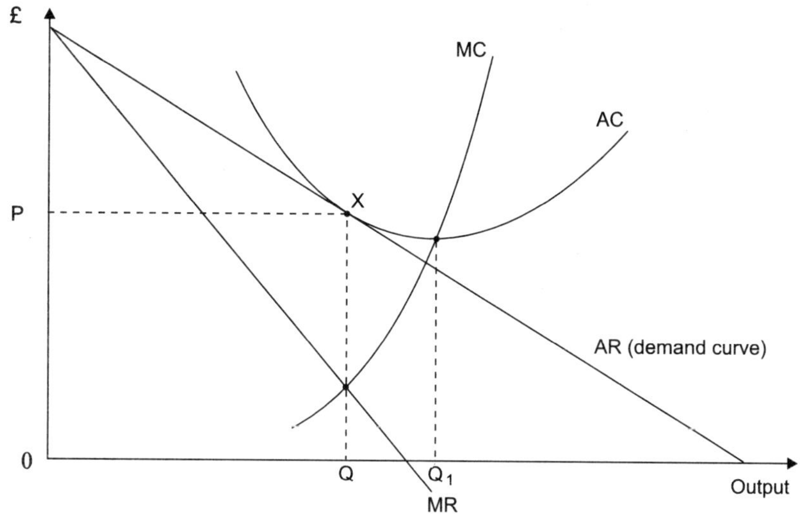

Figure 3.15: Equilibrium of a monopoly firm earning normal profits

In this situation, the monopoly will make a loss by producing at output higher than Q, and so it will have to produce at an output level which is well below the capacity at which its average costs are minimised (output Q_1).

Monopolies are usually able to earn 'monopoly' or supernormal profits in the **long run** as well as the short run, and the situation illustrated in Figure 3.15 will be **rare** for a monopoly, although (as we shall see later) it is a long-run equilibrium situation for firms in the type of market structure known as monopolistic competition.

In perfect competition, a firm should not be able to earn supernormal profits in the long-run because they would be 'competed away' by new entrants to the industry. A monopoly firm can however earn **supernormal profits** in the long-run as well as in the short-run, because there are **barriers to entry** which prevent rivals entering the market.

6.4 Monopolist earning supernormal profits

Figure 3.16 shows the position of the monopolist earning supernormal profits in the short run. SMC is the short-run marginal cost curve and SAC represents short-run average costs.

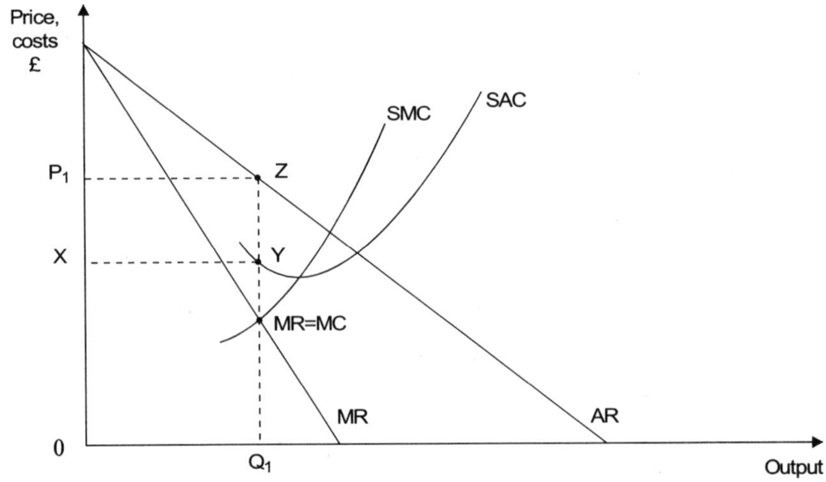

Figure 3.16: Monopolist's short-run equilibrium

In Figure 3.16, the monopolist's profit is maximised at output Q_1, where marginal cost (MC) equals marginal revenue (MR), and the price charged is the average revenue P_1. The monopolist is earning supernormal profits represented by the rectangular area P_1 ZYX.

The monopolist will charge a higher price than a perfectly competitive firm, and produce less output. The output of the monopolist will be at a level where AC is not at a minimum.

In Chapter 1 we looked at market failure – one market failure is monopoly power. We will look at the arguments for and against monopoly in the section below.

6.5 Arguments in favour of monopolies

A firm might need a monopoly share of the market if it is to achieve maximum economies of scale. Economies of scale mean lower unit costs, and lower marginal costs of production. The consumer is likely to benefit from these cost efficiencies through lower prices from the monopoly supplier. Economies of scale shift the firm's cost curves to the right, which means that it will maximise profits at a higher output level, and quite possibly at a **lower selling price** per unit too.

So-called **natural monopolies** exist because of a very high ratio of fixed costs to variable costs. Such a cost structure makes it very likely that significant economies of scale will exist.

Monopolies can afford to spend more on research and development, and are able to exploit innovation and technological progress much better than small firms.

Monopolies may find it easier than small firms to raise new capital on the capital markets, and so they can finance new technology and new products. This may help a country's economy to grow.

Monopolies will make large profits in the short-term, but in many cases their profits will eventually encourage rival firms to break into their market, by developing rival products which might have a better design, better quality or lower price. It can therefore be argued that **temporary monopolies can stimulate competition**, and are in the longer term interests of consumers.

There is also an argument that firms which show entrepreneurial flair and innovation deserve rewarding for the risks they have taken and the new products they have made. They should therefore be rewarded by legal protection of the monopoly through the award of **patent rights**. Monopolies can spend more on research and development and will therefore tend to be innovative.

6.6 Arguments against monopolies

Arguments against monopolies include the following.

(a) The profit-maximising output of a monopolist is likely to be at a price and output level which give it **supernormal profits**. This is a benefit for the monopoly producer at the expense of the consumer.

(b) The profit-maximising output of a monopoly is at a point where **total market output is lower and prices are higher** than they would be if there were a competitive market instead of a monopoly.

(c) **Monopolies do not use resources in the most efficient way possible.** Efficient use of resources can be defined as combining factors of production so as to minimise average unit costs. The profit-maximising output of a monopoly is not where average costs (AC) are minimised (at the lowest point of the firm's AC curve), and so monopolies are not efficient producers.

(d) Monopolists can carry out restrictive practices, such as price discrimination, to increase their supernormal profits.

(e) The higher prices and supernormal profits encourage firms in competitive markets to want to become monopolies, and they can do this by trying to create **product differentiation**, by introducing differences between their own products and the products of rival competitors. These differences might be real product design or quality differences, or imaginary differences created by a brand name and a brand image. This can be beneficial for producers, but at the expense of consumers.

(f) Because they are not threatened by competition and can earn supernormal profits, **monopolies might become slack about cost control**, so that they fail to achieve the lowest unit costs they ought to be capable of. They may also adopt a complacent attitude to innovation, instead of investing in it.

(g) Monopolies might stifle competition, by taking over smaller competitors who try to enter the market or by exploiting barriers to entry against other firms trying to enter the market.

(h) If a monopoly controls a vital resource, it might make decisions which are damaging to the public interest. This is why the government often chooses to put vital industries under state control (for example, health care, the fire service and the nuclear power industry at the time of writing).

(i) There might be diseconomies of scale in a large monopoly firm.

6.7 Barriers to entry

Definition

> **Barriers to entry** are factors which make it difficult for suppliers to enter a market.

Barriers to entry can be classified into several groups.

(a) **Product differentiation barriers.** An existing monopolist or oligopolist would be able to exploit his position as supplier of an established product that the consumer/ customer can be persuaded to believe is better. A new entrant to the market would have to design a better product, or convince customers of the product's qualities, and this might involve spending substantial sums of money on research and development, advertising and sales promotion.

(b) **Absolute cost barriers.** These exist where an existing monopolist or oligopolist has access to cheaper raw material sources or to know-how that the new entrant would not have. This gives the existing monopolist an advantage because his input costs would be cheaper in absolute terms than those of a new entrant.

(c) **Economy of scale barriers.** These exist where the long run average cost curve for firms in the market is downward sloping, and where the minimum level of production needed to achieve the greatest economies of scale is at a high level. New entrants to the market would have to be able to achieve a substantial market share before they could gain full advantage of potential scale economies, and so the existing monopolist would be able to produce its output more cheaply.

(d) The amount of **fixed costs** that a firm would have to sustain, regardless of its market share, could be a significant entry barrier.

(e) **Legal barriers.** These are barriers where a monopoly is fully or partially protected by law. For example, there are some legal monopolies (nationalised industries perhaps) and a company's products might be protected by patent (for example computer hardware or software).

6.8 Allocative inefficiency and X-inefficiency

One of the arguments against monopolies is that they are inefficient compared with firms in conditions of perfect competition because, unlike perfectly competitive firms, they do not produce at an output level that minimises average costs. Instead, they restrict production and raise price to the level that **maximises profit**. As a result, less is produced and consumed than would be the case under perfect competition. The resources that would have been used are diverted elsewhere, to produce things that households actually want less than the monopolist's product. This implies **that monopolies are inefficient in allocating resources**. This is called **allocative inefficiency.**

A second and different criticism of monopolies is that they are wasteful of costs, and spend more than they need to. The lack of competition, perhaps, makes monopolies

complacent, and **resources are not used with maximum efficiency**. This type of over-spending inefficiency is called **X– inefficiency.**

The difference between allocative inefficiency and X-inefficiency is illustrated in Figures 3.17 and 3.18.

(a) **Figure 3.17**. If a monopolist maximises profit at output level Q_2, there is allocative inefficiency because the firm would produce more at lower cost at output Q_1. (This diagram also illustrates **technical** (or productive) inefficiency, which exists when a firm does not achieve the lowest possible cost per unit of output.)

(b) **Figure 3.18**. If a monopolist has an average cost curve AC_1, when it ought to use resources more efficiently and have an average cost curve AC_2, there is X-inefficiency.

(a) *Allocative inefficiency*

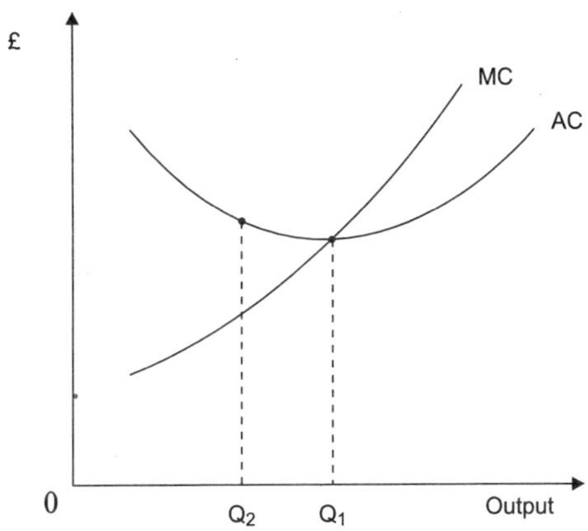

Figure 3.17

(b) *X-inefficiency*

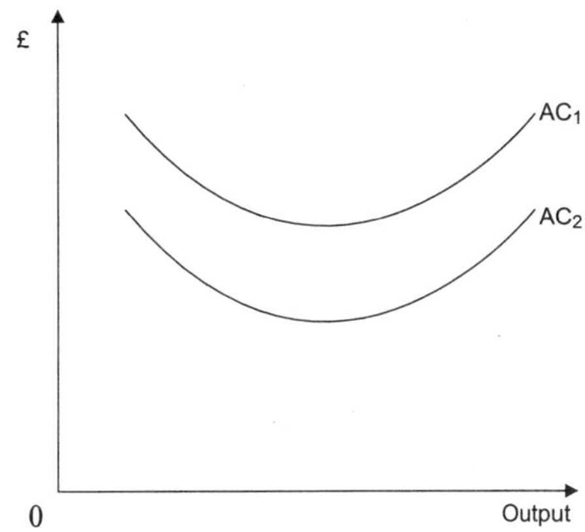

Figure 3.18

All monopolies might be accused of some X-inefficiency, but there has been a view that **state owned monopolies** have a tendency to be more X-inefficient than monopolies which are private companies. This may be because they have different objectives from those of private sector organisations.

7 MONOPOLISTIC COMPETITION AND NON-PRICE COMPETITION

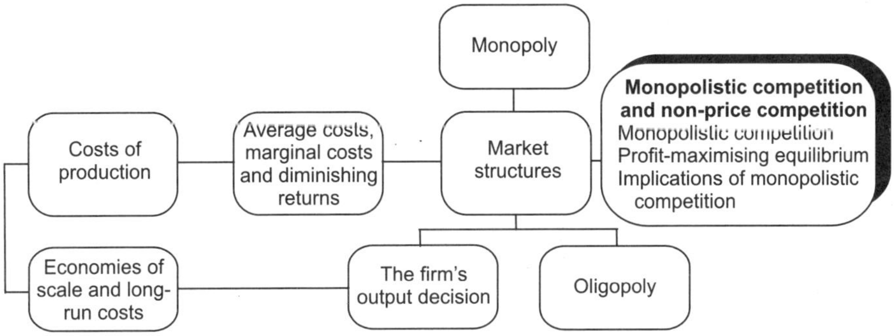

7.1 Monopolistic competition

Definition

> **Monopolistic competition** is a market structure in which firms' products are comparable rather than homogeneous. **Product differentiation** gives the products some market power by acting as a barrier to entry.

A firm operating in conditions of **monopolistic competition** has a downward sloping demand curve like a monopoly (the quantity of output demanded responds to the price at which the firm is prepared to sell). The downward sloping demand curve is possible because of product differentiation created by the firm. Also, unlike a monopoly firm, it is unable to utilise barriers to entry against other firms. (Indeed, the firm already competes with rivals, which can take retaliatory competitive action if the firm makes big profits.)

Firms in monopolistic competition (as well as oligopoly, which we discuss later in this chapter) will **try to avoid competition on price** in order to preserve their position as price maker. They will often resort to **non-price competition** instead, perhaps through advertising and sales promotion, or through **product differentiation**. With product differentiation, suppliers try to create differences between their products and other similar products. These differences might be real (for example, design differences) or largely imaginary and created mainly by advertising and brand image (for example, 'designer label' clothing and washing powders).

> **Activity 12** **(10 minutes)**
>
> See if you can think of other examples of product differentiation.

7.2 Profit-maximising equilibrium

A firm which operates in conditions of monopolistic competition will have a **short-run** equilibrium, in which it can make **supernormal profits** and a **long-run** equilibrium in which it cannot. In the **long-run**, the monopolistic competitor **cannot** earn supernormal profits since there are no **entry barriers**. Its short-run supernormal profits will be **competed away** by new entrants. As a result of competition, the demand curve will move to the left and the firm will eventually be able to achieve normal profits only.

The **short-run equilibrium** for a firm in monopolistic competition is illustrated in Figure 3.19 below. This is the same as the equilibrium of a monopoly firm earning supernormal profits. The firm makes supernormal profits of (P – A) × Q units, shown by the area of the rectangle PQBA.

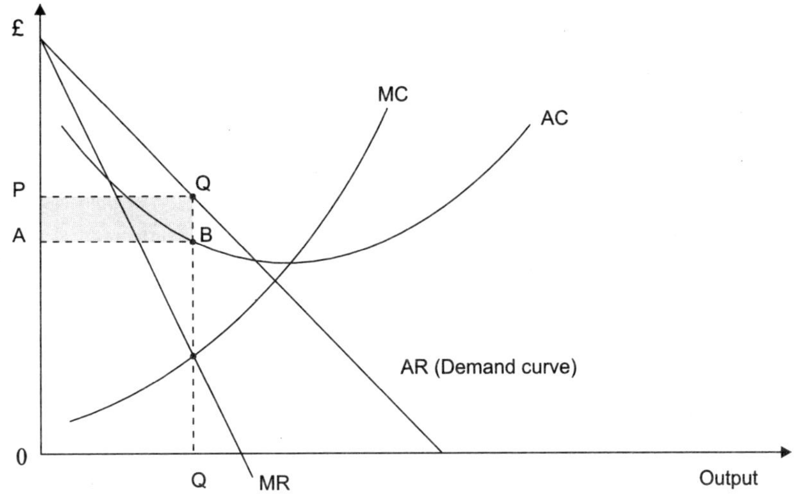

Figure 3.19: The short-run equilibrium of a firm in monopolistic competition

The **long-run equilibrium** for a firm in monopolistic competition is illustrated by Figure 3.20. This is the same as the equilibrium of a monopoly firm which earns no supernormal profits, and so normal profits only.

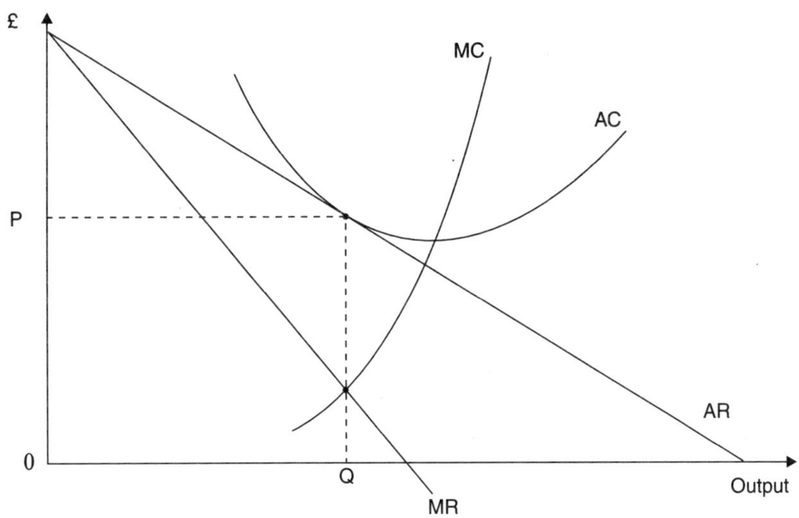

Figure 3.20: The long-run equilibrium of a firm in monopolistic competition

Price is higher and output lower than in perfect competition for the same reasons described earlier when comparing monopoly with perfect competition.

7.3 Implications of monopolistic competition

Because profit-maximising output is lower compared to perfect competition and is at a point where average costs are not minimised, monopolistic competition, like monopoly, is arguably more **wasteful of resources** than perfect competition.

Since firms in monopolistic competition cannot expand their output to the level of minimum average cost output without making a loss, the **excess capacity theorem** predicts that industries marked by monopolistic competition will always tend to have excess capacity. (Check this in Figure 3.20, where profit is maximised at output Q, and output Q is lower than the output level where AC would be minimised.)

It can be argued that it is wasteful to produce a wide variety of differentiated versions of the same product. If a single version of the same product were made, firms might be able to achieve economies of scale with large-volume production (and so shift their cost curves to the right).

Some methods that are used to create product differentiation are a waste of rcsources. Advertising costs are arguably an example of this, although some would argue that promotional activity actually adds utility to a product.

There is reason to argue that monopolistic competition is **not** so wasteful of resources.

(a) Some product differentiation is 'real', where there are technical differences between similar goods from rival firms. Consumers therefore have more to choose from when there is product differentiation. Their requirements are likely to be satisfied better than if there were just a single, basic, low-price good, without any choice.

(b) If product differentiation is entirely imaginary, created by brand image and advertising when the goods of rival firms are exactly the same, rational buyers should opt for the least-cost good anyway.

Activity 13 **(10 minutes)**

Now draw a diagram yourself showing the long-run profit-maximising equilibrium of a firm in monopolistic competition.

Compare your diagram with Figure 3.20 in this chapter.

Note. Monopoly and monopolistic competition are often confused. Make sure you are clear of the difference!

8 OLIGOPOLY

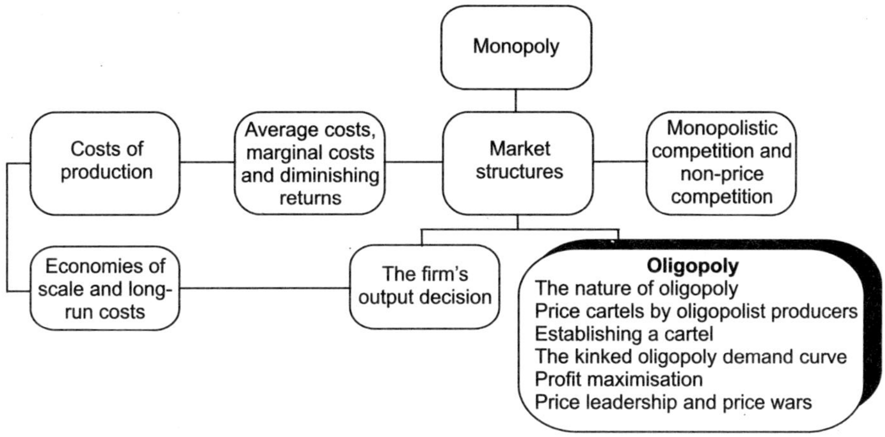

8.1 The nature of oligopoly

Definition

> An **oligopoly** is a market structure where a few large suppliers dominate.

Oligopoly differs from **monopoly** in that there is more than one firm in the market and from **monopolistic competition** because in oligopoly the number of rival firms is small. An oligopoly consisting of only two firms is a **duopoly**.

Oligopolists may produce a homogeneous product (oil, for example) or there may be **product differentiation** (cigarettes and cars, for example).

The essence of oligopoly is that **firms' production decisions are interdependent**. One firm cannot set price and output without considering how its rivals' response will affect its own profits. How an oligopolist will actually set his output and price depends on what assumption firms make about their competitors' behaviour.

8.2 Price cartels by oligopolist producers

A **price cartel** or **price ring** is created when a group of oligopoly firms combine to **agree** on a price at which they will sell their product to the market. The market might be willing to demand more of the product at a lower price, while the cartel agreement attempts to impose a higher price (for higher unit profits) by restricting supply to the market to a level which is consistent with the volume of demand at the price they wish to charge.

Each oligopoly firm could increase its profits if all the big firms in the market charge the same price as a monopolist would, and split the output between them. This is known as **collusion**, which can either be tacit or openly admitted.

Cartels are illegal but difficult to prevent. There might still be price leadership. This occurs when all firms realise that one of them is initiating a price change that will be of benefit to them all, and so follow the leader and change their own price in the same way.

Figure 3.21 shows that in a competitive market, with a market supply curve S_1 and demand curve D, the price would be P_1 and output Q_1. A cartel of producers might agree to fix the market price at P_2, higher than P_1. But to do so, the cartel must also agree to cut market supply from Q_1 to Q_2, and so fix the market supply curve at S_2.

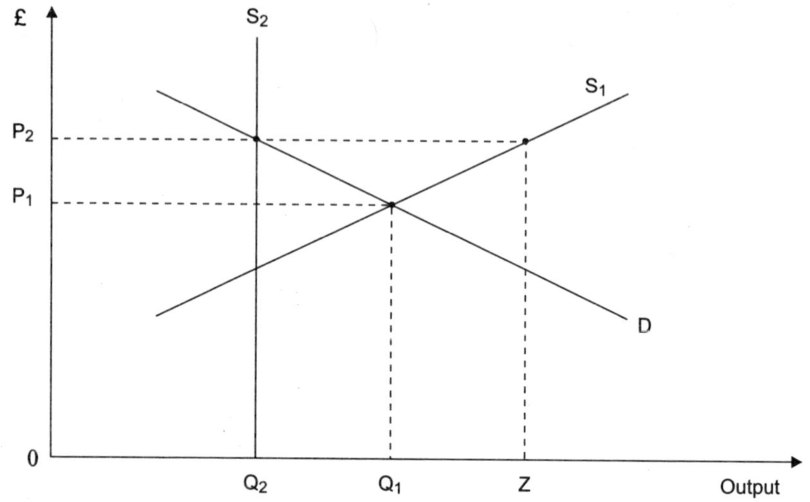

Figure 3.21: Price cartel

8.3 Establishing a cartel

Establishing a cartel depends on two factors.

- The firms in the cartel must be able to control supply to the market.
- The firms must agree on a price and on the output each should produce.

In Figure 3.21, if the market price is fixed at P_2, firms would want to supply output Z in a free market. This cannot be allowed to happen; otherwise market price P_2 could not be sustained.

The main **weakness** with cartels is that each firm is still seeking the best results for itself, and so there is an incentive for an individual firm to break the cartel agreement by secretly increasing its output and selling it at the fixed cartel price. However, if all firms increased their output in this way, the cartel would collapse because the high price could not be sustained without a restricted output, and excess supply on the market would force down the price.

This has been the common experience of the oil-producing countries of the Organisation of Petroleum Exporting Countries. Attempts to agree on a restricted output quota for each country in order to push up oil prices have often broken down because some member countries exceeded their quota, or sold below the cartel's agreed price.

The **success** of a price cartel will depend on several factors.

(a) Whether it consists of most or all of the **producers** of the product.

(b) Whether or not there are **close substitutes** for the product. For example, a price cartel by taxi drivers might lead to a shift in demand for transport services to buses, cars and trains.

(c) The ease with which supply can be **regulated**. In the case of primary commodities, such as wheat, rice, tea and coffee, total supply is dependent on weather conditions and even political events in the producing country.

(d) The **price elasticity** of demand for the product. An attempt to raise prices by cutting output might result in such a large a fall in demand and such a small rise in price that the total income of producers also falls (price elasticity is greater than 1).

(e) Whether producers can agree on their **individual shares** of the total restricted supply to the market. This is often the greatest difficulty of all.

8.4 The kinked oligopoly demand curve

Price cartels do not always exist in an oligopoly market. So how does an oligopoly firm which is **competing** with rival oligopoly firms decide on its price and output level? A feature of oligopoly markets, remember, is that each firm's pricing and output decisions are influenced by what its rivals might do.

When demand conditions are stable, the major problem confronting an oligopolist in fixing his price and output is judging the response of his competitor(s) to the prices he has set. An oligopolist is faced with a downward sloping demand curve, but the nature of the demand curve is dependent on the reactions of his rivals. Any change in price will invite a competitive response. This situation is described by the **kinked oligopoly demand curve** in Figure 3.22, in which the oligopolist is currently charging price P, for output OQ, which is at the kink on the demand curve DD.

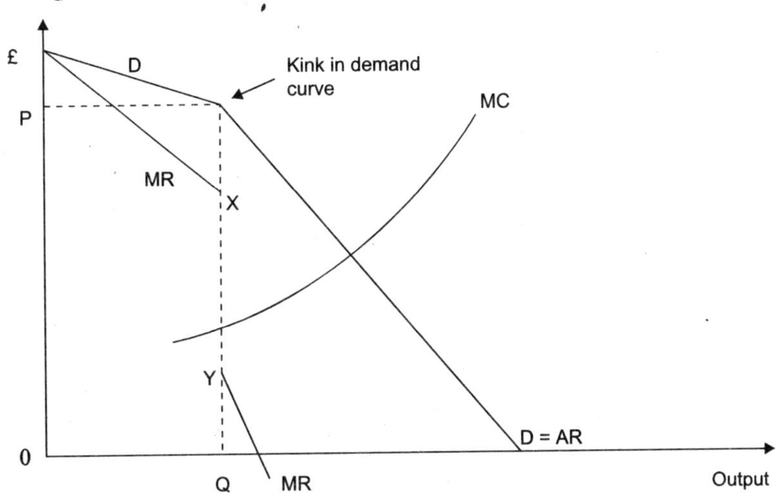

Figure 3.22: Kinked oligopoly demand curve

The kinked demand curve is used to explain how an oligopolist might have to **accept** price stability in the market.

(a) If the oligopolist were to **raise** his prices above P, his competitors would keep their price **lower** and so many consumers would buy from them instead. An example is the difficulty which individual petrol companies have in raising the price of petrol at garages. If competitors do not raise their prices too, the firm usually soon has to restore its prices to their previous level. The demand curve would therefore be quite **elastic** at these higher prices.

(b) If, on the other hand, the oligopolist were to **reduce** his prices below P, competitors would probably **do the same**. Total market demand might rise, but the increase in demand for the oligopolist's products would probably be quite low. Demand is thus likely to be **inelastic** at prices below P hence the kink in the demand curve.

The marginal revenue (MR) curve is **discontinuous** at the output level where there is the kink in the demand curve. The kink in the demand curve explains the nature of the marginal revenue curve MR. At price P, output OQ, the MR curve falls vertically because at higher prices the MR curve corresponds to the more elastic demand curve, and at prices below P the MR curve corresponds to the less elastic demand.

8.5 Profit maximisation

A firm maximises its profit at the point where MR = MC. The more inelastic the demand curve is below price P, the longer the discontinuous portion (XY) of the MR curve will be. There is thus a wide range of possible positions for the MC curve that produce the same profit maximising level of output.

The oligopolist's cost structure can change, with worsening or improved efficiencies, but as long as the MC curve cuts the MR curve through its vertical portion XY, the oligopolist's price and output decision should not alter. Hence, there will be price and output stability, with cost changes for the oligopoly firm, which change its MC curve, not affecting output and price.

Only if marginal costs rise far enough for the MC curve to pass through the MR curve above point X in Figure 3.22 is there a case for raising price, and only if MC falls far enough to pass through the MR curve below point Y is there a case for lowering price.

In general, oligopoly prices will rise only if all the firms follow the lead of a rival in raising its price, so that the AR curve shifts outwards. The kink rises to the new common price level, which is again stable. The converse holds for price falls, perhaps occurring because of technological advance.

8.6 Price leadership and price wars

In oligopoly markets there is a tendency for one firm to set the general industry price, with the other firms following suit. This is called **price leadership**. It is one source of stability in a market where there may be cartels which tend to be undercut, and price wars.

When demand conditions change, the situation becomes somewhat different and price stability might no longer exist.

(a) If total market demand falls, oligopolists might try to increase their share of the market by cutting prices.

(b) Similarly, if one oligopolist begins to lose his share of the market, he might try to restore it by cutting prices. The consequence would be a price war. In the UK in recent years there have been price wars by supermarkets and oil companies in selling petrol, for example. The effect of price wars is usually beneficial to consumers, but they are of limited duration because it is not in the interests of oligopolists to sustain them for long.

Economists sometimes model the strategies of oligopolists and market participants in other types of market structure using **game theory**, which involves examining participants' strategies according to what they stand to gain or lose from each strategy.

Chapter roundup

- It has been emphasised that economic costs are different from accounting costs, and represent the opportunity costs of the factors of production that are used.
- A firm's output decisions should be seen in both the short-run, when some factors of production are fixed and the long-run, when all factors of production can be varied.
- In the short-run, a firm's average cost (SRAC) curve is U-shaped, due to diminishing returns beyond a certain output level. In the short-run, a firm will maximise its profits where MR = MC.
- Profit maximisation is assumed to be the goal of the firm in most economic textbooks, and a great deal of economic theory. Theorists suggest a range of alternative objectives – survival, sales maximisation, managerial ability and non-economic objectives.
- In the long run, a firm's SRAC curve can be shifted, and a firm's minimum achievable average costs at any level of output can be depicted by a long run average cost (LRAC) curve.
- The shape of the LRAC depends on whether there are increasing, constant or decreasing returns to scale. There are some economies of scale, and even if increasing returns to scale are not achievable indefinitely as output rises, up to a certain minimum efficient scale of production (MES) there will be increasing returns to scale. Firms will reduce their average costs by producing on a larger scale up to the MES.
- Whether there are constant or decreasing returns to scale beyond the MES will vary between industries and firms. Similarly, whether economies of scale are significant will vary between industries.
- Technological progress results in shifts in the LRAC, and since technology changes are continual, a firm's LRAC can probably never be 'stabilised' and unchanging for long.
- If economies of scale are significant, there is a strong argument in favour of growth by firms, which might occur either through organic growth (building up the firm's own resources) or through mergers and takeovers.
- Before going on, make sure that you understand two things.
  - The concepts of fixed and variable costs and their relationship to average and marginal costs.
  - The relationships between price, average revenue and marginal revenue

Chapter roundup (continued)

- Perfect competition is a theoretical market structure in which no supplier has an advantage over another.
- In monopoly, there is only one firm, the sole producer of a good which has no closely competing substitutes.
- Monopolistic competition is a market structure in which firms' products are comparable rather than homogeneous. Product differentiation gives the products some market power by acting as a barrier to entry.
- Oligopoly differs from monopoly in that there is more than one firm in the market and from monopolistic competition because in oligopoly the number of rival firms is small.

Quick quiz

1 Explain the distinction between long-run and short-run costs.

2 What is the law of diminishing returns?

3 How can the prices of some products affect the supply of others?

4 Why might there be diseconomies of scale?

5 Which of the following is an example of an external economy of scale?

A Increased wage costs due to falling unemployment in the region.

B The employment of specialist managers by a firm to cope with higher output levels.

C The extension of low-cost telecommunication links to an area of the country not previously served by such links.

D Cheaper finance in recognition of the firm's increased share of the market and therefore its stability.

6 Which of the following cannot be true. In the short-run as output falls?

A Average variable costs falls
B Average total cost falls
C Average fixed cost falls
D Marginal costs falls

7 The tendency for unit costs to fall as output increases in the short run is due to the operation of:

A Economies of scale
B The experience of diminishing marginal returns
C Falling marginal revenue
D Increasing marginal returns

8 Which of the following cannot be true in the short-run as output rises?

A Average variable cost rises
B Average total cost rises
C Average fixed cost rises
D Marginal cost rises

9 Harold Ippoli employs 30 people in his factory which manufactures sweets and puddings. He pays them £5 per hour and they all work maximum hours. To employ one more person he would have to raise the wage rate to £5.50 per hour. If all other costs remain constant, the marginal cost of labour is:

A £20.50
B £15.00
C £5.50
D £0.50

10 Which of the statements below best defines the difference between the short - run and the long-run?

A Labour costs are fixed in the short run and variable in the long-run.

B Economies of scale are present in the long run but not in the short-run.

C At least one factor of production is fixed in the short run but in the long-run it is possible to vary them all.

D None of the factors of production is fixed in the short-run.

11 In what way does monopoly differ from perfect competition?

In a monopoly:

A Products are differentiated
B Supernormal profit is possible
C There are barriers to entry
D There are economies of scale

12 How can a firm in perfect competition make supernormal profits?

13 What is price discrimination?

14 Distinguish allocative inefficiency from X-inefficiency.

15 Which of the following defines the long-run equilibrium position of a firm operating under conditions of perfect competition?

A MC = MR, AC < AR, MR < AR
B MC = MR, AC = AR, MR < AR
C MC > MR, AC = AR, MR = AR
D MC = MR, AC = AR, MR = AR

16 What are the implications of the kinked oligopoly demand curve for price and output by an oligopoly firm?

17 Which of the following statements best describes long run equilibrium in a market where there is monopolistic competition?

A Marginal revenue equals average cost.

B There is excess capacity in the industry since firms reduce average costs by expanding output.

C Firms will earn supernormal profits because price exceeds marginal cost.

D Price equals marginal cost, but does not equal average cost.

18 The oligopolist is *least* likely to compete through:

A Advertising
B Improving product quality
C Cutting price
D Providing incidental services as an 'add-on' to the basic good

Answers to quick quiz

1 The distinction between the short-run and the long-run is that in the long-run, all resource inputs are variable. In the short-run, probably only the amount of labour input is variable.

2 If one or more factors of production are fixed, but the input of another is increased, the extra output generated by each extra unit of input will eventually begin to fall.

3 At the level of output at which marginal cost equals marginal revenue

4 Diseconomies of scale are problems of size and tend to arise when the firm grows so large that it cannot be managed efficiently. Communications may become difficult, motivation may deteriorate because of alienation and senior management may find it difficult to identify the information they need in the vast volumes available.

5 C This is an external economy of scale.

A is a diseconomy of scale.
B is an internal economy of scale.
D is an internal economy of scale.

6 C Factual knowledge. The key to this question is to draw a diagram of the cost curves.

7 D The benefits of specialisation and the division of labour.

Economies of scale only operate in the long-run.
B results in rising unit costs in the short-run.
C is nothing to do with costs.

8 C Average fixed cost must continue to fall as output rises in the short term. This is a mathematical fact.

9 A

	£
Cost of 31 people (at £5.50 per hour)	170.50
Cost of 30 people (at £5.00 per hour)	150.00
Marginal cost	20.50

10 C

11 C All firms produce homogenous goods under perfect competition. Under a monopoly there is only one producer so the concept of product differentiation is not applicable. Both market forms permit supernormal profit (however, only the monopoly can make supernormal profit indefinitely). Economies of scale may be possible under any market form, though they are, perhaps, less likely under perfect competition.

12 In the short-run, the number of firms in the market is fixed. If the prevailing market price is above the lowest point on a firm's average total cost curve, it will make supernormal profits. This will continue until new entrants are attracted into the market and drive the market price down by increasing supply.

13 Price discrimination exists when the same product is sold at different prices in different markets or market segments.

14 A monopolist will produce at a lower level of output and therefore higher cost than a perfectly competitive firm. There is thus inefficient allocation of resources in a monopoly. X-inefficiency arises because monopolists need not control their costs in order to survive. They tend to be inefficient in their use of resources.

15 D For long-run equilibrium, MC = MR = AC = AR.

16 The kinked demand is a descriptive device which illustrates the tendency to stability of prices in oligopoly markets. Oligopolists avoid price competition since a price cut will be matched by competitors and produce little lasting benefit.

17 B For long-run equilibrium in monopolistic competition, MR = MC and AR = AC, but it is *wrong* to say that MR = AC or that AR = MC Since AR = AC, the firm does *not* earn any supernormal profits. There is excess capacity because at the profit-maximising output, average cost is not at a minimum. AC is minimised at a higher output. Since firms could produce more output at a lower AC, we would say that there is excess capacity in the industry.

18 C Oligopoly is usually characterised by price stability, as illustrated by the so-called kinked oligopoly demand curve. Oligopolists are unlikely to cut prices, and are more likely to resort to non-price competition such as advertising and sales promotion, innovation and technical differences and incidental services.

Answers to activities

1 (a) and (b) are correct; (c) is incorrect. An example might help. Suppose a firm has made 100 units of output, and now goes on to produce one more. The costs might be as follows.

	Cost of 100 units	*Cost of 101 units*
	£	£
Total variable cost	200	202
Total fixed cost	100	100
Total cost	300	302
Average cost	£3.00	£2.99

Marginal cost = 302p – 300p = 2p.

2 (a) Accounting profit

	£
Revenue	160,000
Costs	125,000
Profit	35,000

(b) Economic profit

	£	£
Revenue		160,000
Accounting costs	125,000	
Opportunity cost of owner's time – extra salary forgone from alternative employment (20,000 – 12,000)	8,000	
Rental of factory (opportunity cost of £80,000)	11,000	
Opportunity cost of other capital tied up in the business (10% of £120,000)	12,000	
		156,000
Economic profit		4,000

3 (a) True. Average total cost (AC) comprises average fixed cost (AFC) and average variable cost (AVC). AFC falls as output rises, and the fall may be sufficient to outweigh a possible increase in AVC. In such a case, AC will fall while AVC rises.

(b) False. It is *average* fixed costs per unit that fall as output increases. *Marginal* fixed costs = 0.

4 Diminishing returns occur when the marginal physical product of extra units of labour starts to decline. This begins to happen at output W, when the rate of increase in total output starts to decline as the number employed continues to increase.

5

Output	*Total revenue (TR)*	*(a) Marginal revenue* $TR_n - TR_{(n-1)}$	*Total costs (TC)*	*(b) Marginal costs* $TC_n - TC_{(n-1)}$	*Total profit TR – TC*
	£	£	£	£	£
0	–	–	110	–	(110)
1	50	50	140	30	(90)
2	100	50	162	22	(62)
3	150	50	175	13	(25)
4	200	50	180	5	20
5	250	50	185	5	65
6	300	50	194	9	106
7	350	50	229	35	122(max)
8	400	50	269	50	131(max)
9	450	50	325	56	125
10	500	50	425	100	75

(a) Marginal revenue is the additional revenue which results from the sale of the last unit of output.

The figures in the table above show that marginal revenue is a constant £50 at all levels of output given. This means that average revenue (price) must also be a constant £50. The firm's demand curve is perfectly elastic, indicating that the firm is operating in a perfectly competitive market.

(b) The fixed costs of the firm are those costs which do not vary with output. The level of fixed costs are therefore the total costs of £110 at the output level of zero.

Marginal cost is the change in total cost arising from the production of the last unit of output. The marginal cost for each level of output is shown in the table.

(c) As stated in (a) above, the firm is operating in a perfectly competitive market. The firm will seek to maximise profits by producing at a level of output at which marginal cost equals marginal revenue. It can be seen from the table that this occurs at output level 8. Total profit (total revenues minus total costs) at this levels of output is £131.

6 (a) Large firms attract *better quality employees* if the employees see better career prospects than in a small firm.

(b) Specialisation of labour applies to management, and there are thus *managerial economies*; the cost per unit of management will fall as output rises.

(c) *Marketing economies* are available, because a firm can make more effective use of advertising, specialist salesmen, and specialised channels of distribution.

(d) Large companies are able to devote more resources to *research and development* (R & D). In an industry where R & D is essential for survival, large companies are more likely to prosper.

Large companies find raising finance easier and can often do so more cheaply. Quoted public limited companies have access to a stock exchange for new share issues. They are also able to borrow money more readily.

7 (a) There is a huge number of buyers, and many sellers too. For any given model of car, a particular dealer is likely to be a price taker.

(b) Communication is generally good. Product features are well known and list prices are freely available. And discount levels too are widely commented on, in the press and by word of mouth.

(c) Consumers don't always act rationally. Some might be attracted to a car with a higher price, even if it is no better than other cheaper cars. Some may not shop around at different dealers even though it could save them money.

(d) The product is very far from homogeneous.

(e) Entry to the market is not easy, whether we are talking about manufacturers of motor cars (very high start-up costs), or dealers.

(f) Transport costs are *not* absent. On the contrary, significant geographical price differentiation is possible because of the high transport costs involved.

8 (a) True. The firm can sell whatever output it produces at the market price.

(b) False. (a) above implies that the demand curve is perfectly elastic.

9 True. Price is at average revenue (AR) which is equal to MC.

10 D The firm is producing and selling at a level of output where marginal cost is equal to marginal revenue. It is therefore already maximising its profit or minimising its loss. In fact, its monthly total revenue is £40 × 200 units = £8,000. This covers the variable costs and makes a contribution of £800 towards its fixed costs. Ceasing production would cause this contribution to be lost. There would be no point to reducing price since under perfect competition it can sell as much as it can produce at the prevailing market price. If the firm increased production, it would find that its marginal cost rose.

11 At the point where MR = 0. Further sales will lead to negative MR, and hence a reduction in total revenue.

12 One example would be in the sale of petrol, where from time to time petrol suppliers advertise particular performance-enhancing or protective features, but any petrol would make the car go.

13 Refer back to Figure 3.20.

Chapter 4 :

CREDIT CREATION AND THE BANKING SECTOR

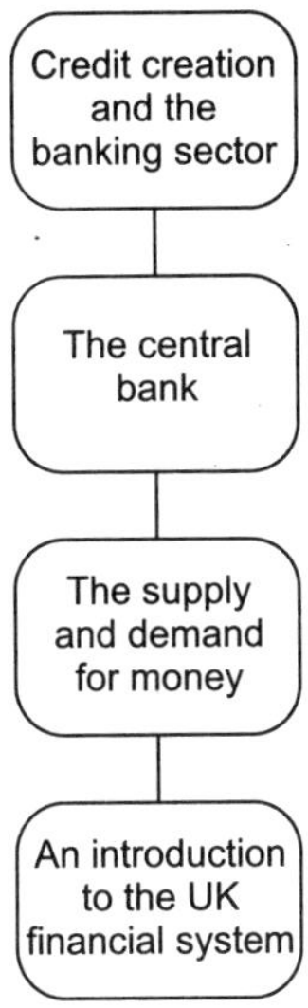

Introduction

In this chapter, we look closer at four issues. First, we discuss the **role of the banks** in the **financial system** and in particular how they create **credit** and provide **liquidity**. Second, we discuss the role of the central bank, and how it influences the functioning of the financial system. Third, we look at the supply and demand for money. Finally, we turn our attention to the UK financial system.

Your objectives

In this chapter you will learn about:

(a) Credit creation and the banking system

(b) The role of the central bank

(c) The supply and demand for money

(d) An introduction to the UK financial system

1 CREDIT CREATION

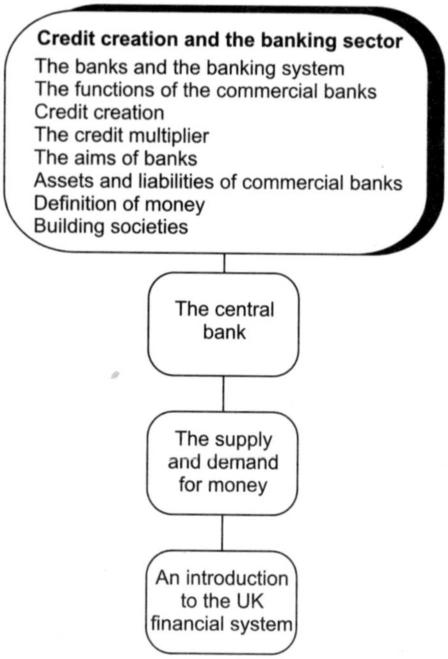

1.1 The banks and the banking system

The term 'bank' is generic and there are different types of banks that operate within a banking system. You will probably have come across a number of terms which describe the types.

(a) **Clearing banks** operate the clearing system for settling payments (eg payments by cheque by bank customers).

(b) The term **retail banks** is used to describe the traditional High Street banks. The term **wholesale banks** refers to banks which specialise in lending in large quantities to major customers. The clearing banks are involved in both retail and wholesale banking but are commonly regarded as the main retail banks.

(c) **Investment banks** (which used to be referred to as **merchant banks**) offer services, often of a specialised nature, to corporate customers.

(d) **Commercial banks** make commercial banking transactions with customers. They are distinct from the country's central bank.

Activity 1 **(5 minutes)**

In the balance sheet of a retail bank, which one of the following items do you think would constitute the largest asset?

(a) Customers' overdrafts and bank loans
(b) Customers' deposits
(c) Land and buildings

1.2 The functions of the commercial banks

(a) **Providing a payments mechanism**. The clearing system is the major payments mechanism in the UK, and it enables individuals and firms to make payments by cheque. The banks are also a source from which individuals and firms can obtain notes and coin.

(b) **Providing a place for individuals, firms and government to store their wealth**. Banks compete with other financial institutions to attract the funds of individuals and firms.

(c) **Lending money** in the form of loans or overdrafts.

(d) **Acting as financial intermediaries** by accepting deposits and lending, and in doing so transforming the risk characteristics and maturity characteristics of the lending.

(e) **Providing customers with a means of obtaining foreign currency, or selling foreign currency**, whenever they require it. Banks play a central role in the foreign exchange markets.

The banks also provide a wide range of other **commercial services** to customers.

(a) Advising and assisting companies, for example advising firms in a takeover bid and assisting companies to issue shares on the stock market.

(b) Providing assistance to exporters and importers, for example helping exporters to obtain payment from buyers abroad, and helping importers to pay for goods they buy from foreign suppliers

(c) Leasing

(d) Debt factoring services

(e) Executorship and trustee services

(f) Acting as insurance brokers for insurance companies by selling some insurance policies

(g) Selling insurance policies of their own, notably life assurance policies

(h) Selling pensions

(i) Share registration and share dealing services

(j) Unit trust business

(k) Giving investment advice

1.3 Credit creation

Definition

> The **bank multiplier** or **credit multiplier** is the name given to banks' ability to create credit, and hence money, by maintaining their cash reserves at less than 100% of the value of their deposits.

When someone deposits money in a bank, the banks are able as a result to 'create' credit of a much greater magnitude than the amount of money originally deposited.

Suppose, for example, that in a country with a single bank, customer deposits total £100,000. The bank, we will assume, re-lends all these deposits to other customers. The customers will use the money they have borrowed to buy goods and services and they will pay various firms and individuals for these purchases. If the firms and individuals receiving payment then put the money into their own accounts with the bank, the bank's deposits will have doubled.

It is this fact that most additions to bank lending end up as money in someone's bank account, adding to total customer deposits with the banks, that give banks this special **ability to create credit**. This is an ability that is also shared in the UK by building societies, since building society deposits are included in definitions of the money supply (M_2 and M_4).

EXAMPLE: CREDIT CREATION

Illustrating the process with some figures may be helpful. We shall assume for simplicity that there is only one bank in the banking system, and that all money lent by the bank is re-deposited by various customers.

A customer depositing £1,000 in cash with the bank **creates an asset**, in the sense that the bank, in return for the deposit, gives the customer a promise to pay on demand, or subject to notice, the £1,000 deposited. The promise is, of course, an account opened under the name of the client.

To the bank, the deposit is a **liability**. However, the deposit provides funds for the bank to acquire **assets**. We shall begin by assuming that the bank holds these assets entirely in the form of cash.

If the bank keeps the full £1,000 and does nothing with it, then it would simply operate as a 'cloakroom' in which the client's money is deposited. However, if the bank believes that the client is unlikely to claim the full £1,000 for some time, there will be some incentive to use the money rather than to keep it idle. One possibility would be to lend it; the bank would be taking a risk that it will not have the cash when its customer wants to have it back, but at the same time it would expect to make a profit by charging interest on the sum of money so lent.

On one hand the deposit of the £1,000 creates the opportunity for the bank to make a profit in the form of the interest that it can charge on the money it lends (the incentive being all the stronger if the bank is paying interest on the deposits it accepts), but on the other hand there is a risk that when the money is out on loan the client may claim it back. The bank will then be unable to meet its obligation to repay the cash to the client unless it can recall the loan instantly, which is unlikely.

As long as the bank feels that the likelihood is small that its depositors will demand a substantial proportion of their deposits in cash, then it faces an acceptable risk in lending some of the money. In other words, the bank strikes a balance between the desire to play safe by holding the cash and the desire to make profits by lending.

In the table below (with hypothetical figures to illustrate the underlying principles), it is assumed that the bank has decided on the basis of past experience and observation to keep 50 pence in cash for every £1 deposited, and then lend out the other 50 pence. In other words, the bank in this example is operating a **50% cash ratio**. At step (1) below, the bank has £1,000 in cash. This is enough to support total liabilities of £2,000 and maintain a 50% cash ratio. If the bank now lends £1,000, and if all of that £1,000 is then spent by the borrowers but ends up back with the bank as deposits of other customers, the new situation for the bank will be as in (2) below.

Bank's liabilities (= customer deposits)	*Bank's assets (= cash or loans to customers)*
(1) £1,000 deposits	£1,000 cash
(2) £2,000 deposits	£1,000 cash £1,000 loans

There is a doubling effect in relation to the money supply.

1.4 The credit multiplier

If the bank decided that the **50% cash ratio** was too conservative and reduced it to 25%, then for £1,000 cash deposited with the bank, deposits could be expanded fourfold. It is important to understand that banks in the process of lending are also potentially creating money because clients either borrowing or receiving the proceeds of borrowers' expenditure can use their deposits to make money transactions. In a modern economy most money transactions are by cheque or other bank transfer such as direct debits or standing order, thus transferring bank deposits from person to person or from firm to firm. Consumers and producers thus use the liabilities of a private institution as money.

The fact that banks do not need to keep a 100% cash reserve ratio automatically implies that they have the capacity to create money out of nothing. The size of this credit expansion depends primarily on the size of their cash reserve ratio.

We can summarise the quantitative side of credit creation in banks as follows.

$$\text{Deposits} = \frac{\text{Cash}}{\text{Cash ratio}} \text{ or } D = \frac{c}{r}$$

The smaller the cash ratio or **credit multiplier**, the bigger the size of the deposits that a given amount of cash will be able to support and hence the larger the money supply.

This theoretical description of the credit multiplier applies only to some extent in practice. If a bank decides to keep a cash reserve ratio of 10%, and it receives additional deposits of £1,000, the total increase in bank deposits will not be £1,000 ÷ 10% = £10,000, but considerably less than this.

Activity 2 **(10 minutes)**

Suppose that all the commercial banks in an economy operated on a cash reserve ratio of 20%. How much cash would have to flow into the banks for the money supply to increase by £80 million?

There are constraints on the growth of a bank's deposits (and on the growth of the deposits of all banks in total).

(a) Cash leaks out of the banking system into less formal accumulations.

(b) Customers might not want to borrow at the interest rates the bank would charge.

(c) Banks should not lend to high-risk customers without good security.

A **cash ratio** or similar **fractional reserve system** might be imposed on banks by the government. Until 1971, a mandatory cash ratio of 8% was applied to the London clearing banks. Between 1971 and 1981 banks were required to maintain 12½% reserve asset ratio requirement. Although not intended as a direct monetary control (on credit growth), in effect it applied a credit multiplier limit of eight – ie every initial £1 increase in bank deposits would result in up to £8 more in deposits.

1.5 Liquidity, profitability and security: aims of the banks

A commercial bank has three different and potentially conflicting aims which it must try to keep in balance. These are as follows.

(a) **Profitability.** A bank must make a profit for its shareholders. The biggest profits come from lending at higher interest rates. These are obtained with long-term lending and lending to higher risk customers.

(b) **Liquidity**. A bank must have some liquid assets. It needs notes and coin (till money) to meet demands from depositors for cash withdrawals. It also needs to be able to settle debts with other banks. For example, if on a particular day, customers of the Barclays Bank make payments by cheque to customers of Lloyds Bank totalling £200 millions, and customers of Lloyds Bank make payments by cheque to customers of Barclays totalling £170 millions, Barclays will be expected to pay Lloyds £30 million to settle the net value of transactions. This is done by transferring funds between the bank accounts of Barclays and Lloyds, which they keep with the Bank of England (as 'operational deposits'). A bank might also need to have some 'near liquid' assets which it can turn into liquid assets quickly, should it find itself with a need for more liquidity. Near-liquid assets earn relatively little interest. A bank will try to keep the quantity of such assets it holds to a safe minimum.

(c) **Security**. People deposit their money with banks because they are regarded as stable and secure institutions. A bank might lend to some high-risk customers, and suffer some bad debts, but on the whole, a bank will be expected to lend wisely and securely, with a strong likelihood that the loans will be repaid in full and with interest. If it did not, people might put their money somewhere else instead, not with the bank. This is why banks usually give careful consideration to the reliability of the borrower. Often, in doubtful cases, they will ask for security for a loan or overdraft. Security means that in the event of a default on loan repayments by the borrower, the bank can realise the security by selling the secured asset or assets and using the sale proceeds to pay off the debt.

1.6 Assets and liabilities of commercial banks

The distribution of assets for all UK commercial banks aggregated together at a particular point in time is summarised in the table below.

UK commercial banks' assets

	%
Cash	0.5
Balance with Bank of England	0.2
Market loans	24.0
Bills of Exchange	1.8
Investments	6.7
Advances	62.0
Miscellaneous	4.8
	100.0

The triple aspects of bank lending – profitability, liquidity, and security – are evident in a commercial bank's **asset structure.**

(a) About 0.5% to 2% or so of a retail bank's assets might be till money (notes and coin) and deposits with the Bank of England. Most of these assets are held to meet the need for immediate liquidity, and earn no interest.

(b) Some assets are 'near-liquid' which means that they can quickly be converted into liquid deposits.

  (i) The most important near-liquid assets are loans to the money markets and other money market securities.

  (ii) Other near-liquid assets are bills, mainly eligible bank bills. Bills are short-term debt instruments. Eligible bills are Bills of Exchange that the Bank of England would be prepared to buy when the banking system is short of money. Most eligible bills are issued by top-class banks who are granted eligible status by the Bank of England.

  (iii) Banks also hold some gilt-edged securities, mainly British government stocks. These can be sold on the stock market should a bank wish to obtain immediate liquid funds, but often, banks will buy gilts on the stock market with a fairly short-term to maturity, and then hold them until they mature and the government redeems the debt.

  Near-liquid assets – market loans, Bills of Exchange and gilt-edged security investments – might represent around 25% to 30% of a retail bank's assets.

(c) The biggest returns are earned by banks on their longer term **illiquid assets** – ie their overdrafts and bank loans to customers. Advances to customers are the biggest proportion of a retail bank's assets (over 70%) and the rate of interest on the loans varies according to the perceived risk of the customer as well as current interest rates.

(d) Banks' assets include the normal type of fixed assets found in any large organisation – eg property and equipment. However, the value of these operational assets is small in relation to the size of loans, even for the big clearing banks.

Sterling sight and time deposits of the retail banks account for most of their **liabilities.** Most sterling deposits are provided by the UK private sector (individuals and firms). **Other currency deposits** are the other main type of liability, consisting of deposits held by customers of UK banks in US dollars, euros and so on. In the UK there are no exchange control regulations currently in operation, and so private individuals as well as commercial firms and financial institutions are allowed to maintain foreign currency accounts. The bulk of other currency deposits, however, are held by overseas customers of UK banks.

1.7 Definition of money

Although we have talked about money in the context of the flow of funds we have not used a precise definition of money so far. The Bank of England uses two definitions of money, narrow money (known as M_0) and broad money (known as M_4). The precise definition of the two measures is as follows.

Definition

> **M_0**: Notes and coins in circulation
>
> **M_4**: M_0 Plus sterling deposit accounts with barks and building societies.

Other less important definitions used include M_1, M_2 and M_3 which all contain M_0 but are differentiated by the type of deposits they include.

1.8 Building societies

The building societies of the UK are **mutual** organisations whose main assets are mortgages of their members, and whose main liabilities are to the investor members who hold savings accounts with the society.

The distinction between building societies and banks has become increasingly blurred, as the societies have taken to providing a range of services formerly the province mainly of banks, and banks have themselves made inroads into the housing mortgage market. Some building societies now offer cheque book accounts, cash cards and many other facilities that compete directly with the banks.

The growing similarity between retail banks and building societies is recognised by the inclusion of building society deposits in the broader monetary aggregate M_4. The building society sector has shrunk in size as a number of the major societies have either converted to public limited companies and therefore become banks or have been taken over by banks or other financial institutions.

2 THE ROLE OF THE CENTRAL BANK

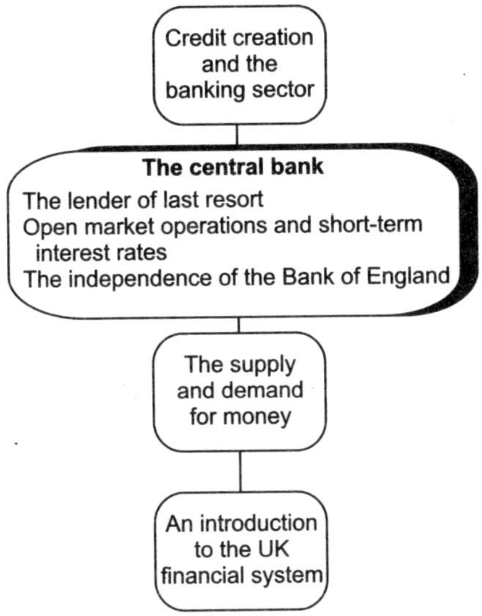

A central bank is a bank which acts on behalf of the government. The central bank for the UK is the Bank of England. The Bank of England ('the Bank') is a nationalised corporation run by a Court of Directors, consisting of the Governor, Deputy Governor, and some Executive Directors and part-time Directors.

Functions of the Bank of England

(a) It acts as **banker to the central Government** and holds the 'public deposits'. Public deposits include the National Loans Fund, the Consolidated Fund and the account of the Paymaster General, which in turn includes the Exchange Equalisation Account (see (a) below).

(b) It is the **central note-issuing authority** in the UK.

(c) It is the **manager of the National Debt** –it deals with long- and short-term borrowing by the central Government and the repayment of central Government debt.

(d) It is the manager of the Exchange Equalisation Account (ie the UK's **foreign currency reserves**).

(e) It acts as adviser to the Government on **monetary policy**.

(f) It acts as agent for the Government in carrying out its monetary policies. Since May 1997, it has had operational responsibility for **setting interest rates** at the level it considers appropriate in order to meet the Government's inflation target.

(g) It acts as a **banker to the commercial banks**. The commercial banks keep a bank account with the Bank of England.

(h) It acts as a **lender to the banking system**. When the banking system is short of money, the Bank of England will provide the money the banks need – at a suitable rate of interest.

Supervision of the banking system is the responsibility of the Financial Services Authority.

2.1 The central bank as lender of last resort

In the UK, the short-term money market provides a link between the banking system and the Government (Bank of England) whereby the Bank of England lends money to the banking system, when banks which need cash cannot get it from anywhere else. A recent example was when the stricken Northern Rock approached the Bank for funds needed to cover immediate liabilities.

(a) The Bank will supply cash to the banking system on days when the banks have a cash shortage. It does this by buying eligible bills and other short-term financial investments from approved financial institutions in exchange for cash.

(b) The Bank will remove excess cash from the banking system on days when the banks have a cash surplus. It does this by selling bills to institutions, so that the short-term money markets obtain interest-bearing bills in place of the cash that they do not want.

The process whereby this is done currently is known as **open market operations** by the Bank. This simply describes the buying and selling of eligible bills and other short-term assets between the Bank and the short-term money market.

2.2 Open market operations and short-term interest rates

Definition

> **Open market operations** are the Bank of England's dealings in the capital market. The Bank uses open market operations to control interest rates.

Open market operations provide the Bank of England with a method of control over short-term interest rates. They are thus an important feature of the Government's monetary policy, which the Bank implements on its behalf.

When bills are bought and sold, they are traded at a discount to their face value, and there is an implied interest rate in the rate of discount obtained. Discounts on bills traded in open market operations have an immediate influence on other money market interest rates, such as the London Inter-Bank Offered Rate (LIBOR), and these in turn influence the 'benchmark' base rates of the major banks.

Because the eligible bills and other assets which the Bank of England acquires in its money market operations are short-term assets, a proportion mature each day. The market is then obliged to redeem these claims and must seek further refinancing from the bank. This continual turnover of assets gives the Bank of England the opportunity to determine the level of interest rates day by day.

2.3 The independence of the Bank of England

The Bank is an adviser to the Government, but not an agent of the Government. How much independence of action does the Bank have?

Proponents of **independence for central banks** argue that independence can prevent the worst government monetary excesses, which in some cases result in **hyperinflation**.

High levels of existing public expenditure commitments combined with electoral pressures (along with other factors) build in strong underlying inflationary pressures. An independent central bank is seen as an essential counterweight to the potentially reckless decisions of politicians. As well as avoiding the worst excesses, a strong central bank is regarded as vital for the shorter term stability of domestic prices and of the currency, and so is important to overseas trade. Any government wishing to reduce an already high rate of inflation will, however, have to listen carefully to the advice of its central bank if it is to have any real success.

Those arguing against independence point out that the central bank is an unelected body and therefore does not have the open responsibility of politicians. Danger in this respect is minimised by the formal publication of decisions and recommendations of the central bank.

Further, it is claimed that central bank views on monetary policy could be in conflict with other economic objectives of the government. For example, excessively strict pursuit of monetary policy in order to pursue an inflation target might result in prolonged recession and heavy under-utilisation of resources.

In May 1997, the new Labour government of the UK announced important changes to the role of the Bank of England. As already mentioned, the Chancellor of the Exchequer handed over to the Bank the power to set interest rates. Rates are set by a **Monetary Policy Committee** including the Governor of the Bank, his two deputies and four outsiders, but no politicians. The Committee sets interest rates with the aim of meeting the inflation target set by Government.

The 1997 changes did not make the Bank of England fully independent, as the UK Government can still override the Bank in an emergency. The role of the Bank of England also falls short of that of many other central banks in that responsibility for setting inflation or monetary targets rests with government.

One of the more independent central banks is the European Central Bank which is designed to be totally free of political interference. It came into existence at the end of 1998, ready for the European single currency.

3 THE SUPPLY AND DEMAND FOR MONEY

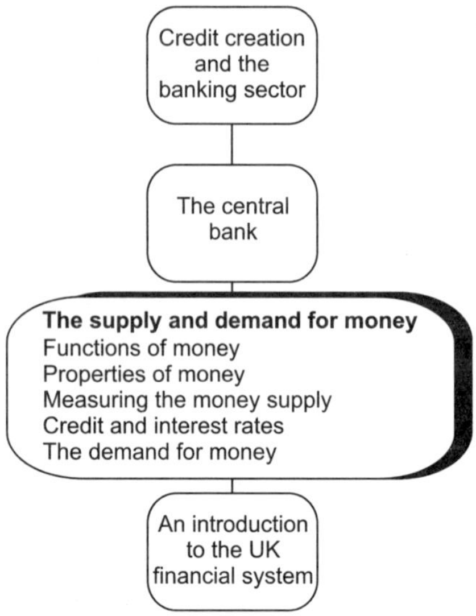

3.1 Functions of money

Money as we know it today is a strange thing in that we value it highly but its intrinsic worth is, generally, negligible. We can solve this puzzle by understanding that the importance of money lies in what it does for us rather than what it actually is. Money enables a modern economy to function; most importantly, without it we should be reduced to the time-consuming and inefficient process of barter. However, this is not all that money can do. In Chapter 1 we identified four different functions of money.

- A means of exchange
- A unit of account
- A standard of deferred payment
- A store of value

Revisit Chapter 1 if you need to remind yourself of the functions of money.

3.2 Properties of money

In order to be able to perform the functions mentioned above, it is necessary that money should possess certain qualities or properties.

Acceptability

Money must be accepted as such without question if it is to be useful. This has important implications.

First, money should be scarce; it will not maintain its value if people can easily obtain more for themselves without economic activity. The episode in *Douglas Adams' Hitch-Hiker* series in which a society of hairdressers and telephone sanitisers adopts leaves as its currency illustrates this point. Leaves grow on trees, while it is not merely proverbial but essential that money does not. Forgery is a serious threat to the scarcity and hence the acceptability of money.

Second, money should be recognisable and establishing recognition should not damage or destroy it.

Durability

Money's function as a store of value requires that it should be durable and not dwindle or deteriorate over time. When gold and silver coins were commonly used as money, wear eroded the amount of metal present in each coin, gold and silver both being soft metals. Similarly, even though cigarettes have been used as money, tobacco does not really make satisfactory money as it is an organic substance and subject to decay.

Convenience

Money must be easy to use. This implies portability and transferability: it should be possible to carry useful quantities of physical money with ease and to transfer ownership to another simply by handing it over. Money that exists as credit balances need not be carried and may be transferred by means such as cheques and Internet bank transfers.

Homogeneity

Money should be available in units of consistent and measurable value. It should also be divisible, so that larger and smaller units are available. Both of these properties are present in notes and coin in their various denominations. A disadvantage of using commodities such as sheep or grain as money is the inevitable variation in quality. With homogeneity

3.3 Measuring the money supply

The money supply is the total amount of money in the economy. It is also referred to as the money stock.

It is important that an economy should have enough money to enable economic activity to take place. As economic growth takes place, the money supply must increase so that there is no shortage. However, it is important that the growth in the money supply should not be too rapid if inflation is to be avoided. Measuring the money supply is therefore an important aspect of economic management.

Narrow money and broad money

We are used to thinking of money in terms of notes and coin but as was mentioned earlier in this chapter, a wide range of assets, such as money market deposits and eligible bills are so liquid that, effectively, they are equivalent to money. It is not always easy to decide whether a particular financial asset is money or not and it is now considered appropriate to distinguish between narrow money and broad money.

Financial assets must have a high degree of liquidity to be regarded as narrow money. A definition of narrow money is 'money balances which are readily available to finance current spending, that is to say for transactions purposes' (*UK Treasury Economic Progress Report*).

Broad money extends the range of assets that are regarded as money to include money held in the form of savings. 'It provides an indicator of the private sector's holdings of relatively liquid assets – assets which could be converted with relative ease and without capital loss into spending on goods and services' *(UK Treasury Economic Progress Report).*

Narrow money can be defined in different ways, depending on how narrowly 'liquidity' is defined; similarly, broad money can be defined in a variety of ways. Even the broadest definition of money will exclude some financial assets. There will never be a clear dividing line between what is narrow money, what is broad money, and what is not money at all.

Measuring the UK money supply

The Bank of England uses two main measures of the money supply, M_0 and M_4.

(a) M_0 is the narrowest definition of money, the great majority of which is made up of notes and coin in circulation outside the Bank of England.

(b) M_4 is a broad definition of money, including deposits held for savings as well as spending purposes.

			£bn
M_0	=	Notes and coin in circulation outside the Bank of England	32.8
	+	banks' operational deposits with the Bank of England	0.1
			32.9
M_4	=	M_4 private sector holdings of:	
		notes and coin	27.6
	+	banks' retail deposits	485.3
	+	building societies' shares and deposits	124.6
	+	other interest bearing deposits (including Certificates of Deposit)	281.3
			918.8

Physical notes and coins form a very small part of the larger aggregates.

3.4 Credit and interest rates

Credit for our purposes here concerns lending and borrowing money, rather than with buying goods on trade credit.

The functions of credit can be seen from the point of view either of the borrower or the lender.

(a) For the borrower, the reason for borrowing money is to be able to purchase goods or services now that he might not otherwise be able to afford. The borrower wants to buy now and pay later.

(b) For the lender, the reason for lending money is that there is nothing that he now particularly wants to spend his money on, and by lending it, he can earn some interest.

Credit involves the transfer of money from a lender to a borrower, in exchange for a promise to return it at some future time and to pay interest meanwhile.

Credit is a scarce commodity, priced through interest rates. Although there are many different interest rates in an economy, including building society mortgage rates, banks' base rates and yields on gilt-edged securities, they tend to move up or down together.

(a) If some interest rates go up, for example the banks' base rates, it is quite likely that other interest rates will move up too, if they have not gone up already.

(b) Similarly, if some interest rates go down, other interest rates will move down too.

Interest rates and the money supply

In the past, attempts have been made to prevent inflation by direct controls on the supply of money such as requiring the clearing banks to make large deposits of funds with the central bank. This approach assumes that the money supply can be controlled exogenously, or from outside the process of commercial lending and borrowing. Direct controls did not work very well and the alternative endogenous view of control now prevails. Under this approach, the creation of credit is controlled within the system, through the structure of interest rates, higher rates tending both to reduce demand for new credit and to reduce discretionary expenditure by increasing the cost of existing loans.

The term structure of interest rates

The various interest rates can be grouped into three broad classes, according to the length of the loan period.

- Short-term interest rates
- Medium-term interest rates
- Long-term interest rates

Longer-term financial assets should in general offer a higher yield than short-term lending. There are several reasons for this.

(a) The investor must be compensated for tying up his money in the asset for a longer period of time. If the government were to make two issues of 9% Treasury Stock on the same date, one with a term of five years and one with a term of twenty years (and if there were no expectations of changes in interest rates in the future) then the liquidity preference of investors would make them prefer the five-year stock.

(b) The only way to overcome the liquidity preference of investors is to compensate them for the loss of liquidity; in other words, to offer a higher rate of interest on longer-dated stock.

(c) There is a greater risk in lending longer-term than shorter-term for two reasons.

(i) **Inflation**. The longer the term of the asset, the greater is the possibility that the rate of inflation will increase, so that the fixed rate of interest paid on the asset will be overtaken by interest yields on new lending now that inflation is higher.

(ii) **Uncertain economic prospects**. The future state of the economy cannot be predicted with certainty. If an organisation wishes to borrow money now for, say, fifteen years, there is no certainty about what might happen to that organisation during that time. It might thrive and prosper or it might run into economic difficulties for one reason or another.

Investors will require a higher return to compensate them for the increased risk.

(d) Note, however, that two other factors also affect the cost of borrowing.

(i) The risk associated with the perceived ability of the borrower to fulfil the terms of the loan

(ii) Whether or not the loan is secured by a mortgage on an asset

Nominal and real rates of interest

Nominal rates of interest are rates expressed in money terms. If interest paid per annum on a loan of £1,000 is £150, the rate of interest would be 15%. The nominal rate of interest might also be referred to as the money rate of interest, or the actual money yield on an investment.

Real rates of interest are the rates of return that investors get from their investment, adjusted for the rate of inflation. The real rate of interest is therefore a measure of the increase in the real wealth, expressed in terms of buying power, of the investor or lender. Real rates of interest are lower than nominal rates when there is price inflation. For example, if the nominal rate of interest is 12% per annum and the annual rate of inflation is 8% per annum, the real rate of interest is the interest earned after allowing for the return needed just to keep pace with inflation.

The relationship between the inflation rate, the real rate of interest and the money rate of interest is:

$(1+ \text{real rate of interest}) \times (1+ \text{inflation rate}) = 1+ \text{money rate of interest}$

We may rearrange this to find the real rate of interest in the example above.

$$\frac{1+\text{money rate}}{1+\text{inflation rate}} = 1 + \text{real rate}$$

$$\frac{1.12}{1.08} = 1.037$$

The real rate of interest is thus 3.7%.

The real rate of interest is commonly measured approximately, however, as the difference between the nominal rate of interest and the rate of inflation. In our example, this would be 12% – 8% = 4%.

Variations in the general level of interest rates over time

Interest rates on any one type of financial asset will vary over time. In other words, the general level of interest rates might go up or down. The general level of interest rates is affected by several factors.

(a) **The need for a real return.** It is generally accepted that investors will want to earn a 'real' rate of return on their investment, that is, a return which exceeds the rate of inflation. The suitable real rate of return will depend on factors such as investment risk.

(b) **Uncertainty about future rates of inflation**. When investors are uncertain about what future nominal and real interest rates will be, they are likely to require higher interest yields to persuade them to take the risk of investing, especially in the longer-term.

(c) **Changes in the level of government borrowing**. When the demand for credit increases, interest rates will go up. A high level of borrowing by the government is likely to result in upward pressure on interest rates.

(d) **Higher demand for borrowing from individuals**. If individuals want to borrow more, for example because they feel confident about their level of future earnings, then interest rates will tend to rise.

(e) **Monetary policy**. Governments control the level of interest rates in order to control inflation.

(f) **Interest rates abroad**. An appropriate real rate of interest in one country will be influenced by external factors, such as interest rates in other countries and expectations about the exchange rate.

3.4 The demand for money

The classical theory

The classical theory of money is based on the view that money is used only as a medium of exchange and people require it only in order to settle transactions in good and services. This leads to the quantity theory of money, which holds that changes in the level of prices are caused predominantly by changes in the supply of money.

There is a logic behind the classical quantity theory and it relates to the basic transactions assumption. If it is true that money is used only for transactions relating to goods and services, it follows that an excess of money will lead to increased attempts to spend it. Similarly, a shortage of money will have the effect of reducing demand. If the economy is utilising its productive resources to the full (that is, if there is full employment) it will not be possible to increase output. Any increase in demand will therefore cause prices to rise by the action of market forces. Similarly, any reduction in demand will cause prices to fall.

This theory is very satisfactory in explaining past experience of price rises and falls over long periods, as during the nineteenth century. In the first half of the nineteenth century there was large scale economic expansion, but the money supply was based on the gold standard and expanded only slowly: prices generally fell. In the second half of the century there were extensive increases in the supply of gold as a result of mining in Australia and America. The growth of economic activity, and hence output, did not match the growth in the gold supply and prices rose.

The modern view

The classical theory does not, in fact, fully explain the role of money in the economy. *Keynes* argued that money is held not only for transactions but also for precautionary and for speculative reasons. The precautionary motive means that people choose to keep money on hand or in the bank as a precaution for when it might suddenly be needed. The speculative motive means that people choose to keep money on hand to take advantage of any profitable opportunity to invest in bonds that may arise (or they may sell bonds for money when they fear a fall in the market prices of bonds).

The precautionary motive is really just an extension of the transactions motive. However, the speculative motive for holding money is rather different and has important implications for interest rates.

The reason for holding money instead of investing in bonds is that interest rates are expected to go up. If interest rates go up, bond prices will fall. For example, if the current **market price** of bonds which pay 5% interest on face value is £100, and interest rates doubled to 10%, the market value of the bonds would fall, perhaps to £50. This is because the interest paid on a bond is fixed at a percentage of **face value**. The ratio between the income paid and the **market value** adjusts to the current prevailing interest rate by means of changes in the market value. So if interest rates are expected to go up, any bonds held now will be expected to lose value, and bond holders would make a capital loss. Thus, it makes sense to hold on to money, for investing in bonds later, after interest rates have gone up.

What causes individuals to have expectations about interest rate changes in the future? *Keynes* argued that each individual has some expectation of a normal rate of interest. This concept of a normal interest rate reflects past levels and movements in the interest rate, and expectations of the future rate level, obtained from available market information.

Keynes argued further that people will need money to satisfy the transactions motive and precautionary motive regardless of the level of interest. It is only the speculative motive that alters the demand for money as a result of interest rate changes.

(a) If interest rates are high, people will expect them to fall and will expect the price of bonds to rise. They will therefore purchase bonds in anticipation of a capital gain and will therefore have low liquidity preference.

(b) If interest rates are low but are expected to rise, this implies that bond prices are likely to fall. People will therefore hold liquid funds in order to be able to invest in bonds later on. Their liquidity preference will be high.

The conclusion is that the demand for money will be high (liquidity preference will be high) when interest rates are low. This is because the speculative demand for money will be high. Similarly, the demand for money will be low when interest rates are high, because the speculative demand for money will be low.

4 AN INTRODUCTION TO THE UK FINANCIAL SYSTEM

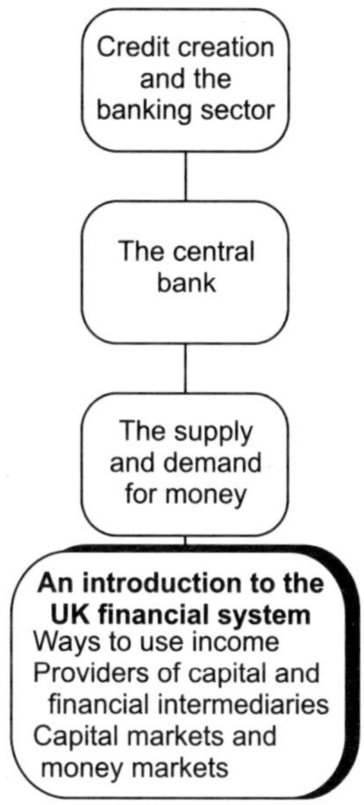

4.1 Ways to use income

Money is used for a wide variety of purposes, but we can analyse these purposes into a few important categories. A large part of household income, for example, can be described simply as being spent on consumption. This category includes all the goods and services purchased by the household, including foodstuffs and clothing; transport and housing costs; furniture and major household items such as cars; and luxury goods and services. Another major destination for much household income, is taxation. Individuals have very little influence over the extent of this element of expenditure, unlike consumption, much of which is discretionary. Finally, if anything is left, a proportion of income may be devoted to savings.

Each of these categories of expenditure has an important economic role. Consumption expenditure provides the revenue for the firms that organise economic activity; taxation finances government expenditure and savings provide both the capital for firms to invest and loans to households and government.

In the rest of this section we will be looking at some of the financial institutions that deal in capital for investment and loans

4.2 Providers of capital and financial intermediaries

We may think of three basic categories of providers of capital.

(a) **Private individuals**, as mentioned above, may have spare income or other funds that they wish to invest as a form of saving.

(b) **Firms**, similarly, may wish to invest funds that are not immediately required to finance their own business operations.

(c) **Government** may use some of its revenue to finance activities that it wishes to promote. Often, this kind of government spending provides funds direct to the intended recipient, but sometimes it is carried out through the capital and money markets.

There are also important groups of institutional investors that both fall into the category of firms with their own funds to invest and act as financial intermediaries between suppliers and users of funds.

(a) **Pension funds**. Pension funds invest the pension contributions of individuals who subscribe to a pension fund, and of organisations with a company pension fund.

(b) **Insurance companies**. Insurance companies invest premiums paid on insurance policies by policy holders.

(c) **Investment trusts**. The business of investment trust companies is investing in the securities of other companies and the government. In other words, they trade in investments.

(d) **Unit trusts**. Unit trusts are similar to investment trusts, in the sense that they invest in stocks and shares of other companies. A unit trust will set up portfolios of stocks or shares in a range of companies or gilts; frequently a portfolio will have a special characteristic, such as having all of its shares in property companies or mining companies. The trust will then create a large number of small units of low nominal value, with each unit representing a stake in the total portfolio. These units are sold to individual investors and investors will benefit from the income and capital gain on their units in the portfolio.

(e) **Venture capital**. Venture capital providers specialise in raising funds for new business ventures, such as management buy-outs. These organisations are therefore providing capital for fairly risky ventures. A venture capital organisation that has operated for many years in the UK is Investors in Industry plc, usually known as '3i'. In recent years, many more venture capital organisations have been set up, for example by large financial institutions such as pension funds.

(f) **Banks**. Banks can be approached directly by firms and individuals for medium-term and long-term loans as well as short-term loans or overdrafts. Private borrowers will tend to obtain funds from clearing banks, while merchant banks, who typically deal in larger amounts on wholesale terms, will be more likely to provide finance to larger firms. The major clearing banks, many merchant banks and foreign banks operating in the UK are increasingly willing to lend medium-term capital, especially to well established companies.

(g) **Building societies**. Traditionally, building societies are **mutual funds**, owned by their investors, and established to provide long-term loans for house purchase. Many UK building societies have demutualised and are, effectively, banks.

The role of financial intermediaries in capital markets is illustrated in Figure 4.1 below.

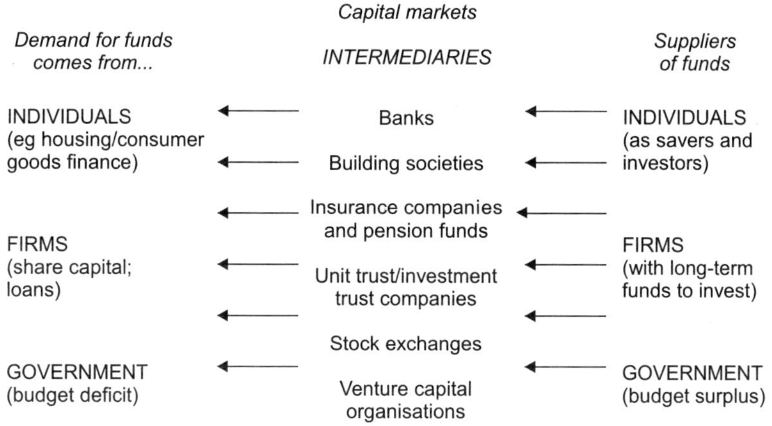

Figure 4.1: Role of financial intermediaries

The Northern Rock crisis – a case study

Northern Rock plc is a British bank, best known for becoming the first bank in 150 years to suffer a bank run after having had to approach the Bank of England for a loan facility during the credit crisis in 2007.

Compared to other mortgage lenders and banks Northern Rock had a very low amount of customers depositing money with them in the form of savings and a high proportion borrowing off them in the form of mortgages.

This low capital base meant that in order to offer large volumes of mortgages to consumers was much of it had to borrow money on the LIBOR money markets. This lending is typically done over fairly short period (usually about 3 months). Also traditionally the LIBOR interest rate is slightly lower than the Bank of England Base Rates, meaning that they could usually borrow money from LIBOR, then sell mortgages at, say Base Rates, and make a profit.

The above model changed dramatically as the US sub prime crisis unfolded. As more and more banks and financial institutions announced heavy losses through their investments in sub prime securities, the large banks became very suspicious of each other and became reluctant to lend each other money. As a result a result the LIBOR rate shot up.

This increased LIBOR rate meant that the Northern Rock was borrowing expensively in the short term and lending out cheaply in the long term. Obviously this situation was unsustainable. Within a short period of time Northern Rock had to approach the Bank of England and ask to borrow more capital as a 'lender of last resort'. This approach to the BoE was very rare, with the last suspected loan made in the 1970's. Though the exact numbers are unknown the Bank of England is suspected to have lent Northern Rock over £25bn.

4.3 Capital markets and money markets

There is a wide range of markets for dealing in capital. We can divide them into two main types.

(a) **Capital markets** are financial markets for **raising** and **investing** largely long-term capital.

(b) **Money markets** are financial markets for lending and borrowing largely short-term capital.

What do we mean by **long-term** and **short-term** capital?

(a) By **short-term capital,** we mean capital that is lent or borrowed for a period which might range from as short as overnight up to about one year, and sometimes longer.

(b) By **long-term capital,** we mean capital invested or lent and borrowed for a period of about five years or more, but sometimes shorter.

(c) There is a **grey area** between long-term and short-term capital, which is lending and borrowing for a period from about one or two years up to about five- years, which is not surprisingly referred to as **medium-term** capital.

The Stock Exchange

The London Stock Exchange is an organised capital market that plays an important role in the functioning of the UK economy. It is the main capital market in the UK.

(a) It makes it easier for large firms and the government to raise long-term capital, by providing a market place for borrowers and investors to come together.

(b) The Stock Exchange publicises the prices of quoted (or 'listed') securities, which are then reported in daily national newspapers such as the Financial Times. Investors can therefore keep an eye on the value of their stocks and shares, and make buying and selling decisions accordingly.

(c) The Stock Exchange tries to enforce certain rules of conduct for its listed firms and for operators in the market, so that investors have the assurance that companies whose shares are traded on the Exchange and traders who operate there are reputable. Confidence in the Stock Exchange will make investors more willing to put their money into stocks and shares.

The Alternative Investment Market (AIM), which opened in 1995, is a market where smaller companies which cannot meet the more stringent requirements needed to obtain a full listing on the Stock Exchange can raise new capital by issuing shares. Like the Stock Exchange main market, the AIM is also a market in which investors can trade in shares already issued. It is regulated by the Stock Exchange.

The price of shares on a stock market fluctuate up and down.

(a) The price of shares in a particular company might remain unchanged for quite a long time; alternatively, a company's share price might fluctuate continually throughout each day.

(b) The general level of share prices, as measured by share price indices such as the All-Share Index and the FTSE 100 Index, may go up or down each minute of the day.

The indices of share prices on the Stock Exchange act as indicators of the state of investor confidence in the country's economy. For example, if investors believe that interest rates are too low to curb inflation, they may sell shares and move their funds to other countries, causing a decline in share prices.

Activity 3 **(5 minutes)**

From your reading of business pages (which should be a central feature in anyone's study of economics) what factors have you noticed as having an influence on share prices?

The gilt-edged market

The gilt-edged market is a further major capital market in the UK. The government borrows over the medium- and longer-term by issuing government stocks (called 'gilt-edged stock'). Trade in second-hand gilts will continue until the debt eventually matures and the government redeems the stock.

Gilts may be issued either by selling them direct to dealers, or by selling them to the Bank of England first, and then releasing them gradually ('on tap') to the market at a suitable time.

The primary gilts market is the market for the sale of new gilt issues. There is an active market in second-hand gilts with existing holders selling their holdings of gilts to other investors in the gilts market.

The money markets

The UK money markets are operated by the banks and other financial institutions. Although the money markets largely involve wholesale borrowing and lending by banks, some large companies and the government are also involved in money market operations. The money markets are essentially shorter-term debt markets, with loans being made for a specified period at a specified rate of interest.

The money markets operate both as a primary market, in which new financial claims are issued and as a secondary market, where previously issued financial claims are traded.

Amounts dealt in are relatively large, generally being above £50,000 and often in millions of pounds. Loans are transacted on extremely 'fine' terms – ie with small margins between lending and borrowing rates – reflecting the economies of scale involved. The emphasis is on liquidity: the efficiency of the money markets can make the financial claims dealt in virtually the equivalent of cash.

There are several markets.

(a) **The primary market** is the market where, as already described, the Bank of England carries out 'open market operations' in short-term financial instruments in order to ensure the liquidity of the banking system and to exert influence over interest rates.

(b) **The interbank market** is the market in which banks lend short-term funds to one another. The principal interest rate in this market is the London Inter-Bank Offer Rate or LIBOR, which is used by individual banks to establish their own base interest rates and interest rates for wholesale lending to large borrowers.

(c) The **building society market** is where building societies can obtain funds in large amounts if needed.

(d) **The local authority market** is a market in which local authorities borrow short-term funds from banks and other investors, by issuing and selling short-term 'debt instruments'.

(e) **The finance house market** covers the short-term loans raised from the money markets by finance houses (eg hire purchase finance companies).

(f) **The inter-company market** refers to direct short-term lending between companies, without any financial intermediary. This market is very small, and restricted to the treasury departments of large companies, and has largely been superseded by the sterling commercial paper market.

(g) **The Certificate of Deposit market** is a market for trading in Certificates of Deposit, a form of deposit which can be sold by the investor before maturity.

(h) **The sterling commercial paper market** is a market in which companies issue debt securities carrying interest, known as commercial paper (CP) with a maturity of up to one year, or medium-term notes (MTNs) with a period of between one and five years.

A distinction is sometimes made between the primary market and all the other money markets which are referred to collectively as the parallel markets or 'unofficial' markets.

Chapter roundup

- Banks (and building societies) create **credit** when they lend or grant overdrafts, and their activities thus contribute significantly to the increase in the money supply. In practice, the size of the **credit multiplier** is restricted by 'leakages' and by central bank controls over the liquidity and capital structure of banks.
- The **central bank** has various functions. These include acting as a **banker to the central government** and to the **commercial banks**. The Bank of England has responsibility for controlling sterling inflation by setting interest rates.
- In practice, there is a variety of **interest rates**. To make a profit, institutions that borrow money to re-lend, or that accept deposits which they re-lend (eg banks) must pay lower interest on deposits than they charge to customers who borrow.
- Money functions as a means of exchange, a unit of account, a standard of deferred payment and a store of value. To do these things it must be acceptable, durable, convenient and homogeneous.
- The narrow money supply (M_0 in the UK) consists largely of notes and coin. The broad money supply (M_4 in the UK) includes deposits held for savings as well.
- Interest rates on long-term loans should be higher than on short-term loans because of the greater risk and commitment involved.
- Inflation must be taken into account when considering interest rates.
- The demand for money is created by three motives: transactions, precautionary and speculative.
- Income can be used for consumption, saving and paying taxes. Individuals, firms and government all make investments. Some firms are also financial intermediaries.
- Capital markets deal in longer-term finance, while shorter-term finance is dealt with in the money markets.

Quick quiz

1 Define the credit multiplier.

2 What three aims must a commercial bank keep in balance?

3 List the likely functions of a central bank.

4 If tho banking system has liquid reserves of £225bn and seeks to maintain a reserve ratio of 13%, what will broad money supply be?

   A £17bn
   B £1,731bn
   C £2,925bn
   D £292,599bn

5 The ability of the banks to create credit is constrained by all the following except:

A Leakages of cash out of the banking system
B A reduced reserve ratio
C Low demand for loans
D Prudent lending operations

6 What are the four functions of money?

7 Do building societies' shares and deposits form part of M_0 or M_4?

8 What is the relationship between the inflation rate, the real rate of interest and the money rate of interest?

9 What are the motives behind the demand for money?

10 In which market is LIBOR set?

Answers to quick quiz

1 The credit multiplier (or bank multiplier) is the name given to banks' ability to create credit, and hence money, by maintaining their cash reserves at less than 100% of the value of their deposits.

2 Liquidity, profitability and security

3 Setting interest rates
Banker to the government
Central issuer of banknotes
Manager of the national debt
Manager of the nation's foreign currency reserves
Banker to the clearing banks
Supervision of the banking system

4 B £225bn × credit multiplier = total deposits (broad money) therefore £225bn × (1/0.13) = £1,731bn

5 B A falling reserve ratio will increase the credit multiplier

6 Money is a means of exchange, a unit of account, a standard of deferred payment and a store of value.

7 M_4

8 (1 + real rate of interest) × (1 + inflation rate) = 1 + money rate of interest

9 Transactions, precautionary and speculative motives

10 The London interbank market

Answers to activities

1 The answer is (a). Item (b) is not an asset of the bank – it is a liability (a sum of money owed by the bank to its customers). It might be tempting to choose item (c), if you think about the large number of High Street sites owned by the retail banks, but in fact the value of this asset is dwarfed by the banks' lending.

2 Call the extra cash £C. Then:

$$\frac{C}{20\%} = 80 + C$$

$$C = 20\% \times (80 + C)$$

$$0.8C = 16$$

$$C = £20 \text{ million}$$

If an extra £20 million is deposited, the total money supply will rise to £20 million ÷ 20% = £100 million. This includes the initial £20 million, so the increase is £80 million.

3 Share prices respond to:

(a) Factors related to the circumstances of individual companies – eg news of a company's annual profits, or a proposed takeover bid

(b) Factors related to the circumstances of a particular industry – eg new government legislation or regulations for an industry, such as new laws on pollution controls or customer protection measures

(c) Factors related to the circumstances of the national economy – eg changes in interest rates, the latest official figures for the balance of trade, or price inflation.

Chapter 5 :

FINANCIAL INSTITUTIONS

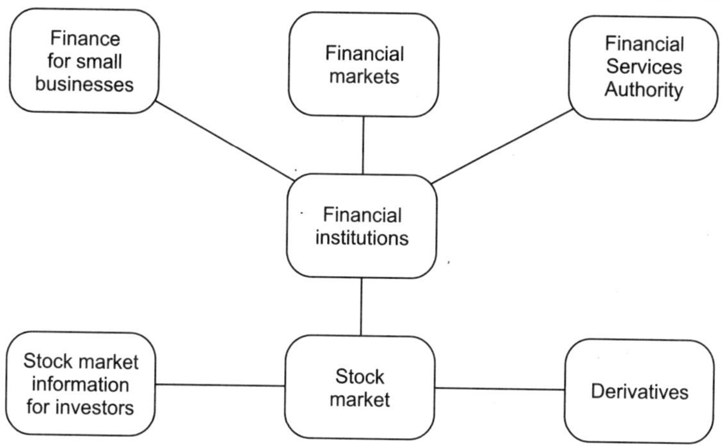

Introduction

This chapter is concerned with the institutions that specialise in the financial services needed in a sophisticated economy. Their main role is to organise and facilitate the flows of money needed to make economic activity possible. Much of their work concerns the linking together of providers and users of financial capital and the first three sections of this chapter deal with various aspects of this role. We then move on to consider a more specialised aspect of finance, the use of derivatives, both as a kind of insurance and as a way to speculate on future price changes. The chapter conclude with two short sections dealing with the role of the UK Financial Services Authority and the special problems of financing small businesses.

Your objectives

In this chapter you will learn about:

(a) The nature of investment

(b) Government and corporate borrowing

(c) How interest rates are managed

(d) How stock markets work, including the efficient markets hypothesis and the workings of the London Stock Exchange

(e) How investors measure companies' success

(f) How derivatives work

(g) What the Financial Services Authority does

(h) The problems of small company finance

1 FINANCIAL MARKETS

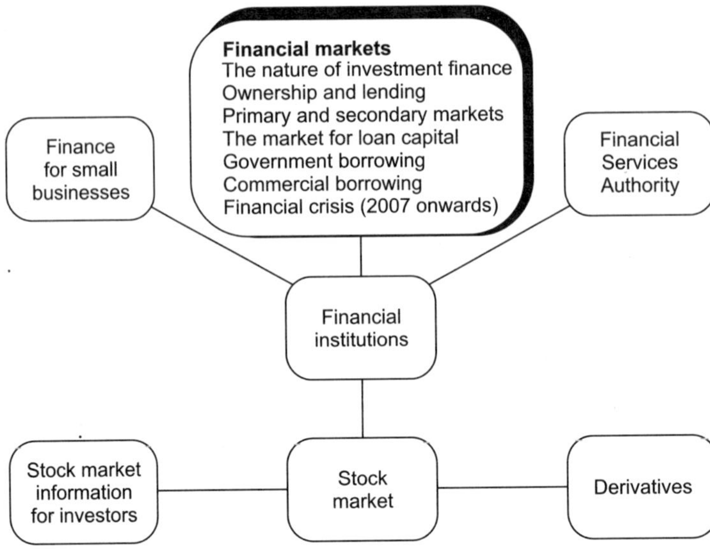

Money is an essential part of all economic systems that develop beyond the use of barter. A modern economy is fundamentally dependent on a vast network of institutions that organise the flows of money required to make business possible. The functions of money are discussed in general terms elsewhere in this Course Book; here we will take a slightly different approach and identify two main aspects of the role of money. The first aspect is the way that money is used in routine transactions to pay for goods and services of all kinds which we have already explored in earlier chapters. The second aspect is the use of money for investment. This aspect is more complex, in that it concerns business's need for capital, or money to finance the acquisition of productive assets, and the role of money provided on credit as the basis of most trade. It is with this second aspect, the role of finance, that we will be concerned with in this chapter.

1.1 The nature of investment finance

The basic transactions involved in investment finance are the transfer of funds from investors to the firms that can use them profitably and the return of the eventual profits back to the investors. Proper arrangements must be incorporated into the system to prevent fraud and to ensure that the degree of risk involved in a given investment is matched by the rewards it offers. Fraud is dealt with by regulation, while the relationship between risk and return is dealt with by the action of market forces. The greater the risk perceived in a given use of funds, the higher the reward that will be demanded. Money can thus be said to have a price, which is the return required for making it available for use in a given economic activity.

A further important aspect of the provision of finance is the degree of liquidity the transaction provides to the investor. Funds are liquid if they can be rapidly moved from one investment to another; they are illiquid if they are committed to a specific purpose for a long period of time. Generally, investors will require a higher return on illiquid assets than on liquid ones, so the price of money will reflect both risk and liquidity.

Since there are large numbers of firms and potential investors and they are largely unknown to one another, there is a vital role to be played by financial intermediaries.

These organisations receive investors' money and supply it to the firms that can make use of it. They provide both financial expertise and an administrative service. Their expertise lies in their judgement of where to apply the funds they obtain and their administrative role lies in the way they aggregate and account for the relatively small amounts provided by individual investors. A very good example of this basic kind of financial activity is provided by the traditional building society or mutual fund, which receives many small deposits from individual savers and makes large loans to enable people to buy their homes. The depositors require a high degree of security for their savings and a reasonable return, while the borrowers are able to offer security for their loans in the form of mortgages over their properties.

Other institutions and methods have been developed to provide a wide range of methods for investment, lending and borrowing, many of them far more complex than the simple building society deposit and loan model.

1.2 Two investment relationships: ownership and lending

Fundamentally, there are two ways to invest in economic activity. The first is to purchase some element of ownership, the second is to make a loan. These two routes to investment differ substantially in their legal form and in the nature of the risk and reward they involve. The simplest form of **ownership** appears in the case of the sole trader or partnership, where individuals use their own money to finance their own economic activity. They accept all of the risk inherent in their business ventures and are entitled to enjoy all of the rewards. They may enjoy great success or they may lose everything. Nobody else is involved.

From this model developed the **limited liability** corporation, which is the basis of almost all modern private sector business organisations. This enables large numbers of investors to pool their funds in order to finance large-scale operations. Ownership is divided into shares and the number of shares purchased governs both the risk assumed and the entitlement to reward. Liability for the debts of the corporation is limited to the amounts the investors originally agreed to subscribe for their shares and the profits of the business are divided in the same proportions.

Lending involves no element of ownership. Risk is limited to the sum lent and reward is governed by the terms of the loan. Within these basic parameters, the loan mechanism can take many forms. Banks and other financial institutions will make loans on any practical scale to both businesses and private individuals. Individuals and organisations can make loans to corporations through the mechanism of bond purchase. And financial institutions make loans among themselves in a rapidly moving market for liquid funds.

Traditionally, investment is recognised by the issue of a document: purchase of shares would be recognised by the issue of a share certificate, while making a loan would be acknowledged by the issue of one of a number of kinds of certificate such as bills and bonds. Collectively, all of these kinds of document are referred to as **securities**. Since they represent significant financial assets, strict rules have been developed concerning their sale and purchase and the changes that must be made in any record of their lawful possession. In modern times, electronic trading has largely made the physical documents obsolete, but the investments they represent are still known as securities.

Activity 1 **(5 minutes)**

When the Eurotunnel, the Channel Tunnel company, could no longer pay the interest due on its enormous borrowings, it proposed that the lenders should convert their bonds into shareholdings. Why do you suppose it made this suggestion?

1.3 Primary and secondary markets

The existence of a large number of investors and investment opportunities available makes the development of a market for finance inevitable. In the simplest sense, some financial institutions, such as banks, perform the functions of a market by themselves, in that they match the supply of finance and the demand for it at an agreed price. A wide range of other, more developed, markets exists, each tending to specialise in particular kinds of funding. Each of these markets consists of group of institutions dealing with one another, both on their own accounts and as agents for external providers and users of funds. Within this institutional setting we may distinguish two slightly different kinds of activity: a primary market and a secondary one. A primary market brings together original providers of funds and the end users of those funds, while a secondary market allows providers of funds to buy and sell their financial assets.

The great value of a secondary market to the financial system is the liquidity it provides by allowing investors to realise their investment at short notice. The liquidity this provides encourages investment and thus promotes economic activity. The secondary market has another important economic function, in that it acts as an important signalling system: the market price for existing shares reflects the judgement of the market participants about the viability and prospects of the companies involved. This helps to guide the flow of funds to their most efficient economic use.

The basic distinction between primary and secondary markets can be applied to all of the markets that make up the financial system.

In the UK, the London Stock Exchange (LSE) provides both primary and secondary markets in investments of many kinds. Thus, one function of the LSE is to provide a primary market for shares in limited liability companies. A new company offers its shares for sale and investors buy them through the facilities provided by the Stock Exchange. Other Stock Exchange mechanisms provide a secondary market, allowing investors to buy and sell existing securities among themselves.

We will discuss the LSE in more detail later in this chapter.

1.4 The market for loan capital

Much loan capital is provided by direct loans from banks to businesses. However, there are also extensive primary and secondary market-based dealings in loans, using a wide range of financial instruments. In the UK, most of this activity centres on the LSE.

1.5 Government borrowing

The Debt Management Office

Governments also participate in the financial markets. When a government spends more money than it raises in revenue, it borrows the shortfall. In the UK, this fiscal deficit is known as the Public Sector Net Cash Requirement (PSNCR).

A prime responsibility of the Debt Management Office (DMO) of the Treasury is to borrow money to finance the PSNCR. The DMO will borrow money in the short-term by issuing Treasury bills and in the long-term through the issuance of UK Government bonds.

Treasury bills

A Treasury bill is a short-term debt instrument issued by the DMO. It represents an obligation to pay a set amount of money, normally in 91 days' time. It pays no interest, but is issued at a discount to its face value. The difference between the discounted issue price and the face value of the bill compensates lenders for providing funds. The DMO sells Treasury bills by tender every Friday, in minimum denominations of £25,000. The DMO also sells bills denominated in euros, by monthly tender.

Gilt characteristics

UK Government bonds are known colloquially as gilts, since the stock certificates formerly issued were printed on gilt-edged paper. In the UK, the market in government debt is known as the gilt-edged market.

Gilts are issued to provide for longer-term government borrowing; they may be issued for a fixed term or undated. Over the life of the bond the holder receives interest, often referred to as the 'coupon', since at one time a coupon attached to the bond had to be surrendered to obtain payment. In the UK, the convention is for the coupon rate to be paid on a semi-annual basis in equal instalments. Gilts pay gross and holders are liable for income tax on their bond income. The cheque paying the coupon is known as a warrant.

Gilt-edged stocks are classified with respect to their maturity dates. The official Debt Management Office definitions are given below.

(a) Shorts are gilts with less than seven years until redemption.
(b) Mediums are gilts with between seven and fifteen years until redemption.
(c) Longs are gilts with over fifteen years until redemption.

Note that both the LSE and *Financial Times* classify shorts as those with up to five years to run until redemption and mediums as those with between five and fifteen years to run until redemption.

On maturity the loan (the principal) is repaid.

The gilts market

There is an active secondary market in gilts, so they are a very liquid investment as well as being a very secure one.

The price of a gilt is quoted in terms of the amount an investor must pay in order to obtain £100 nominal value of the stock. Where the market price is greater than £100 the gilt is said to be priced above par. This happens if the bond pays an attractive coupon compared with current interest rates. Where the market price is less than £100 the gilt is said to be priced below par.

Because government stock is regarded as being risk-free, the only factor that influences the price of gilts is the future cash-flows they guarantee to the holder. The market price of the bond is the present value of those cash-flows, discounted at the current rate of interest. The important implication of this is that as interest rates rise (or fall), bond prices fall (or rise).

EXAMPLE: FIXED INTEREST BONDS

A government bond paying 6½% is due to mature in one year's time. The risk free interest rate is 8%. What is the market value of the bond? Assume that the final coupon payment will be for a full year's interest.

Time	*Cash-flow*	*8% Discount factor*	*Present value*
1	£106.50	0.926	£98.62

What would be the market value of the bond if the interest rate were 4%?

Time	*Cash-flow*	*4% Discount factor*	*Present value*
1	£106.50	0.962	£102.45

This simple example illustrates an important rule of thumb about fixed interest bonds of all kinds: when interest rates fall, their prices rise and *vice versa*.

1.6 Commercial borrowing

Corporate bonds

In much the same way that governments finance their deficits through the use of debt, companies wishing to spend more than they currently have available may also borrow money through the issuance of corporate bonds. Due to the increased risk of default, these bonds will yield more than government debt. Once again this illustrates one of the key maxims of investment – greater risk requires greater reward. In order to mitigate the effect of risk on the cost of borrowing, companies have the ability to issue debt that is secured against the company's assets. This offers some protection for the creditors' investment in the event of a default, since the security can be seized and sold.

In addition to security, the issuers of a bond may attach various rights to the issue in order to encourage investors to buy their securities.

For example, a conversion right gives bondholders the power, at a specified date or dates in the future, to convert their bonds into shares in the company concerned. The number of shares to be received and the price to be paid, if any, will be fixed at the time of the issue of the bond. Depending on the movement in the underlying share price, this conversion right may be very valuable indeed. The trade-off in this sort of issue is that the coupon will often be much lower than the market would otherwise expect on a bond from that particular company.

Most corporate bonds are issued with a fixed coupon rate, like gilts, and their market value is largely determined in the same way. However, since corporate bonds are riskier than gilts, the market adds a risk premium to the basic discounted cash-flow price.

Commercial paper

A discount security can be defined as a non-interest bearing debt instrument, issued at a discount to the nominal value, which is then redeemed at face value (par) at maturity. We have already seen discount securities in the form of Treasury bills. A further example is provided by 'commercial paper' (CP).

CP is short-term debt issued by a company; it will normally mature twelve months or less after it is issued. As a discount security, CP will pay no interest, instead trading at a discount to nominal value. The discount will reflect credit risk and time to maturity. CP is normally unsecured and is therefore only attractive as an investment if it is guaranteed by a bank or issued by companies with a very high credit rating.

Eurobonds

In essence, a Eurobond is a debt instrument issued by a borrower (typically a government or a large company) normally, or predominantly, domiciled outside of the country in whose currency it is denominated. For example, a US dollar Eurobond could be issued anywhere in the world except for the US. As such, a better name for it might be an 'international bond'. Eurobonds frequently carry no security, other than the name and credit rating of the issuer.

Certificates of deposit

Certificates of deposit (CDs) are issued by banks to acknowledge the receipt of large sums of money from investors. The sums involved are usually in the order of hundreds of thousands of pounds. These deposits are made for the medium-term: six to eighteen months would be typical, though deposits for several years are common. The CD records the sum, the term of the deposit and the rate of interest payable. Interest may be drawn during the life of the CD or at its end; the latter course brings the benefit of compound interest. There is an active secondary market in CDs.

Bills of Exchange

The system of Bills of Exchange has been in existence for many centuries and exists primarily as a secure means of moving large sums of money, typically in connection with trading transactions. A Bill of Exchange is *drawn* by a *drawer* upon a *drawee*. Typically, the drawer will be a supplier and the drawee a customer who has received goods or services. When the drawee *accepts* the bill by signing it, he enters into an unconditional obligation to pay the sum stated on the bill. Most bills are written so that they are inherently negotiable and the right to receive the payment can be sold to a third party. After such a sale, the purchaser enjoys an unconditional right to collect payment, even if a dispute arises between the drawer and the drawee. The payment may fall due on a stated date or *at sight*: that is, when the holder presents it to the drawee for payment.

In past times, Bills of Exchange offered a much more convenient and secure means of moving money about than actually transporting notes and coin. The common method of using them would be for the drawer to draw a bill on his bank. The reputation and credit of the drawee bank would then allow the bill to be sold to another bank and the funds thus realised.

Today, Bills of Exchange are still widely used in international trade. The importer draws a bill upon his bank in much the same way as writing a cheque and gives it to the supplier. Because long periods of credit may be offered, the bill is more useful than a cheque, in that the supplier can obtain payment for it immediately from his own bank. The payment would be at a discount, which compensates the paying bank for providing the credit given in the original sale. The process of selling a Bill of Exchange is therefore known as *discounting*. The two banks involved then settle the payment between themselves when it falls due. The importer obtains a period of credit, the exporter obtains the funds due and the banks earn appropriate sums for their services in the form of fees and the discount on the bill.

1.7 The financial crisis of 2007 and onwards

The financial crisis of 2007 and onwards was a crisis which was arguably triggered by a liquidity shortfall in the United States banking system caused by the overvaluation of property assets. It resulted in the collapse of large financial institutions, the bailout of banks by national governments and downturns in housing and stock markets around the world.

The collapse of a global housing bubble, which peaked in the US in 2006, caused the values of securities tied to property pricing to plummet thereafter, damaging financial institutions globally. Stock markets suffered large losses during late 2008 and early 2009, due to a number of factors such as questions regarding bank solvency, declines in credit availability, and damaged investor confidence.

Economies worldwide slowed during this period as credit tightened and international trade declined. Critics argued that credit rating agencies and investors failed to accurately price the risk involved with mortgage-related financial products, and that governments did not adjust their regulatory practices to address 21st century financial markets. Governments and central banks responded with unprecedented fiscal stimulus, monetary policy expansion, and institutional bailouts.

2 STOCK MARKETS

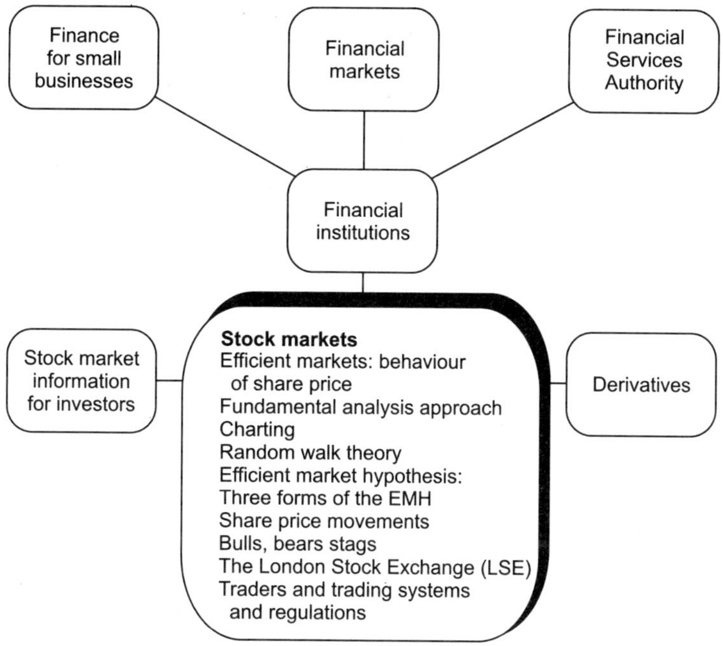

Stock markets, such as the London Stock Exchange (LSE) provide both primary and secondary markets in investments. We will discuss the way the LSE works later; first we must consider the theoretical background to the prices of share and other securities.

2.1 Efficient markets and the behaviour of share prices

There are three different approaches to understanding share price movements.

- Fundamental analysis
- Technical analysis
- Random walk theory

2.2 The fundamental analysis approach to share values

The fundamental theory of share value suggests that the market price of a share represents a valuation of its estimated future dividends. Thus, the value of a share will be the discounted present value of all future expected dividends on the share, discounted at the shareholders' cost of capital.

The logical basis of fundamental analysis seems to be valid. In practice however, share price movements are affected by day to day fluctuations, reflecting three main influences.

- Supply and demand in a particular period
- Investor confidence
- Market interest rate movements

Investment analysts want to be able to predict these fluctuations in prices, but fundamental analysis might be inadequate as a technique. Some analysts therefore rely on technical analysis of share price movements.

2.3 Technical analysis

Technical analysts (or 'chartists', from their extensive use of graphs) attempt to predict share price movements by assuming that past price patterns will be repeated. At times, this approach can be spectacularly successful, but there is no real theoretical justification for it. Academic studies have found that the results it obtains are generally no better or worse than those obtained from a simple 'buy and hold' strategy based on a well-diversified share portfolio.

This may be explained by research that has found that there are no regular patterns or cycles in share price movements over time: they follow a random walk.

2.4 Random walk theory and the efficient market hypothesis

The key feature of random walk theory is that, although share prices may have an intrinsic or fundamental value, this value will be altered as new information becomes available. Also, the behaviour of investors is such that the actual share price will fluctuate from day to day around the intrinsic value. Research was carried out in the late 1960s to explain why share prices in the stock market display a random walk. This research led to the development of the efficient market hypothesis (EMH).

The EMH suggests that the stock market price of a share reflects all available relevant information about companies, earnings, dividend policy and so on. This means that an individual investor cannot, in the long run, obtain greater than average returns from a diversified share portfolio.

If the stock market is efficient at processing information, share prices should vary in a rational way.

(a) If a company makes an investment with a positive net present value (NPV), shareholders will get to know about it and the market price of its shares will rise in anticipation of future dividend increases.

(b) If a company makes a bad investment, shareholders will find out and so the price of its shares will fall.

(c) If interest rates rise, shareholders will want a higher return from their investments, so market prices will fall.

It has been argued that the UK and US stock markets are efficient capital markets since three conditions prevail.

(a) The prices of securities bought and sold reflect all the relevant information which is available to the buyers and sellers. That is, share prices change quickly to reflect all new information about future prospects.

(b) No individual dominates the market.

(c) Transaction costs of buying and selling are not so high as to discourage trading significantly.

2.5 Three forms of the EMH

Three forms of the EMH are advanced.

Weak form efficiency

The weak form hypothesis suggests that share prices take into account all relevant information about past price movements and their implications. Share prices do not change in anticipation of new information. Since new information arrives unexpectedly, share prices will move up and down without a predictable pattern, and past price movements are unlikely to be repeated.

Semi-strong form efficiency

Semi-strong form efficiency means that current share prices reflect all relevant publicly available knowledge, including information about past price movements and their implications.

Semi-strong efficiency will mean that investors will not gain an advantage through studying company accounts or economic forecasts, since share prices will already have taken account of this information.

Strong form efficiency

Strong form efficiency means that in addition to information about past price changes and other relevant publicly available knowledge, share prices also reflect all information available from specialists' or experts' insider knowledge.

This theory suggests, therefore, that an expert, such as an investment manager, should be able to use his privileged access to additional information about companies to earn a higher rate of return than an ordinary investor. Unit trusts should, according to this theory, perform better than the average investor. Research has suggested, however, that this expert skill does not actually exist.

2.6 How efficient are stock markets in reality?

Evidence so far collected suggests that stock markets show at least weak form efficiency and tend to show semi-strong form efficiency. In other words, current share prices reflect all or most publicly available information about companies and their securities. Research in both the UK and the USA has suggested that market prices anticipate mergers several months before they are formally announced, and the conclusion drawn is that the stock markets in these countries exhibit at least semi-strong efficiency.

2.7 Explaining share price movements

If the market is efficient, then share prices should vary in a rational way; however, despite the evidence referred to above, various types of anomaly appear to support the views that irrationality often drives the stock market.

(a) Seasonal and month of the-year effects, day-of-the-week effects and also hour-of-the-day effects seem to occur, so that share prices might tend to rise or fall at a particular time of the year, week or day.

(b) There may be a short-run overreaction to recent events.

(c) Individual shares or shares in small companies may be neglected.

2.8 The London Stock Exchange (LSE)

The LSE is an organised capital market based in London. It is the main capital market in the UK and plays an important role in the functioning of the UK economy.

(a) It enables large firms and the government to raise long-term capital, by providing a market place for borrowers and investors to come together.

(b) The LSE publicises the prices of quoted (or 'listed') securities, which are then reported in daily national newspapers such as the *Financial Times*. Investors can therefore keep an eye on the value of their stocks and shares, and make buying and selling decisions accordingly.

(c) The LSE tries to enforce certain rules of conduct for its listed firms and for operators in the market, so that investors have the assurance that companies whose shares are traded on the Exchange and traders who operate there are reputable. Confidence in the LSE will make investors more willing to put their money into stocks and shares.

Smaller companies that cannot meet the stringent requirements needed to obtain a full listing on the Stock Exchange can raise new capital by issuing shares on the Alternative Investment Market (AIM), which opened in 1995. Like the Stock Exchange main market, the AIM is a market in which investors can also trade in shares already issued. It is regulated by the Stock Exchange.

2.9 Traders: the role of member firms of the LSE

All member firms of the LSE are broker-dealers. Before the deregulation of the LSE in 1986, investors wishing to buy or sell shares did so through a broker. The brokers were the customers' agents and did not themselves actually deal in securities: that was the role of dealers (called jobbers), who bought and sold securities among themselves. The operation of the market thus required two kinds of specialists. One of the reforms of 1986 was to allow firms to have dual capacity and act as both brokers and dealers. A broker-dealer is both able to act as agent for customers and to buy and sell on its own account with other dealers in order to execute the required trades.

Some broker-dealers can elect to take on additional responsibility as market makers.

2.10 Trading systems

As already mentioned, one of the most important functions of the LSE is to provide a secondary market in investment securities. Such a secondary market can be operated in several ways: the main approaches used on the LSE are the order driven (or auction) market and the quote driven (or dealer) market.

In an order driven market, investors present their orders to buy or sell a particular investment and the market trading system matches buyers and sellers at compatible prices. Information about open orders is contained in the market 'order book'. An order driven market works well with securities that are traded frequently and regularly, such as the shares of major companies. On the LSE, about 150 shares fall into this category and are traded on an electronic trading platform known as the Stock Exchange Trading System, or SETS. Prices of securities that trade on SETS are, therefore, purely driven by the buyers and sellers in the market themselves.

A quote driven market requires market makers to provide prices at which investors can deal. In such a market, the dealer posts 'bid' and 'offer' (or 'ask') prices. The bid price is the price at which the dealer will buy stock and the offer price is the price at which the dealer will sell stock. Usually the bid price will be lower than the offer price, giving a bid-ask spread. Prices quoted by the market maker will usually be firm, that is, guaranteed, up to a particular transaction size. For such a market to operate efficiently, up-to-date prices at which market makers are willing to trade need to be made available to other market participants. On the LSE, this function is performed by the Stock Exchange Automated Quote system, or SEAQ. SEAQ provides prices for securities that are not sufficiently liquid to trade on the SETS order driven system. It lists the prices quoted by at least two competing market makers.

2.11 Bulls, bears and stags

Notwithstanding the wide applicability of the EMH, many investors trade because they have firm opinions about the future movement of individual share prices or of share prices in general.

(a) Bulls believe that prices will rise. Their strategy is to buy in anticipation of a capital gain.

(b) Bears believe that prices will fall. Their strategy is to sell in order to avoid a capital loss.

If bulls or bears deal in large enough volumes, their beliefs can be self-fulfilling through the simple operation of the market forces of supply and demand. Extensive selling of a security is likely to drive its price down, because supply will exceed demand. Similarly, extensive buying of a security is likely to drive its price up for the converse reason. These effects are well-understood on stock markets. Investors mounting a take-over bid will build up their stock holding in as much secrecy as possible in order to avoid a rapid price rise. In an unstable market, bears can profit by selling a stock in order to drive its price down and repurchasing it later at the lower price.

Note: On June 16, 2010, the Chancellor of the Exchequer, George Osborne, announced plans to abolish the FSA and separate its responsibilities between a number of new agencies and the Bank of England. For more details see section 5 below.

Activity 2 **(5 minutes)**

In 1980, Nelson Bunker Hunt and his brother Herbert bought large quantities of silver as hedge against inflation. Eventually, they controlled one-third of the world's supply. What was the great danger to the brother's financial position?

Stags, like bulls, anticipate a price rise, but in the special case of an initial public offering of shares by a new entrant to the stock market. Such offers are usually made at an attractively low price so as to ensure that they are fully taken up: this is a less risky approach than setting a high price in the hope of maximising receipts. Also, such offers are usually guaranteed by merchant banks: it is in their interest not to be required to take up unsold shares, so their advice will favour an attractive price. A further consideration is that an unsuccessful offer will damage the reputations of the company and its advisers. Thus, it is normal for the price of newly floated shares to rise significantly when trading begins. Stags take advantage of this by subscribing to the offer for as many shares as they can and selling them as soon as the market stabilises at a higher price.

2.12 The regulation of the LSE

Investors will only provide funds if they trust the recipients to honour the bargain. It is in the interests of both providers and users of funds to promote the highest standards of probity and care. Over the years there have been many frauds perpetrated on investors and a large body of law and regulation has been developed to deter dishonest practices. Stock exchanges such as the LSE are themselves active in the strict regulation of investment business.

Overall supervision of investment business is the responsibility of Financial Services Authority (FSA), which acts as external regulator for Recognised Investment Exchanges, of which the LSE is one. There are thus two layers of regulation: the requirements laid down by the FSA and the rules by which the LSE satisfies those requirements.

The LSE rules amount to a moderately sized book. They are concerned with the activities of the member firms and the way they carry on their business. Strict standards are laid down to govern such matters as qualifications for membership; how transactions are conducted and recorded; making payments; and control of the pattern and rate of activity on the market.

Formerly, the LSE rules also regulated the stock-market related activities of the companies whose securities are traded on it. This role has now been taken over by the FSA in its capacity as UK Listing Authority. The listing rules are particularly concerned with the corporate governance of listed companies and those seeking a listing.

3 STOCK MARKET INFORMATION FOR INVESTORS

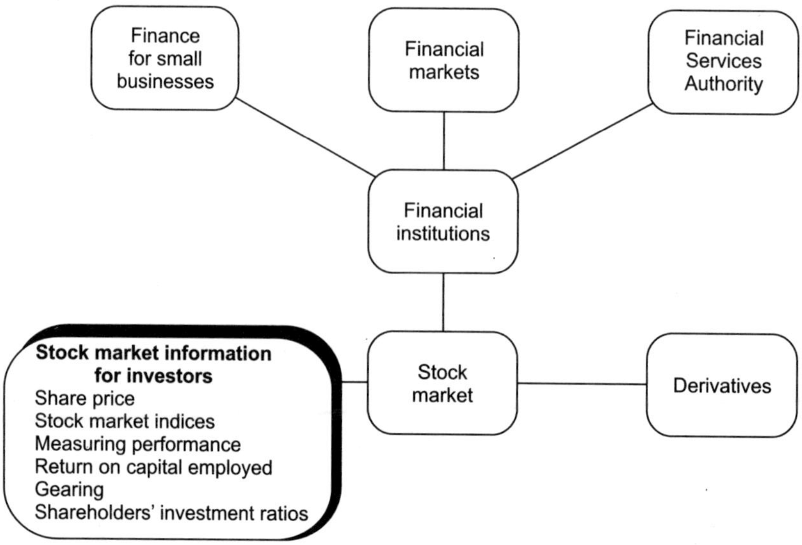

3.1 Share prices

Investors and traders need to know the market price of any security in which they are interested and how it fluctuates up and down. The market value of a quoted company can be measured if its share price and the number of shares in issue are multiplied together. Price information for traded securities is therefore widely published in the financial press and within the communications systems of the markets concerned. Market traders will have access to prices minute-by-minute on a system such as SETS; the public will rely on the financial press and the Internet, both of which will relay information after a delay. Typically, the information listed below will be available for each security in the financial press.

(a) The price at the close of business on the previous day

(b) The overall movement in price during the day

(c) The price one year previously, for comparison

(d) Measures of financial performance such as yield and earnings per share (these measures are explained below)

3.2 Stock market indices

The general level of share prices is also important, since it indicates the degree of confidence investors have in prospects for the economy. Overall share price performance may be measured by calculating an index. All stock markets have their own particular indices and may have more than one.

The LSE has several share price indices, the most prominent being the Financial Times-Stock Exchange 100 (FTSE 100), the Financial Times-Actuaries All Share index (FT-A) and the FTSE MID 250. The FTSE 100 indexes the share price performance of the 100 largest companies traded on the LSE, while the FTSE MID 250 covers the next 250 companies by size. Reasonably enough, the FT-A covers the performance of all of the companies traded.

In the USA the Dow Jones index, monitors 30 leading US stocks while the Standard & Poor's index follows the top 500 American stocks. Also in the USA, the NASDAQ market (which takes its name from the National Association of Securities Dealers Automated Quotations system) provides an entirely screen-based stock exchange with no central physical location and has its own indices in the NASDAQ composite, the NASDAQ 100 and the NASDAQ Financial 100. The Nikkei-Dow is the most-quoted index for Japan, while the Morgan-Stanley index shows the average performance of stock markets globally.

3.3 Measuring performance

Investors' information needs extend well beyond knowledge of prices: they also require detailed information on current and past performance. This is provided by the analysis of companies' published accounts. A key problem is how to extract information that has meaning; often, figures in a set of accounts only acquire meaning when they are subjected to a process of comparison. There are various comparisons that could be made. Here are some examples.

(a) Comparisons of the current year's results with the previous year, to establish whether performance or the financial situation has improved or worsened

(b) Comparisons of the current year's results with those of similar companies in the same industry, to establish whether the company appears to be doing better or worse than competitors

(c) Comparisons against a 'standard' or 'benchmark' level of performance

One way of making comparisons is by calculating ratios between the figures in the accounts. A ratio calculated from the current year's accounting figures can then be compared with the ratio achieved in the previous year, or by a competitor company. Accountants calculate and use a wide range of ratios in their work but we will discuss only a few that are of particular interest to investors.

3.4 Return on capital employed

Profitability is obviously a very important consideration. However, it is impossible to assess profits or profit growth properly without relating them to the amount of capital that was employed in making them. The most important profitability ratio is therefore return on capital employed (ROCE), which states the profit as a percentage of the amount of capital employed.

$$\text{ROCE} = \frac{\text{Profit before interest and taxation}}{\text{Capital employed}} \times 100\%$$

Capital employed = Shareholders' equity plus non-current liabilities
(*or* total assets less current liabilities)

The underlying principle is that we must **compare like with like,** and so if capital means share capital and reserves plus non-current liabilities and debt capital, profit must mean the profit earned by all this capital together. This is usually taken as profit before interest and tax. This figure is used rather than net profit since interest is the return for loan capital and because there might be unusual variations in the tax charge from year to year that would not affect the underlying profitability of the company's operations

3.5 Gearing

Capital gearing (or leverage) is an important aspect of a company's long-term capital structure. The company's assets and operations are financed by its long-term capital, which can be thought of as being of two types.

(a) Ordinary share capital (also known as equity)

(b) Prior charge capital, which is long-term debt and any preference shares that may have been issued

Like loan capital, preferred share capital has a prior claim over profits before interest and tax, ahead of ordinary shareholders.

The capital gearing ratio is a measure of the proportion of a company's capital that is prior charge capital.

$$\text{Capital gearing} = \frac{\text{Total prior charge capital}}{\text{Shareholders' equity} + \text{total prior charge capital}} \times 100\%$$

(Total capital)

As with the debt ratio, there is **no absolute limit** to what a gearing ratio ought to be, though a company with a gearing ratio of more than 50% would probably be said to be highly geared.

The implications of high or low gearing

Gearing influences both the ability to raise further capital and the risk inherent in investing in a company.

Many companies are highly geared and successful. However, the higher its gearing, the greater the possibility that a company may have difficulty in raising further loan capital, unless it can also boost its shareholders' capital, either with retained profits or by a new share issue.

The gearing ratio is an attempt to quantify the risk involved in holding equity shares, both in terms of the company's ability to remain in business and in terms of expected ordinary dividends from the company. A high level of prior charge capital means that large interest (or preference dividend) payments must be paid out of profit. The more highly geared the company, the greater the risk that little (if anything) will be available to fund dividends to the ordinary shareholders.

3.6 Shareholders' investment ratios

There are several ratios that are particularly helpful to equity shareholders and other investors in assessing the value and quality of an investment in the ordinary shares of a company.

Earnings per share

$$\text{Basic EPS} = \frac{\text{Net profit/(loss) attributable to ordinary shareholders}}{\text{Weighted average number of ordinary shares outstanding during the period}}$$

Earnings per share (EPS) is the amount of net profit for the period that is attributable to each ordinary share in issue during all or part of the period. If the number of shares in issue has changed during the year, a weighted average is used.

Dividend cover

$$\text{Dividend cover} = \frac{\text{Earnings per share}}{\text{Dividend per (ordinary) share}}$$

Dividend cover shows the proportion of earnings that is distributed to shareholders and the proportion that will be retained in the business to finance future growth. A dividend cover of 2, for example, would indicate that the company had paid 50% of its distributable profits as dividends, and retained 50% in the business. Retained profits are an important source of funds for most companies, so the dividend cover can in some cases be quite high.

Dividend yield

Dividend yield is the actual cash return a shareholder is currently expecting on the shares of a company.

$$\text{Dividend yield} = \frac{\text{Dividend on the share for the year}}{\text{Current market value of the share (ex div)}} \times 100\%$$

(a) The dividend per share is taken as the dividend for the previous year.

(b) Ex-div means that the share is valued as though it does not have the right to any dividend that might be about to be paid.

Shareholders look for both income and capital growth from their investments, so dividend yield is an important aspect of a share's performance.

Price/earnings ratio

P/E ratio is calculated as $\frac{\text{Share price}}{\text{Earnings per share}}$

Notice that this ratio uses current share market price, not nominal value. It is market price that is important here.

A share's P/E ratio reflects the market's view of the company's future rather than its current performance. A high P/E ratio indicates strong shareholder confidence in the company and its future prospects, while a lower P/E ratio indicates lower confidence.

You will encounter shareholders' ratio again in your study of capital investments in Chapter 6.

Activity 3 **(5 minutes)**

Microsoft shares rose in price from its stock market launch in 1986 until 1999, yet the company paid its shareholders no dividends at all in this period. Why were shareholders happy to buy shares in a company that provided no income?

4 DERIVATIVES

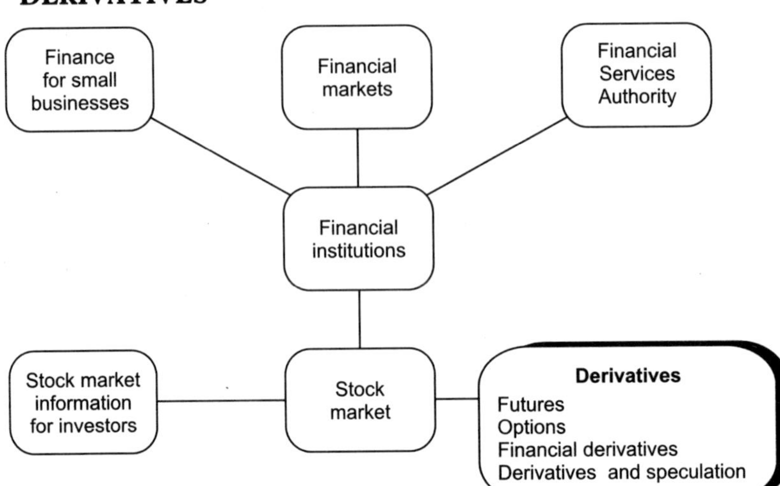

Everything we have discussed in this chapter so far has been concerned with investing money in yield-producing securities of one kind or another. We must now move on and consider another aspect of the work of financial markets: the trade in derivatives.

Derivatives are so called because their value is derived from that of an underlying security or physical commodity. Their importance lay originally in their usefulness in the management of risk and this is still a major aspect of their use. However, they have achieved notoriety from their use as a means of speculating on future price movements.

In essence, derivatives can be thought of as a kind of insurance against adverse price changes in the future. A business is concerned about the effect such a change might have, so it pays a premium to have the risk borne by someone else – typically a bank of some kind. A contract entered into in order to limit losses is called a hedge and the use of derivatives in this way is called hedging.

Let us look at a very common kind of derivative: the future.

4.1 Futures

Futures have their origins in the markets for commodities such as wheat, coffee and minerals. The prices of all commodities tend to fluctuate seasonally and are also subject to large changes because of unpredictable events such as storms, drought, wars and political unrest. To avoid the uncertainty arising from large swings in prices, producers and users of these commodities would agree quantities and prices in advance. Such forward contracts protected the seller against a fall in market price, with its consequent loss of revenue, and the buyer against a rise in price, with its consequent increase in expense. To achieve this desirable result of avoiding adverse price movements, both parties gave up the possibility of receiving the gain that would follow a market price movement in their favour. Forward contracts encouraged investment in productive capacity and benefited buyers and sellers alike by enabling them to plan for the future.

The difficulty with this kind of simple forward contract is that it involves a buyer and seller who actually wish to deliver and receive the specified quantities of the underlying commodity involved. There is a problem of matching the exact requirements of buyer and seller; this is the sort of problem that markets and the financial institutions operating in them exist to solve. The solution is the futures contract, often known, more simply, as a 'future'.

Commodities futures are forward contracts that are standardised in terms of quantity, quality and delivery date. Rather than individual producers and users expending a great deal of energy on establishing contact and negotiating with one another, they are able to go straight to a financial intermediary and buy or sell the underlying commodity at a fixed price for future delivery. Buyer and seller are protected against the risk of adverse price movements by the contract, as before, and so is the intermediary, by the simple method of being both seller and buyer. The intermediary is paid for the service it provides by dealing with buyer and seller at different prices and by charging fees for the arrangement.

Futures contracts, being in standard forms, are actively traded on futures exchanges by financial institutions. Market prices for future trade are thus available for buyers and sellers of the underlying commodity who wish to limit their exposure to price movements. Active trade makes it possible to adjust the effective life of a contract despite there being a fixed date for delivery. When the insurance is no longer required, the contract can be sold at the prevailing market price and thus brought to an end. This is called 'closing out' the contract and, in fact, very few traded contracts run for their intended lives: they are closed out beforehand at the prevailing market price. Naturally, that price reflects the risk assumed by the institution providing the insurance.

4.2 Options

We can see the insurance-like nature of derivatives even more clearly in the case of options. Like futures, options have been traded for centuries. They differ from futures in that they provide the right, but not the obligation, to either purchase or sell an underlying asset at a date and price fixed at the start. An option to sell is called a 'put' option, while an option to buy is known as a 'call' option. In either case, a premium is paid to acquire the option. The fixed option price is called the 'strike' price.

Let us consider a supplier who purchases a put option for a commodity such as sugar. If the market price for sugar falls below the strike price, the supplier will exercise his option and require the other party to the option to purchase the goods at the strike price, thus avoiding having to sell at the lower market price. His only loss is the cost of the option premium. If the market price rises, the supplier will forgo the option and simply sell his sugar on the open market, once again losing the cost of the premium, but benefiting from the higher price obtained. A buyer can use a call option in an essentially similar way to insure against price rises. In both cases, the financial intermediary selling the option gains the option premium in exchange for assuming the risk of having to deal in the underlying commodity at a disadvantageous price.

4.3 Financial derivatives

The usefulness of commodity derivatives for managing risk has led to the development of equivalent products for use in financial markets. Simple examples occur in relation to interest and foreign exchange rates. Companies that wish to limit their exposure to adverse changes in these rates can use forward contacts, futures and options in exactly the same way as producers and purchasers of commodities, since interest rates and exchange rates are effectively the prices of domestic and foreign currency respectively.

A further widely used kind of financial derivative is the share option. Like any other option, it gives a right, but not an obligation, to buy or sell the underlying item, in this case a share. Share options are widely used in executive remuneration schemes as a way of encouraging the senior managers to promote the interests of the shareholders. The company gives the managers options to purchase its shares at a future date and at what it expects to be an attractive price. The greater the success of the company in the intervening period, as measured by its share price, the greater the reward the managers will receive from exercising their options. If all goes well, the shareholders benefit from the rise in share price, while the managers are able to buy their shares and immediately sell them at a profit.

4.4 Derivatives and speculation

The essence of the use of derivatives as a form of insurance is to reduce the risk of loss. However, the future also holds the possibility of gain and it is possible to use derivatives to speculate as well as to insure against possible loss. Let us take the example of a simple future contract for the sale of a commodity. Suppose a trader believes that the actual market price of the commodity will fall below the currently available strike price for the same point in the future and enters into a future contract to sell the commodity. This is called 'going short' on the commodity, or, simply, 'shorting' it. If the actual market price does fall below the strike price, our trader will be able to buy the required amount on the open market and make a profit by fulfilling his contract at the strike price. Part of the attractiveness of this idea is that to put it into practice it is not actually necessary to be connected in any way with the actual production or handling of the commodity in question: it is a purely financial transaction. The disadvantage of the proceeding for the speculator is that the market price might actually rise above the strike price: he would then make a loss when he delivered on his future contract. Such transactions are therefore attractive to those who believe that they have some kind of inside information relevant to the future movement of prices.

More complex manoeuvres are possible with options of various kinds, some of which, if carried out on a large enough scale, can actually influence the market price in such a way as to serve the ends of the speculators. The use of derivatives is therefore subject to an element of scrutiny by the regulators of the markets where they are traded.

5 THE FINANCIAL SERVICES AUTHORITY

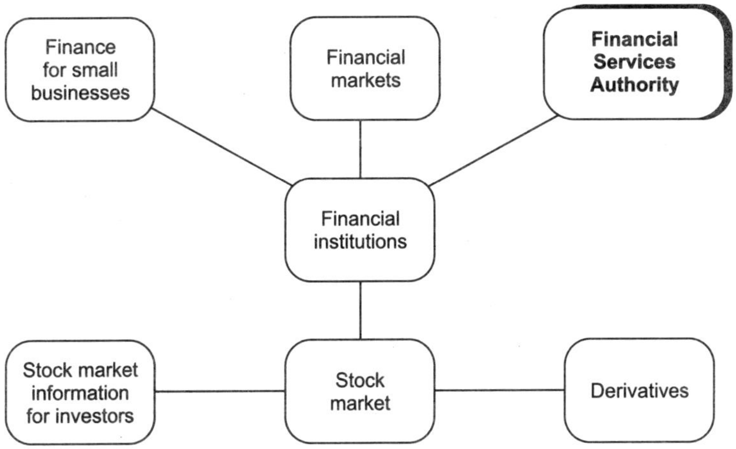

The UK Financial Services Authority (FSA) is an independent, non-governmental body financed by the financial services industry. The Financial Services and Markets Act gives it four statutory objectives:

- Maintenance of confidence in the financial system generally
- Promotion of public understanding of the financial system
- Securing an appropriate level of consumer protection
- Reduction of financial crime

The FSA regulates most financial services markets, exchanges and firms in the UK, including financial advisers, insurance companies, building societies and friendly societies. We have already mentioned its role in relation to the LSE.

A particularly important role played by the FSA is the supervision of all UK banking, a role previously performed by the Bank of England. In this role, the FSA sets standards designed to protect both the banking industry's customers and the banking system itself.

(a) Minimum capital and liquidity requirements are laid down to reduce the risk of default.

(b) A minimum provision for bad and doubtful debts is specified.

(c) Internal systems and controls are monitored to ensure that banks are properly run.

Plans to abolish the FSA

On June 16, 2010, the Chancellor of the Exchequer, George Osborne, announced plans to abolish the FSA and separate its responsibilities between a number of new agencies and the Bank of England. The Consumer Protection and Markets Authority will be responsible for policing the City and the banking system. A new Prudential Regulatory Authority will carry out the prudential regulation of financial firms, including banks, investment banks, building societies and insurance companies. All other responsibilities will be assumed by the Bank of England which will establish a Financial Policy Committee. The transition is expected to be completed by 2012.

Activity 4 **(30 minutes)**

At the time of publication the future of the FSA looked uncertain. Research what has happened to the FSA and what has been put in its place.

6 FINANCE FOR SMALL BUSINESSES

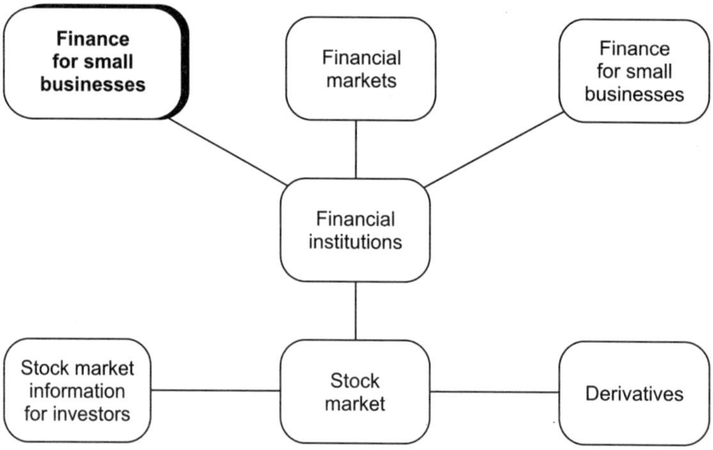

This chapter has been concerned with the way financial markets are able to provide the funds that businesses need to operate. Generally, most of these finance sources are much more accessible to large and well-established companies than they are to small companies. There are several reasons why this is so.

(a) Unlike public companies, private companies cannot issue shares on a stock exchange. Their most important source of new equity is therefore retained profit. However, small companies are unlikely to be very profitable, so this is a very time-consuming route to expansion.

(b) Similarly, it is not practicable for small companies to issue bonds in the market.

(c) A traditional source of finance for all companies has been bank lending. However, banks will not lend to risky companies, except at high interest rates. Also, they will expect their loans to be secured on assets of the company. Small businesses frequently do not have assets of sufficient value to provide the required security. Frequently, therefore, the bank will require that the loan is secured on the personal assets of the company's owner-director. Owner-directors are often unwilling to allow this.

(d) There may be a lack of information about the current performance and future prospects of a small company. Larger companies are more likely to have sophisticated information, planning and control systems and quoted companies are expected to provide large amounts of information to the market. A potential lender might refuse to consider a request for finance unless the borrower is able to provide detailed information.

Successive UK governments have been concerned about the difficulty small businesses have in raising finance and have sponsored a number of schemes to assist them. However, the view of the venture capital industry has tended toward the view that the amount of finance available exceeds the worthwhile opportunities to use it.

Chapter roundup

- Businesses in a modern economy require money to operate and market-based institutions exist to bring together providers and users of capital. Investment in business can be organised through ownership or lending. Investors require investments that are both secure and liquid; they are also concerned that the return from an investment should reflect its risk.
- A primary capital market enables a firm to raise new finance from investors; secondary capital markets provide liquidity to investors by enabling them to sell their securities at a fair value.
- The Debt Management Office organises government borrowing in the UK, raising money by issuing Treasury bills and government bonds. Bonds pay a stated rate of interest on their nominal value, but bills provide a return to their purchasers by being sold at a discount to their face value. Commercial organisations also issue bonds and bills in a similar way. Other commercial debt instruments include certificates of deposit, commercial paper, Eurobonds and Bills of Exchange.
- The three forms of the efficient markets hypothesis suggest that share prices reflect the extent of the information available to the market. Favoured access to information seems to be the only way to make a higher return on investment than that provided by a simple buy-and-hold strategy.
- Traders on the London Stock Exchange provide primary and secondary markets in shares and bonds. An order-driven market system called the Stock Exchange Trading System is used for the most extensively traded securities, while the Stock Exchange Automated Quote system provides a quote-driven system for those that are less widely traded. The LSE is regulated by the Financial Services Authority and has its own extensive body of internal rules.

- Investors use a range of numerical information, including share prices, records of their movements and measures of companies' performance when deciding how to invest their funds. Performance measures include return on capital employed, earnings per share, price/earnings ratio, gearing, dividend yield and dividend cover. The general movement of stock market values is given by indices such as the FTSE 100, the Dow-Jones and the NASDAQ 100. Stock market indices give an indication of the extent of investors' confidence in the wider economy.
- Derivatives such as forward contracts, futures and options allow traders to insure against unfavourable price movements. They are traded on derivatives exchanges and can be based on the price of commodities or purely financial matters such as interest and exchange rates. They are frequently used for speculation and are subject to extensive regulation.
- The UK Financial Services Authority regulates most financial services markets, exchanges and firms in the UK, including the banking industry. On June 16, 2010, the Chancellor of the Exchequer, George Osborne, announced plans to abolish the FSA and separate its responsibilities between a number of new agencies and the Bank of England.
- Small businesses can find it particularly difficult to raise finance. There are several explanations for this, but an important problem seems to be a lack of good investment opportunities rather than a shortage of funds.

Quick quiz

1. What are the two basic investment relationships?
2. What is the difference between a primary investment market and a secondary investment market?
3. A government bond has a coupon rate that is equal to the current risk-free rate of interest. What will happen to the market price of the bond if interest rates fall?
4. What information would be reflected in a security's market price if the strong form of the efficient market hypothesis is true?
5. Does a bull expect share prices to rise or to fall?
6. Who regulates the UK AIM?
7. What effect is high gearing likely to have on a firm's ability to raise debt capital?
8. What does a high P/E ratio suggest about a share?
9. What is the nature of an option?
10. What is the difference between a put and a call option?

Answers to quick quiz

1. Ownership and lending
2. A primary investment market is used to raise new capital; a secondary market provides liquidity to investors by enabling them to sell their securities.
3. It will rise.
4. All relevant information including that available only to specialists or insiders
5. A bull expects share prices to rise.
6. The LSE
7. It will probably limit it, since high gearing means that it already has a large amount of borrowing.
8. A high P/E ratio tells us that the share price is high in relation to its earnings. This suggests that the market thinks it has better than average prospects for the future.
9. An option confers the right, but not the obligation, to either purchase or sell an underlying asset at a fixed date and price in the future.
10. An option to sell is called a 'put' option, while an option to buy is known as a 'call' option.

Answers to activities

1. Lenders are entitled to be paid the agreed rate of interest. If the borrower defaults, the terms of the loan normally allow the lenders to seize the borrower's assets and sell them in order to realise their capital. Realistically, it would have been very difficult to do this with the Channel Tunnel. By converting their bonds into shares, the lenders would acquire an ownership interest and would be entitled to share in any profits the company might eventually make. In the meantime, they would forfeit their right to interest (which they had no chance of receiving anyway), allowing the company to use its cash flow to continue in business.
2. The Hunt brothers' attempt to corner the world silver market eventually fell apart catastrophically when the price of silver actually fell, leaving the brothers with enormous debts.
3. The extent of Microsoft's capital growth more than compensated for the lack of dividends. Shareholders were confident that if they needed cash, they would be able to sell some of their shares at a large profit. The shares were valued at 9.7 cents each on 13 March 1986 and by 31 December 1999, adjusting for stock splits, were valued at $58.375.
4. Your research!

Chapter 6 :
CAPITAL INVESTMENTS

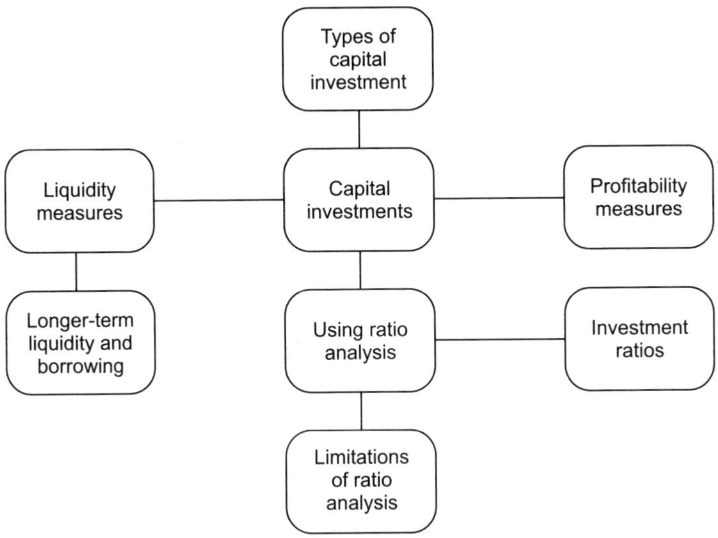

Introduction

This is a very practical chapter. It is intended to give you a good working knowledge of the numerical tools used by investors to assess company performance, so it includes lots of worked examples and exercises for you to try. However, before we plunge into them, we will build on the material in the previous chapter and look in a little more detail at three kinds of equity-based investment.

Your objectives

In this chapter you will learn about:

(a) The nature of investment trusts, unit trusts and open-ended investment companies

(b) How to use financial and accounting information to interpret and evaluate companies' performance and prospects

1 TYPES OF CAPITAL INVESTMENT

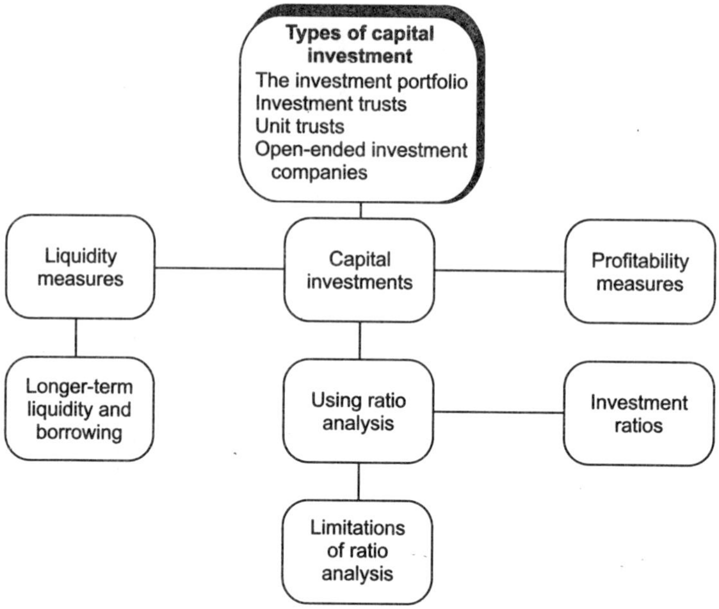

In the previous chapter, we explained two approaches to investing: making a loan or purchasing an ownership interest; and some of the main implications of each. As well as choosing the form of investment they wish to make, investors must also decide on the kind of asset or area of economic activity they will invest in. Most investments will combine these two aspects: lending to a company, for example, enables it to produce and market its particular form of good or service and at the same time, assuming the loan is secured, gives some degree of control over the company's assets. Similarly, buying shares in a commercial property company provides finance for the company's operational role as a landlord and gives an interest in the company's real estate portfolio.

Activity 1 **(5 minutes)**

Can you think of any investments that do not combine assets with economic activity?

1.1 The investment portfolio

The range of potential investments is enormous. Here are some examples.

- Manufacturing
- Government stock
- Mining and quarrying
- Agriculture and fisheries
- Precious metals
- Real property
- Insurance
- Health care

This wide variety reflects the complexity of modern economies and choosing from among the huge number of investments available presents a significant problem to potential investors. In fact, the wise investor will seek to build up a portfolio of investments in order to limit the impact of any lack of success in one company or industry. A well-balanced portfolio will not produce the returns that might be provided by a wildly successful single investment, but neither will it be over-affected by the single investment that suddenly turns sour. However, you should note that even the most carefully constructed portfolio will be subject to the varying success of the wider economy as a whole.

Building a portfolio by purchasing the shares of a wide range of companies is expensive, because of the costs of dealing, and difficult, since to do it well requires a degree of research and analysis. However, several kinds of individual investment are available that allow the investor to gain exposure to a wide portfolio of underlying securities. We will discuss three of these.

- Investment trusts
- Unit trusts
- Open-ended investment companies

1.2 Investment trusts

Investment trusts, despite their name, are public limited companies rather than trusts and their shares are traded in the secondary market. Their business is investing in other companies and, indeed, in other investment trusts. The investor who buys shares in an investment trust thus has an interest in a portfolio of investments as a result of a single purchase. The market price of the trust's shares reflects the market's perceptions of its performance and prospects in the usual way. It is very common for investment trusts to have no employees but to purchase the services of a professional fund management company.

An important feature of the way investment trusts work is that, being companies, they are able to borrow in order to invest. The shareholders can benefit from this gearing so long as the investments made earn more than the net cost of the borrowing, which is entirely possible. However, partly as result of this feature, shares in investment trusts usually trade at a discount to the company's net asset value. That is to say, if the company were to be wound up, the shareholders would receive value greater than the market value of their shareholdings. The fact that they cannot achieve this value by selling their shares on the market reflects the greater risk associated with gearing up.

1.3 Unit trusts

Unlike an investment trust, a unit trust is in fact a trust, with trustees and governed according to the terms of a trust deed. The role of trustee is normally played by a large financial intermediary, such as an insurance company. Each unit trust has its own specified investment objectives and limitations. Typically, these will include aims for income and growth; and the geographical region and the type of industry or asset that will be invested in.

Investment in a unit trust consists of buying units: units are quite different from shares.

(a) Units may only be bought from and sold back to the trust: there is no secondary market. Bid and offer prices are published in the financial press.

The trust will buy back units at the bid price and will sell them at the offer price.

(b) Units are created and liquidated according to demand. The money paid in to the trust to purchase a unit is immediately invested in financial assets, which are sold if the unit holder decides to sell his units. The total number of units in issue is therefore directly related to the value of the assets owned by the trust.

This approach to investment is known as open-ended, since there is no limit to the number of units that can be sold, unlike the shares in a company such as an investment trust.

As with investment trusts, the management of the trust's assets is normally outsourced to an investment management company. The manager will charge an annual management fee to cover the administrative costs associated with running the trust and will make a profit from the bid-offer spread.

1.4 Open-ended investment companies (OEICs)

Open-ended investment companies (OEICs) combine the features of investment trusts and unit trusts. They resemble investment trusts in that they are quoted public companies and investment in them takes the form of purchasing their shares. However, they are open-ended, like unit trusts, in that their shares are issued and cancelled according to demand rather than being bought and sold on the secondary market. New funds are immediately invested and assets are realised in order to return capital to investors who wish to have their shares cancelled. The value of an OEICs shares is thus a precise reflection of the value of the company's assets. An important feature of OEICs is that that are able to act as an 'umbrella' fund, operating a number of sub-funds, each with its own investment objectives. This means that investors can switch their capital between types of investment more easily and at less cost than is possible if they buy units in a unit trust. A single price is quoted for shares, so there is no bid-offer spread; however, the management company will charge a fee of up to six per cent of the initial investment and make a smaller annual charge thereafter.

2 USING RATIO ANALYSIS

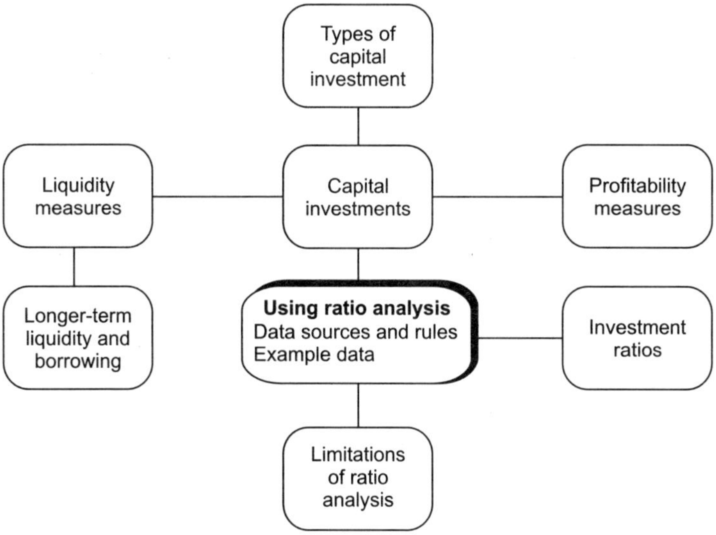

2.1 Data sources and uses

For the remainder of this chapter we will be concerned with the analysis of companies' published financial statements. A wide range of stakeholder groups has a legitimate interest in companies' activities, performance, plans and prospects, so, in all advanced economies, the law requires that companies should publish extensive information about such matters. Financial information lies at the heart of the reporting requirements since companies are vitally important agents of economic activity and existing and potential investors are chiefly interested in financial matters.

A very wide range of standard measures or ratios can be calculated and they are generally accepted as meaningful indicators. However, each individual business must be considered separately: a figure or ratio that is meaningful for a manufacturing company may be completely meaningless for a financial institution. As we have already pointed out, the key to obtaining meaningful information from financial analysis is comparison. This may be comparison over time within the same business to establish whether things are improving or deteriorating, or comparison between similar businesses to see whether the company is better or worse than average within its specific business sector.

It must be stressed that numerical analysis on its own is not sufficient for interpreting company accounts, and that there are other items of information that should be considered, such as those listed below.

(a) Comments in the Chairman's report and directors' report

(b) The age and nature of the company's assets

(c) Current and future developments in the company's markets, at home and overseas

(d) Any other noticeable features of the report and accounts, such as notes describing events after the balance sheet date, a qualified auditors' report and the company's taxation position

EXAMPLE: DATA

In the previous chapter, we looked briefly at some fundamental performance ratios. We will now follow that up by extending our coverage of ratio analysis and examine some other concepts that will help us to understand the nature of company performance and activity. To do this we will make use of the accounts set out below.

BETATEC PLC INCOME STATEMENT
FOR THE YEAR ENDED 31 DECEMBER 20X1

	Notes	*20X1*	*20X0*
		£	£
Turnover	1	3,095,576	1,909,051
Operating profit	1	359,501	244,229
Interest	2	17,371	19,127
Profit on ordinary activities before taxation		342,130	225,102
Taxation on ordinary activities		74,200	31,272
Profit on ordinary activities after taxation		267,930	193,830
Dividend		41,000	16,800
Retained profit for the year		226,930	177,030
Earnings per share		12.8p	9.3p

BETATEC PLC BALANCE SHEET
AS AT 31 DECEMBER 20X1

	Notes	*20X1*	*20X0*
		£	£
Assets			
Non-current assets		802,180	656,071
Current assets			
Inventories		64,422	86,550
Trade receivables	3	1,002,701	853,441
Cash and cash equivalents		1,327	68,363
Total assets		1,870,630	1,664,425
Equity and liabilities			
Called-up share capital	5	210,000	210,000
Share premium account		48,178	48,178
Retained earnings		610,721	383,791
Total equity		868,899	641,969
Non-current liabilities			
10% first mortgage debenture stock 20Y4/20Y9		100,000	100,000
Long-term provisions		20,000	10,000
Total non-current liabilities		120,000	110,000
Current liabilities			
Trade and other payables	4	881,731	912,456
Total current liabilities		881,731	912,456
Total equity and liabilities		1,870,630	1,664,425

NOTES TO THE ACCOUNTS

1 *Turnover and profit*

	20X1	*20X0*
	£	£
(a) Turnover	3	1,909,051
Cost of sales	2,402,609	1,441,950
Gross profit	692,967	467,101
Administration expenses	333,466	222,872
Operating profit	359,501	244,229
(b) Operating profit is stated after charging:		
Depreciation	151,107	120,147
Auditors' remuneration	6,500	5,000
Leasing charges	47,636	46,336
Directors' emoluments	94,945	66,675

2 *Interest*

	20X1	*20X0*
	£	£
Payable on bank overdrafts and other loans	8,115	11,909
Payable on debenture stock	10,000	10,000
	18,115	21,909
Receivable on short-term deposits	744	2,782
Net payable	17,371	19,127

3 *Receivables*

	20X1	*20X0*
	£	£
Prepayments and accrued income	97,022	45,729
	981,581	805,981
Trade debtors	21,120	47,460
Total debtors	1,002,701	853,441

4 *Payables*

	20X1	*20X0*
	£	£
Trade creditors	627,018	545,340
Accruals and deferred income	81,279	280,464
Corporation tax	108,000	37,200
Other taxes and social security costs	44,434	32,652
Dividend	21,000	16,800
	881,731	912,456

5 *Called-up share capital*

	20X1	*20X0*
	£	£
Authorised ordinary shares of 10p each	1,000,000	1,000,000
Issued and fully paid ordinary shares of 10p each	210,000	210,00

3 PROFITABILITY MEASURES

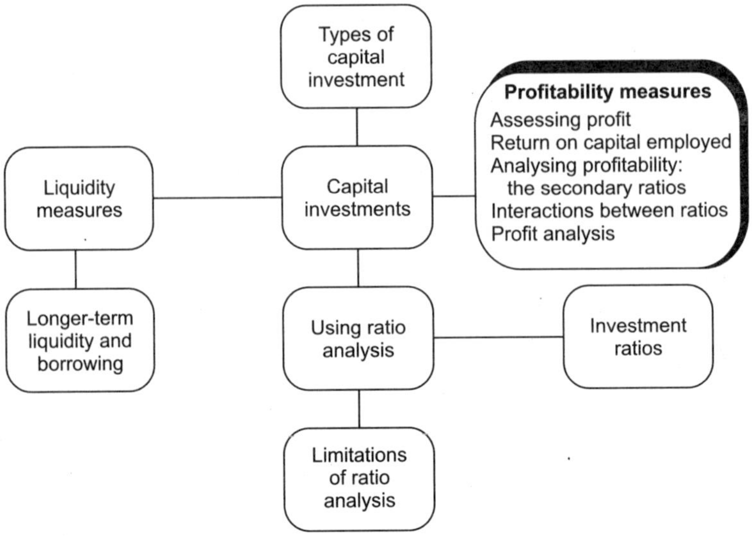

3.1 Assessing profit

We discussed return on capital employed, the most common measure of profitability, in the previous chapter. Let us now revise that topic. In our example above, the company made a profit in both 20X1 and 20X0 and there was an increase in profit on ordinary activities between one year and the next of:

- 52% before taxation
- 39% after taxation

Profit on ordinary activities *before* taxation is generally thought to be a better figure to use than profit after taxation, because there might be unusual variations in the tax charge from year to year which would not affect the underlying profitability of the company's operations.

Another profit figure that should be calculated is profit before interest and tax (PBIT). This is the amount of profit the company earned before having to pay interest to the providers of loan capital. By providers of loan capital, we usually mean longer-term loan capital, such as debentures and medium-term bank loans, which will be shown in the balance sheet as 'non-current liabilities'.

PBIT is therefore:

- Profit on ordinary activities before taxation PLUS
- Interest charges on long-term loan capital

Published accounts do not always give sufficient detail on interest payable to determine how much is interest on long-term finance. We will assume in our example that the whole of the interest payable (£18,115, note 2) relates to long-term finance.

PBIT in our example is therefore:

	20X1	20X0
	£	£
Profit on ordinary activities before tax	342,130	225,102
Interest payable	18,115	21,909
PBIT	360,245	247,011

This shows a 46% growth between 20X0 and 20X1, which is remarkable and brings us to the topic of inflation, which is yet another matter to be cautious about.

In simple terms, inflation is a decline in the purchasing power of money, which shows up as a rise in prices. Before we can assess any aspect of growth revealed by Betatec's financial statements, we need to know what the inflation rate was between the two year ends. The higher it was, the less the real growth that actually took place. We can assess the effect of inflation on any figure for 20X1 by dividing it by (1+i), where i is the inflation rate. Thus if inflation has been running at, say 17%, Betatec plc's inflation adjusted PBIT for 20X1 would be:

$$\frac{£360{,}245}{1.17} = £307{,}902$$

This is an increase of only 25% over 20X0.

The general relationship between the inflation rate (i), the real growth rate (g) and the apparent growth rate (a) is given by the equation below.

$$1+a = (1+i)(1+g)$$

Substituting the figure in our example we obtain: $1.46 = 1.17 \times 1.25$

3.2 Return on capital employed (ROCE)

It is impossible to assess profits or profit growth properly without relating them to the amount of funds (capital) that were employed in making the profits. The most important profitability ratio is therefore return on capital employed (ROCE), which states the profit as a percentage of the amount of capital employed.

Definition

$$\text{ROCE} = \frac{\text{Profit on ordinary activities before interest and taxation}}{\text{Capital employed}}$$

Capital employed = Shareholders' funds plus 'creditors: amounts falling due after more than one year' plus any long-term provision for liabilities and charges (*or* total assets less current liabilities).

The underlying principle is that we must compare like with like, and so if capital means share capital and reserves plus long-term liabilities and debt capital, profit must mean the profit earned by all this capital together. This is PBIT, since interest is the return for loan capital.

In our example, capital employed = 20X1 868,899 + 100,000 + 20,000 = £988,89
20X0 641,969 + 100,000 + 100,000 = £751,969

These total figures are the total assets less current liabilities figures for 20X8 and 20X7 in the balance sheet.

	20X1	*20X0*
ROCE	$\frac{360{,}245}{988{,}899} = 36.4\%$	$\frac{247{,}011}{751{,}969} = 32.8\%$

What does a company's ROCE tell us? What should we be looking for? There are three comparisons that can be made.

(a) The change in ROCE from one year to the next can be examined. In this example, there has been an increase in ROCE by about 10% or 11% from its 20X0 level.

(b) The ROCE being earned by other companies, if this information is available, can be compared with the ROCE of this company. Here the information is not available.

(c) A **comparison** of the ROCE with **current market borrowing** rates may be made.

  (i) What would be the cost of extra borrowing to the company and is it earning a ROCE that suggests it could make sufficient profit to make such borrowing worthwhile?

  (ii) Is the company making a ROCE which suggests that it is getting value for money from its current borrowing?

  (iii) Companies are in a risk business and commercial borrowing rates are a good independent yardstick against which company performance can be judged.

In this example, if we suppose that current market interest rate for medium-term borrowing is around 10%, then the company's actual ROCE of 36% in 20X1 would not seem low. On the contrary, it might seem high.

However, it is **easier to spot a low ROCE than a high one,** because there is always a chance that the company's **fixed assets,** especially property, are undervalued in its balance sheet, and so the capital employed figure might be unrealistically low. If the company had earned a ROCE, not of 36%, but of, say only 6%, then its return would have been below current borrowing rates and so disappointingly low.

3.3 Analysing profitability: the secondary ratios

We often sub-analyse ROCE, to find out more about why the ROCE is high or low, or better or worse than last year. There are two factors that contribute towards a return on capital employed, both related to sales turnover.

(a) **Profit margin.** A company might make a high or low profit margin on its sales. For example, a company that makes a profit of 25p per £1 of sales is making a bigger return on its turnover than another company making a profit of only 10p per £1 of sales.

(b) **Asset turnover.** Asset turnover is a measure of how well the assets of a business are being used to generate sales. For example, if two companies each have capital employed of £100,000 and Company A makes sales of £400,000 per annum whereas Company B makes sales of only £200,000 per annum,

> Company A is making a higher turnover from the same amount of assets (twice as much asset turnover as Company B) and this will help A to make a higher return on capital employed than B. Asset turnover is expressed as 'x times' so that assets generate x times their value in annual turnover. Here, Company A's asset turnover is 4 times and B's is 2 times.

Profit margin and asset turnover together explain the ROCE and if the ROCE is the primary profitability ratio, these other two are the secondary ratios. The relationship between the three ratios is simple.

Definition

> Profit margin × Asset turnover = ROCE
>
> Therefore, $\frac{\text{PBIT}}{\text{Sales}} \times \frac{\text{Sales}}{\text{Capital employed}} = \frac{\text{PBIT}}{\text{Capital employed}}$

In our example:

	Profit margin		*Asset turnover*		*ROCE*
(a) 20X1	$\frac{360{,}245}{3{,}095{,}576}$	×	$\frac{3{,}095{,}576}{988{,}899}$	=	$\frac{360{,}245}{988{,}899}$
	11.64%	×	3.13 times	=	36.4%
(b) 20X0	$\frac{247{,}011}{1{,}909{,}051}$	×	$\frac{1.909{,}051}{751{,}969}$	=	$\frac{247{,}011}{751{,}969}$
	12.94%	×	2.54 times	=	32.8%

In this example, the company's improvement in ROCE between 20X0 and 20X1 is attributable to a higher asset turnover. Indeed the profit margin has fallen a little, but the higher asset turnover has more than compensated for this.

It is also worth commenting on the change in sales turnover from one year to the next. You may already have noticed that Betatec plc achieved sales growth of over 60% from £1.9 million to £3.1 million between 20X0 and 20X1. This is very strong growth, and this is certainly one of the most significant items in the income statement and balance sheet. However, remember our earlier remarks about inflation when considering growth in turnover.

3.4 Interactions between ratios

It might be tempting to think that a high profit margin is good, and a low asset turnover means sluggish trading. In broad terms, this is so. But there is a trade-off between profit margin and asset turnover, and you cannot look at one without allowing for the other.

(a) A high profit margin means a high profit per £1 of sales, but if this also means that sales prices are high, there is a strong possibility that sales turnover will be depressed, and so asset turnover lower.

(b) A high asset turnover means that the company is generating a lot of sales, but to do this it might have to keep its prices down and so accept a low profit margin per £1 of sales.

Consider the following.

Company A		*Company B*	
	£		£
Sales	1,000,000	Sales	4,000,000
Capital employed	1,000,000	Capital employed	1,000,000
PBIT	200,000	PBIT	200,000

These figures would give the following ratios.

Company A:

$$\text{ROCE} = \frac{200{,}000}{1{,}000{,}000} = 20\%$$

$$\text{Profit margin} = \frac{200{,}000}{1{,}000{,}000} = 20\%$$

$$\text{Asset turnover} = \frac{1{,}000{,}000}{1{,}000{,}000} = 1$$

Company B:

$$\text{ROCE} = \frac{200{,}000}{1{,}000{,}000} = 20\%$$

$$\text{Profit margin} = \frac{200{,}000}{4{,}000{,}000} = 5\%$$

$$\text{Asset turnover} = \frac{4{,}000{,}000}{1{,}000{,}000} = 4$$

The companies have the same ROCE, but it is arrived at in a very different fashion. Company A operates with a low asset turnover and a comparatively high profit margin whereas company B carries out much more business, but on a lower profit margin. Company A could be operating at the luxury end of the market, whilst company B is operating at the popular end of the market.

Activity 2 **(5 minutes)**

Which one of the following formulae correctly expresses the relationship between return on capital employed (ROCE), profit margin (PM) and asset turnover (AT)?

A $\text{PM} = \frac{\text{AT}}{\text{ROCE}}$

B $\text{ROCE} = \frac{\text{PM}}{\text{AT}}$

C $\text{AT} = \text{PM} \times \text{ROCE}$

D $\text{PM} = \frac{\text{ROCE}}{\text{AT}}$

3.5 Profit analysis

Depending on the format of the income statement, you may be able to calculate the gross profit margin as well as the net profit margin. Looking at the two together can be quite informative.

For example, suppose that a company has the following summarised income statements for two consecutive years.

	Year 1	*Year 2*
	£	£
Turnover	70,000	100,000
Cost of sales	42,000	55,000
Gross profit	28,000	45,000
Expenses	21,000	35,000
Net profit	7,000	10,000

Although the net profit margin is the same for both years at 10%, the gross profit margin is not.

In year 1 it is: $\frac{28,000}{70,000} = 40\%$

and in year 2 it is: $\frac{45,000}{100,000} = 45\%$

The improved gross profit margin has not led to an improvement in the net profit margin. This is because expenses as a percentage of sales have risen from 30% in year 1 to 35% in year 2.

4 LIQUIDITY MEASURES

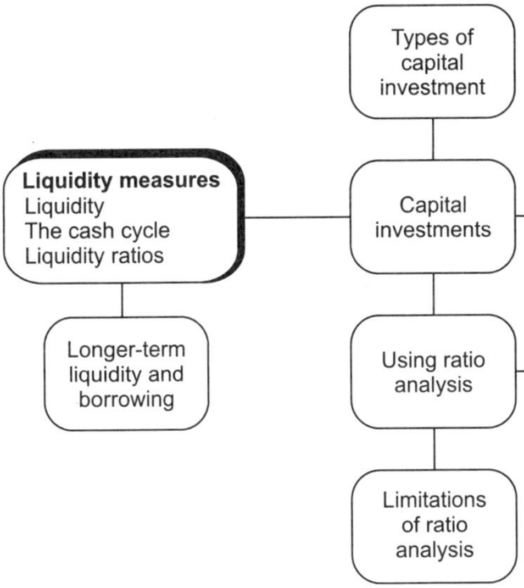

4.1 Liquidity

Profitability is a vital aspect of a company's performance, but, in the short term at least, it is possible to view liquidity as being even more important. It is actually possible to trade at a loss for several years, but the ability to pay debts as they fall due is vital for survival.

Liquidity is a measure of the amount of cash a company can put its hands on quickly. Several different kinds of asset may be regarded as liquid funds.

(a) Cash

(b) Short-term investments for which there is a ready market

(c) Other investments that can be realised rapidly. These may include fixed-term deposits with a bank or building society where the remaining term is short, for example, a six month high-interest deposit with a bank

(d) Trade debtors (because they will pay what they owe within a reasonably short period of time)

(e) Some kinds of stock

In summary, **liquid assets** are current asset items that will or could soon be **converted into cash,** and **cash itself**. Two common definitions of liquid assets are:

(a) All current assets without exception
(b) All current assets with the exception of stocks

A company can obtain liquid assets from sources other than sales, such as the issue of shares for cash, a new loan or the sale of fixed assets. But a company cannot rely on these at all times, and in general, obtaining liquid funds depends on making sales and profits. Even so, profits do not always lead to increases in liquidity. This is mainly because funds generated from trading may be immediately paid out for operating expenses and other costs, invested in assets or paid to shareholders as dividends.

4.2 The cash cycle

To help you to understand liquidity ratios, it is useful to begin with a brief explanation of the cash or working capital cycle. This shows how cash flows out of a business and back into it again as a result of normal trading operations.

Cash goes out to pay for supplies, wages and salaries and other expenses, although payments can be delayed by taking some credit. A business might hold stock for a while and then sell it. Cash will come back into the business from the sales, although customers might delay payment by themselves taking some credit.

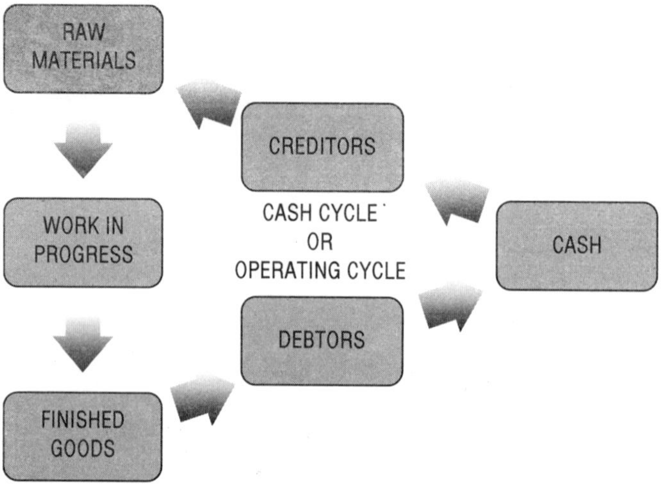

Figure 6.1: The cash cycle

The main points about the cash cycle are as follows.

(a) The **timing of cash-flows in and out of a business does not coincide with the time when sales and costs of sales occur**. Cash-flows out can be postponed by taking credit. Cash-flows in can be delayed by having debtors.

(b) The time between making a purchase and making a sale also affects cash-flows. If stocks are held for a long time, the delay between the cash payment for stocks and cash receipts from selling them will also be a long one.

(c) Holding stocks and having debtors can therefore be seen as two reasons why cash receipts are delayed. The amount of money a business has tied up in stocks and debtors is known as its working capital: if a company invests in working capital, its cash position will show a corresponding decrease.

(d) Taking credit from creditors will help the overall cash position. However, the debts have to be paid eventually and liquidity will fall unless the company can get more cash in from sales and debtors in the meantime.

The liquidity ratios and working capital turnover ratios are used to test a company's liquidity, length of cash cycle, and investment in working capital.

Activity 3 **(5 minutes)**

Butthead Ltd buys raw materials on six weeks credit, holds them in store for three weeks and then issues them to the production department. The production process takes two weeks on average, and finished goods are held in store for an average of four weeks before being sold. Debtors take five weeks credit on average.

Calculate the length of the cash cycle.

4.3 Liquidity ratios

The 'standard' test of liquidity is the **current ratio**. It can be obtained from the balance sheet, and is calculated as follows.

Definition

$$\textbf{Current ratio} = \frac{\text{Current assets}}{\text{Current liabilities}}$$

The idea behind this is that a company should have enough current assets that give a promise of 'cash to come' to meet its future commitments to pay off its current liabilities. Obviously, a ratio in excess of 1 should be expected. Otherwise, there would be the prospect that the company might be unable to pay its debts on time. In practice, a ratio comfortably in excess of 1 should be expected, but what is felt to be comfortable varies between different types of businesses.

Companies are not able to convert all their current assets into cash very quickly. In particular, some manufacturing companies might hold large quantities of raw material stocks, which must be used in production to create finished goods stocks. Finished goods stocks might be warehoused for a long time, or sold on lengthy credit. In such businesses, where stock turnover is slow, most stocks are not very liquid assets, because the cash cycle is so long. For these reasons, we calculate an additional liquidity ratio, known as the **quick ratio** or **acid test** ratio.

Definition

The **quick ratio**, or **acid test ratio** is: $\frac{\text{Current assets less stocks}}{\text{Current liabilities}}$

This ratio should ideally be at least 1 for companies with a slow stock turnover. For companies with a fast stock turnover, a quick ratio can be comfortably less than 1 without suggesting that the company could be in cash flow trouble.

Both the current ratio and the quick ratio offer an indication of the company's liquidity position, but the absolute figures should not be interpreted too literally. It is often suggested that an acceptable current ratio is 1.5 and an acceptable quick ratio is 0.8, but these figures should only be used as a guide.

Different businesses operate in very different ways. Supermarkets, for example, will have low debtors because they sell for cash only, low cash holdings because of frequent banking, medium stock levels because of quick turnover (particularly in view of perishability) and very high creditors, since they are ruthless with their suppliers. Manufacturing businesses, even if they operate just-in-time logistics, are likely to have valuable stocks and fairly high levels of debtors.

Nevertheless, these standard ratios are still useful because, as we have already pointed out, it is their trend over time that is important. From this, one can easily ascertain whether liquidity is improving or deteriorating. If a supermarket has traded very successfully for the last 10 years with a current ratio of 0.52 and a quick ratio of 0.17, then it should be supposed that the company can continue in business with those levels of liquidity. However, if the current ratio were to fall to 0.38 and the quick ratio to 0.09, further investigation into the liquidity situation would be appropriate. It is the relative position that is far more important than the absolute figures.

Don't forget the other side of the coin either. A current ratio and a quick ratio can get bigger than they need to be. A company that has large volumes of stocks and debtors might be over-investing in working capital, and so tying up more funds in the business than it needs to. This would suggest poor management of debtors (credit) or stocks by the company.

5 LONGER-TERM LIQUIDITY AND BORROWING

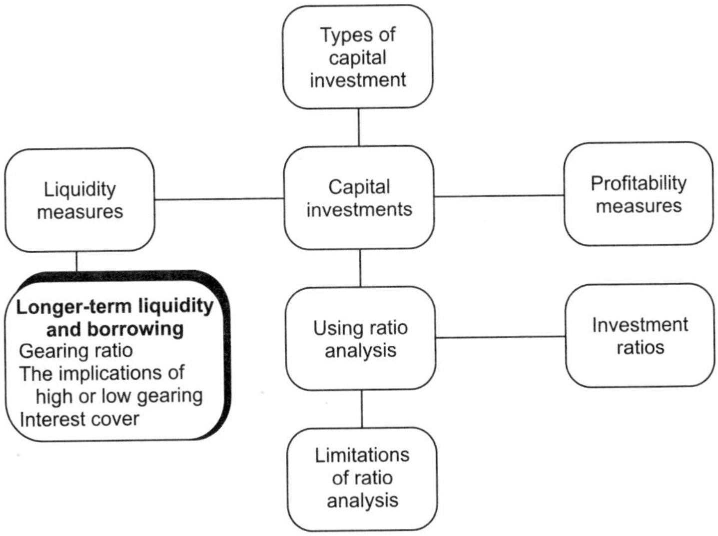

Debt ratios are concerned with how much the company owes in relation to its size, whether it is getting into heavier debt or improving its situation, and whether its debt burden seems heavy or light.

(a) When a company is heavily in debt banks and other potential lenders may be unwilling to advance further funds.

(b) When a company is earning only a modest profit before interest and tax, and has a heavy debt burden, there will be very little profit left over for shareholders after the interest charges have been paid. And so, if interest rates were to go up (on bank overdrafts and so on) or the company were to borrow even more, it could soon be incurring interest charges in excess of PBIT. This might eventually lead to the liquidation of the company.

These are two major reasons why companies should keep their debt burden under control and we will look at two relevant measures of indebtedness: gearing and interest cover. Some of the material in this section has also been touched on in the previous chapter.

5.1 Gearing ratio

As we mentioned in the previous chapter, capital gearing is concerned with a company's long-term capital structure. We can think of a company as consisting of fixed assets and net current assets (ie working capital, which is current assets minus current liabilities). These assets must be financed by long-term capital of the company, which is one of two things

(a) **Share capital and reserves**

(i) Ordinary shares plus reserves

(ii) Preference shares

(b) **Long-term debt capital**

Preference share capital is not debt. It would certainly not be included as debt in the debt ratio. However, like loan capital, preference share capital has a prior claim over profits before interest and tax, ahead of ordinary shareholders. Preference dividends must be paid out of profits before ordinary shareholders are entitled to an ordinary dividend, and so we refer to preference share capital and loan capital as prior charge capital.

The **capital gearing ratio** is a measure of the proportion of a company's capital that is prior charge capital. It is measured as follows.

Definition

$$\text{Capital gearing ratio} = \frac{\text{Prior charge capital}}{\text{Total capital}}$$

(a) **Prior charge capital** is capital carrying a right to a fixed return. It will include preference shares and debentures.

(b) **Total capital** is ordinary share capital and reserves plus prior charge capital plus any long-term liabilities or provisions. In group accounts we would also include minority interests. It is easier to identify the same figure for total capital as total assets less current liabilities, which you will find given to you in the balance sheet.

As with the debt ratio, there is no absolute limit to what a gearing ratio ought to be. A company with a gearing ratio of more than 50% would probably be said to be highly geared. Many companies are highly geared, but if a highly geared company is becoming increasingly highly geared, it is likely to have difficulty in the future when it wants to borrow even more, unless it can also boost its shareholders' capital, either with retained profits or by a new share issue.

5.2 The implications of high or low gearing

We mentioned earlier that measuring gearing is, amongst other things, an attempt to quantify the **degree of risk** involved in holding equity shares in a company, both in terms of the company's ability to remain in business and in terms of expected ordinary dividends from the company. The problem with a highly geared company is that by definition there is a lot of debt. Debt generally carries a fixed rate of interest (or fixed rate of dividend if in the form of preference shares), hence there is a given (and large) amount to be paid out from profits to holders of debt before arriving at a residue available for distribution to the holders of equity. The riskiness involved will perhaps become clearer with the aid of an example.

EXAMPLE: IMPLICATIONS OF GEARING

Below are shown extracts of the financial statements of three different companies.

	Company A	*Company B*	*Company C*
	£'000	£'000	£'000
Ordinary share capital	600	400	300
Profit and loss account	200	200	200
Revaluation reserve	100	100	100
	900	700	600
6% preference shares	–	–	100
10% loan stock	100	300	300
Capital employed	1,000	1,000	1,000
Gearing ratio	10%	30%	40%

Now suppose that each company makes a profit before interest and tax of £50,000, and the rate of corporation tax is 30%. Amounts available for distribution to equity shareholders will be as follows.

	Company A	*Company B*	*Company C*
	£'000	£'000	£'000
Profit before interest and tax	50	50	50
Interest	10	30	30
Profit before tax	40	20	20
Taxation at 30%	12	6	6
Profit after tax	28	14	14
Preference dividend	–	–	6
Available for ordinary shareholders	28	14	8

If in the subsequent year profit before interest and tax falls to £40,000, the amounts available to ordinary shareholders will become:

	Company A	*Company B*	*Company C*
	£'000	£'000	£'000
Profit before interest and tax	40	40	40
Interest	10	30	30
Profit before tax	30	10	10
Taxation at 30%	9	3	3
Profit after tax	21	7	7
Preference dividend	–	–	6
Available for ordinary shareholders	21	7	1

Note the following.

	%	%	%
Gearing ratio	10	30	40.0
Change in PBIT	–20	–20	–20.0
Change in profit available for ordinary shareholders	–25	–50	–87.5

The more highly geared the company, the greater the risk that little (if anything) will be available to distribute by way of dividend to the ordinary shareholders.

(a) The example clearly displays this fact in so far as the more highly geared the company, the greater the percentage change in profit available for ordinary shareholders for any given percentage change in profit before interest and tax.

(b) The relationship similarly holds when profits increase, and if PBIT had risen by 20% rather than fallen, you would find that once again the largest percentage change in profit available for ordinary shareholders (this means an increase) will be for the highly geared company.

(c) This means that where a company is highly geared, there will be greater volatility of amounts available for ordinary shareholders and presumably therefore greater volatility in dividends paid to those shareholders. That is the risk: you may do extremely well or extremely badly without a particularly large movement in the PBIT of the company.

The ability of a company to remain in business was referred to earlier. Gearing is relevant to this. A highly geared company has a large amount of interest to pay annually (assuming that the debt is external borrowing rather than preference shares). If those borrowings are secured in any way (and debentures in particular are secured), then the holders of the debt are perfectly entitled to force the company to realise assets to pay their interest if funds are not available from other sources. Clearly the more highly geared a company the more likely this is to occur if profits fall. Higher gearing may mean higher returns, but it also means higher risk.

5.3 Interest cover

The interest cover ratio shows whether a company is earning enough profit before interest and tax to pay its interest costs comfortably, or whether its interest costs are high in relation to the size of its profits. If the latter, a fall in PBIT would then have a significant effect on profits available for ordinary shareholders.

Definition

$$\textbf{Interest cover} = \frac{\text{Profit before interest and tax}}{\text{Interest charges}}$$

An interest cover of 2 times or less would be low, and this ratio should really exceed 3 times before the company's interest costs are to be considered within acceptable limits.

Returning first to the example of Companies A, B and C, the interest cover was as follows.

	Company A	*Company B*	*Company C*
(a) When PBIT was £50,000	$\frac{50,000}{10,000}$	$\frac{50,000}{30,000}$	$\frac{50,000}{30,000}$
	= 5 times	= 1.67 times	= 1.67 times
(b) When PBIT was £40,000	$\frac{40,000}{10,000}$	$\frac{40,000}{30,000}$	$\frac{40,000}{30,000}$
	= 4 times	= 1.33 times	= 1.33 times

Note. Although preference share capital is included as prior charge capital for the gearing ratio, it is usual to exclude preference dividends from interest charges. We also look at all interest payments, even interest charges on short-term debt, and so interest cover and gearing do not quite look at the same thing.

Both B and C have a low interest cover, which is a warning to ordinary shareholders that their profits are highly vulnerable, in percentage terms, to even small changes in PBIT.

Activity 4 **(5 minutes)**

Returning to the example of Betatec plc above, what is the company's interest cover?

6 INVESTMENT RATIOS

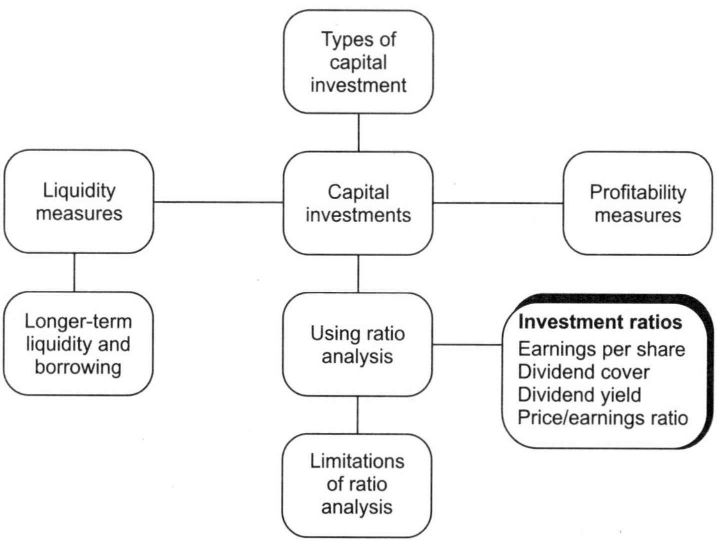

Once again, you will find some material here that is already familiar to you, though not, perhaps in the detail we provide here.

Investment ratios help shareholders and other investors to assess the value and quality of an investment in the ordinary shares of a company. The value of an investment in ordinary shares in a listed company is its market value, and so investment ratios must have regard not only to information in the company's published accounts, but also to the current share price. The market price of the company's shares is used to calculate some of these ratios.

6.1 Earnings per share

Earnings per share (EPS) is often regarded as the most important single measure of a company's performance. It is used to assess the results of a company over a period of time and to compare the performance of one company's shares against that of another's (and also against the returns obtainable from loan stock and other forms of investment). It shows the amount of residual profit available to the holder of one ordinary share.

Definition

$$\textbf{EPS} = \frac{\text{Profit for the year available for ordinary shareholders}}{\text{Number of ordinary shares in issue}}$$

The profit attributable to ordinary shareholders is the profit that is left after all other appropriations have been made, including interest on debt; taxation; and preference dividends (if any). It can be paid out directly in the form of ordinary dividends or retained in the company where it will help to generate increased profits in future periods.

In our example, earnings per share is as follows.

20X1	*20X0*
$\frac{267{,}390}{2{,}100{,}000} = 12.7\text{p}$	$\frac{193{,}830}{2{,}100{,}000} = 9.2\text{p}$

6.2 Dividend cover

Dividend cover is an indicator of how secure shareholders can expect to be in terms of their dividend being paid. It measures the number of times the current dividend could have been paid from available earnings.

Definition

$$\textbf{Dividend cover} = \frac{\text{Earnings per share}}{\text{Net dividend per ordinary share}}$$

In practice, the simplest way to calculate this is by dividing the profit available to ordinary shareholders by the ordinary dividend shown in the profit and loss account.

In our example, dividends per share is as follows.

20X1	*20X0*
$\frac{267{,}930}{41{,}000} = 6.5 \text{ times}$	$\frac{193{,}830}{16{,}800} = 11.5 \text{ times}$

Although earnings per share has increased, dividend cover has fallen. This is because the dividend paid has gone up by 244.1% over this period when the net profit after tax has only increased by 38.2%.

6.3 Dividend yield

Many shareholders are particularly interested in drawing income from their investments. Dividend yield measures the rate of cash return a shareholder can expect on the shares of a company, so it is a particularly important aspect of share performance for such investors. It is obviously far less important when investments are made with a view to capital growth.

Definition

> **Dividend yield** = $\frac{\text{Dividend on the share for the year}}{\text{Current market value of the share (ex div)}} \times 100\%$

(a) The dividend per share is taken as the dividend for the previous year.

(b) Ex-div means that the share is valued as though it does not have the right to any dividend that might be about to be paid. This is so that the price represents a fair value for the underlying longer-term investment.

6.4 Price earnings ratio (P/E ratio)

Definition

> The **price earnings ratio (P/E ratio)** = $\frac{\text{Share price}}{\text{Earnings per share}}$

When investors' confidence is high, they buy shares and share prices tend to rise as a result. This can affect individual shares, a sector, or the whole market. P/E ratio combines a measure of past performance, in the form of EPS, with current price, which reflects belief about the future. The result is a measure that indicates the state of shareholder feeling about future prospects. A high P/E ratio indicates strong shareholder confidence in the company (or sector, or the economy generally) and its future, while a lower P/E ratio indicates lower confidence. The P/E ratio of one company can be compared with other companies in the same business sector and with other companies generally. Suppose that the market price of a share in Betatec plc is 45p per share. The P/E ratio for 20X1 is:

$$\frac{45}{12.7} = 3.5$$

When P/E ratios generally are rising, investor confidence is high and they are driving up prices by large scale buying. The danger here is that economic conditions may not really justify the price boom and a fall may follow.

7 LIMITATIONS OF RATIO ANALYSIS

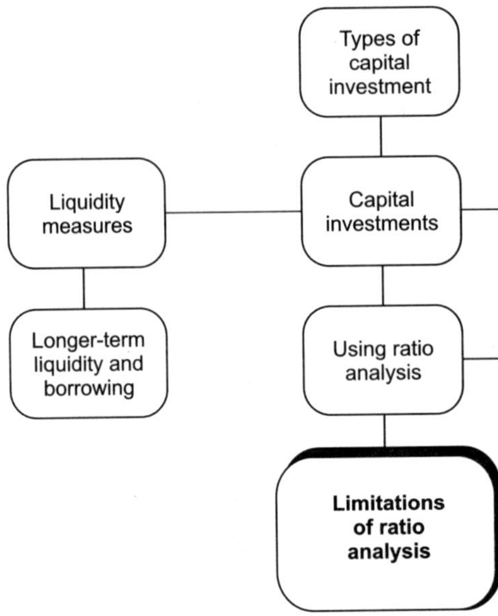

7.1 General limitations

(a) Financial statements are based on historic information, not forecast information. They may be several months out of date by the time that they are published.

(b) Financial statements normally ignore the effects of inflation (although some fixed assets may be measured at current value). This means that trends can be distorted.

(c) Information in published accounts is generally summarised information, so that analysis based on published information alone is likely to be superficial. (However, proper analysis of ratios should identify areas about which more information is needed.)

7.2 Comparing different businesses

It can be useful to compare the ratios of a business with industry averages, or with ratios for another business in the same industry sector. However, such a comparison may be misleading.

(a) Ratios may not always be calculated in the same way. For example, there are several different ways of calculating the return on capital. It can be calculated based on total capital employed or on ordinary shareholders' capital. It can be based on average capital employed, rather than on the closing figure.

(b) The businesses may adopt different accounting policies. For example, if a business that revalues fixed assets is compared with one that measures them at historic cost, ratios such as ROCE, profit margin and gearing will not be strictly comparable.

(c) A small business may not be directly comparable with a large company, because it is probably managed in a completely different way. For example, a large company is likely to be able to take advantage of extended credit terms and trade discounts for bulk buying which may not be available to a smaller business.

(d) Businesses within the same industry sector can operate in completely different markets. for example, one clothes store may sell a very large number of cheap items at low margins, while another may sell a relatively small number of expensive items.

Always remember: ratio analysis is not foolproof. There are many problems in trying to identify trends and make comparisons.

Activity 5 **(30 minutes)**

PATCH LIMITED
SUMMARY INCOME STATEMENTS
FOR THE YEAR ENDED 30 SEPTEMBER 20X1

	20X1	*20X1*
	£'000	£'000
Turnover	2,300	2,100
Cost of sales	1,035	945
Gross profit	1,265	1,155
Expenses	713	693
Net profit before interest and tax	552	462

PATCH LIMITED
SUMMARY BALANCE SHEETS
AS AT 30 SEPTEMBER 20X1

	20X1		*20X0*	
	£'000	£'000	£'000	£'000
Fixed assets		4,764		5,418
Current assets				
Stocks	522		419	
Debtors	406		356	
Cash	117		62	
	1,045		837	
Current liabilities				
Trade creditors	305		254	
Taxation	170		211	
	475		465	
Net current assets		570		372
Long-term loan		(1,654)		(2,490)
		3,680		3,300
Share capital		1,100		1,000
Share premium		282		227
Profit and loss account		2,298		2,073
		3,680		3,300

Relevant industry average ratios

	20X1	*20X0*
Return on capital employed	9.6%	9.4%
Net profit percentage	21.4%	21.3%
Quick ratio/acid test	1.0:1	0.9:1
Gearing (debt/capital employed)	36%	37%

Tasks

Calculate and comment on the following ratios for the two years shown.

(a) Return on capital employed
(b) Net profit percentage
(c) Quick ratio/acid test
(d) Gearing

Chapter roundup

- There is a very wide range of possible investments: wise investors create a diverse portfolio in order to limit the risk of loss. Three kinds of investment offer a ready-made portfolio: investment trusts, unit trusts and OEICs.
- Investment performance is measured partly by numerical techniques, but it is always necessary to look beyond the numbers and assess circumstances, conditions, comments and prospects.
- Profit is usually measured in terms of profit before interest and tax. Using this measure, profitability is assessed using:
  - return on capital employed
  - net profit as a percentage of sales
  - asset turnover ratio
  - gross profit as a percentage of sales
- A business must be liquid if it is to finance working capital in the form of debtors and stocks and be able to pay its debts as they fall due. The cash cycle shows how cash flows in and out of the business in the course of trade. Liquidity is measured by:
  - current ratio
  - quick ratio (acid test ratio)
- Gearing is the ratio of prior charge capital to total capital. It must be controlled so that interest payments are manageable and cash is available for dividends. Debt and gearing are measured by:
  - gearing ratio
  - interest cover
- Investors use investment ratios to help in their assessment of companies' performance and prospects. Investment ratios include earnings per share, dividend cover, dividend yield and the price earnings (P/E) ratio.

Chapter roundup continued

- Ratios provide information through comparison:
  - **trends** in a company's ratios from one year to the next, indicating an improving or worsening position
  - in some cases, against a **'norm'** or **'standard'**
  - in some cases, against the ratios of other companies, although differences between one company and another should often be expected
- Ratio analysis is not foolproof. There are several problems inherent in making comparisons over time and between organisations.

Quick quiz

1 How does an investment trust differ from a unit trust?

2 What is meant by the statement that OEICs can operate as 'umbrella' funds?

3 Apart from ratio analysis, what other information might be helpful in interpreting a company's accounts?

4 What is the usual formula for ROCE?

5 ROCE can be calculated as the product of two other ratios. What are they?

6 What are the formulae for:

   (a) The current ratio?

   (b) The quick ratio?

7 Give the formulae for calculating capital gearing.

8 What does the interest cover ratio reveal about a company?

9 What is the significance of the P/E ratio?

Answers to quick quiz

1 To invest in an investment trust is to buy shares in a public limited company; the price of the shares reflects the market forces of supply and demand affecting them and is usually at a discount to the company's net asset value. Unit trusts are investment funds operated by financial intermediaries. They create and liquidate units according to investor requirements, so the price of a unit reflects the value of the underlying assets.

2 They can operate a number of sub-funds, each with its own investment objectives.

3
- Comments in the Chairman's report and directors' report.
- The age and nature of the company's assets.
- Current and future developments in the company's markets.
- Post balance sheet events, contingencies, qualified audit report and so on.

4 $\dfrac{\text{Profit on ordinary activities before interest and tax}}{\text{Capital employed}}$

5 Asset turnover and profit margin

6 (a) $\dfrac{\text{Current assets}}{\text{Current liabilities}}$

(b) $\dfrac{\text{Current assets less stock}}{\text{Current liabilities}}$

7 Capital gearing ratio $= \dfrac{\text{Prior charge capital}}{\text{Total capital}}$

8 Whether it can pay its interest charges comfortably, leaving funds available for its shareholders.

9 It is an indication of the extent of investor confidence.

Answers to activities

1 Lending money to governments could be said to support economic activity, in that governments produce things that people want, such as education, roads and defence. However, while governments generally possess extensive assets, purchasing government debt confers no rights over those assets. Similarly, buying gold is a popular form of investment. While part of the demand for gold is based on its use as a raw material (in the electronics industry, for example) very large amounts of gold are held in the form of bullion, simply acting as a store of value and never put to any practical use.

2 ROCE $= \dfrac{\text{Profit}}{\text{Capital employed}}$

PM $= \dfrac{\text{Profit}}{\text{Sales}}$

AT $= \dfrac{\text{Sales}}{\text{Capital employed}}$

It follows that ROCE = PM x AT, which can be re-arranged to the form given in option D.

3 The cash cycle is the length of time between paying for raw materials and receiving cash from the sale of finished goods. In this case Butthead Ltd stores raw materials for three weeks, spends two weeks producing finished goods, four weeks storing the goods before sale and five weeks collecting the money from debtors: a total of fourteen weeks. However, six weeks of this period is effectively financed by the company's creditors so that the length of the cash cycle is eight weeks.

4 Interest payments should be taken gross, from the note to the accounts, and not net of interest receipts as shown in the P & L account.

	20X1	*20X0*
$\dfrac{\text{PBIT}}{\text{Interest payable}}$	$\dfrac{360{,}245}{18{,}115}$ = 20 times	$\dfrac{247{,}011}{21{,}909}$ = 11 times

Betatec plc has more than sufficient interest cover. In view of the company's low gearing, this is not too surprising and so we finally obtain a picture of Betatec plc as a company that does not seem to have a debt problem, in spite of its high (although declining) debt ratio.

5 *General comments*

Both turnover and profits have increased over the two years. The company is clearly expanding, although not at an exceptionally fast rate. The growth seems to have been achieved without investing heavily in fixed assets, the fall in this figure presumably being due to depreciation. Shares were issued in 20X8 at a premium, while a sizeable portion of the long-term loan has been paid off. Expansion appears to be financed by share capital and profits.

Return on capital employed

This has increased from 8% in 20X0 to 10.3% in 20X1. It had also gone from being below the industry average in 20X0 to above it in 20X1. These are encouraging signs. As indicated above, the company has not invested significantly in fixed assets to finance its expansion – the assets/capital employed are simply working harder.

Net profit percentage

This has also increased from 22% in 20X0 to 24% in 20X1. In both years it was higher than the industry average. This is obviously good news. Sometimes when a company grows, it is at the expense of lower margins, but this is clearly not the case for Patch Ltd.

Quick ratio or acid test

The quick ratio shows the extent of the assets, excluding stock, available to meet the current liabilities. Stock is excluded because it is not always readily convertible into cash. The quick ratio or acid test is therefore a better indicator of a company's true liquidity than the current ratio, which does not exclude stock. Patch Ltd's quick ratio is healthy (around 1) in both years, and has in fact improved from) 0.9:1 to 1.1:1. While Patch's quick ratio was the same as the industry average in 20X0, it was better than average in 20X1.

These are encouraging signs. Sometimes growth can lead to overtrading to the detriment of liquidity, but Patch Ltd has not fallen into this trap.

Gearing

The gearing ratio is also favourable. This can be calculated in two ways: debt/capital employed and debt/equity. Debt/capital employed shows a fall from 43% in 20X0 to 31% in 20X1. In 20X0 it was higher than the industry average, but in 20X1 it is lower. Calculated as debt/equity, the ratio shows an even more significant decline.

This is reassuring. A highly geared company is more risky than a low geared one in that, if profits are falling, it is more difficult for a highly geared company to meet interest payments. A highly geared company is therefore more likely to go into liquidation.

Conclusion

Patch Ltd's profitability and liquidity are improving and the gearing is at a lower level than last year. In addition the company compares favourably with other companies operating in the same sector.

APPENDIX – CALCULATION OF RATIOS

	20X1	Industry average 20X1	20X0	Industry average 20X0
Return on capital employed	$\frac{552}{5,334} = 10.3\%$	9.6%	$\frac{462}{5,790} = 8.0\%$	9.4%
Net profit percentage	$\frac{552}{2,300} = 24\%$	21.4%	$\frac{462}{2,100} = 22\%$	21.3%
Quick ratio/acid test	$\frac{1,045 - 522}{475} = 1.1:1$	1.0:1	$\frac{837 - 419}{465} = 0.9:1$	0.9:1
Gearing:				
Debt/capital employed	$\frac{1,654}{5,334} = 31\%$	36%	$\frac{2,490}{5,790} = 43\%$	37%
Debt/equity	$\frac{1,654}{3,680} = 45\%$		$\frac{2,490}{3,300} = 75\%$	

Chapter 7 : MACROECONOMICS

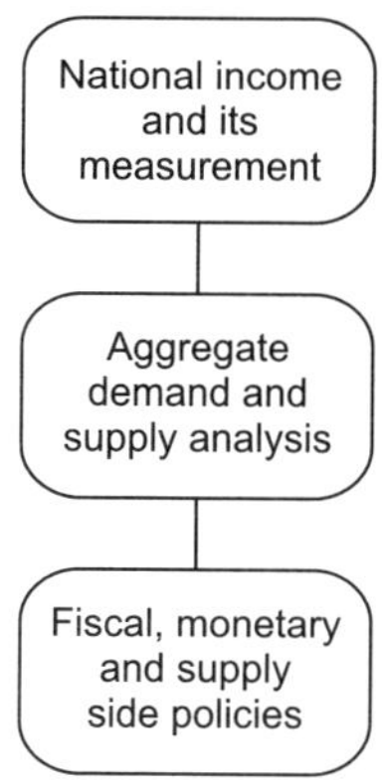

Introduction

Businesses operate in the economy as a whole and changes in the macroeconomic environment can have major implications for them.

Figures for the level of economic activity and economic growth are monitored closely by economists and by financial institutions because they are indicators of the economic health of a country.

In this chapter we begin by looking at how we can measure the total amount of economic activity of a nation.

There are different approaches to measuring economic activity. There are also different measures, with specific definitions. The process of measurement involves some estimates and there are a number of sources of possible inaccuracy in the figures.

In macroeconomics we are looking, not at individual spending decisions, investment decisions, pricing decisions, employment decisions, and output decisions but at spending, investment, price levels, employment and output in the economy as a whole and at total income (national income).

Broadly speaking, macroeconomists divide into the two camps of the Keynesians and the monetarists. These two camps have had differing ideas about how national income can be made to grow, how full employment can be achieved and how booms and slumps of trade cycles can be smoothed out.

The Keynesians and monetarists differ in their views about the causes of inflation, the extent to which inflation creates unemployment and prevents economic growth, and the effectiveness of government measures to stimulate the economy.

The chapters concludes with an overview of the goals of macroeconomic policy and then concentrates on three broad types of policy, fiscal policy, monetary policy and supply side policies used to achieve these goals.

Your objectives

In this chapter you will learn about:

(a) National income accounting
(b) Key measures of national economic output
(c) The circular flow of income in the economy
(d) The three approaches to national income accounting
(e) Aggregate demand
(f) The multiplier
(g) The business cycle
(h) Inflation and its consequences
(i) Unemployment and inflation
(j) Economic policy objectives
(k) Fiscal policy
(l) Monetary policy
(m) Supply side policy

1 NATIONAL INCOME AND ITS MEASUREMENT

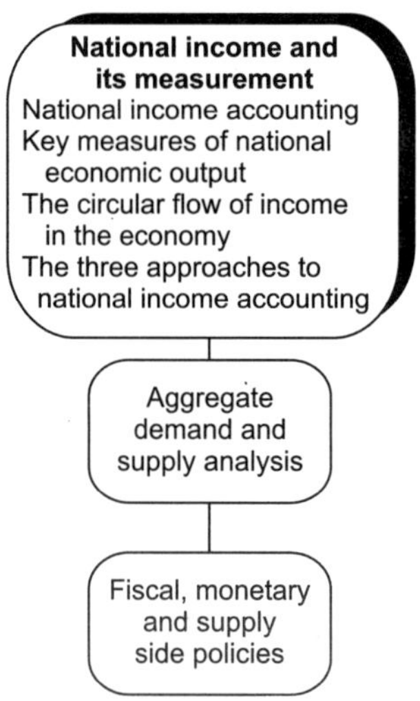

1.1 National income accounting

Definition

> **National income accounting** is the system through which economic activity on a national scale is measured.

Measuring economic activity on a national scale

In order to study and understand the economy, we first need to be able to measure it. In the same way that measurement is an essential part of any scientific study, measuring economic activity is essential for studying macroeconomics.

National output is important for the following reasons.

(a) National output is an aggregate of personal incomes. The bigger the aggregate of personal incomes in a country, the more income its individual inhabitants will be earning on average.

(b) More income means more spending on the output of firms, and more spending (ignoring inflation) means that a higher output of goods and services is required to be produced.

(c) Growth is an economic policy objective of most, if not all, governments.

Aspects of national income accounting

The concept of national income accounting is based on the underlying principle that economic activity in a country can be measured in terms of:

(a) The amount of **output** produced in the country
(b) The **income** received by those producing the output
(c) The amount of **expenditure** incurred by those purchasing the output.

National income accounting can be viewed from these three different aspects.

(a) **Output**

The firms (or government departments and corporations) which **produce** the goods or services in the national economy

(b) **Income**

The factors of production, which **earn** factor incomes

(c) **Expenditure**

The people or organisations that **spend money** to buy the goods and services such as consumers (or **households**), the government and foreign buyers (the **overseas sector**)

Activity 1 **(5 minutes)**

Before proceeding, recall from Chapter 1 what the factors of production are, and what reward is earned by each.

The three approaches to the creation of economic wealth give rise to three ways of measuring national economic output.

- The expenditure approach
- The income approach
- The value added approach (also called the output approach)

National income accounting identity

The national income accounting identity follows from the three approaches to the creation of economic wealth and states that:

Income	=	**Output**	=	**Expenditure**
Total of all factor income earned during the year		The total value of final output created during the year		The total spending on final goods and services during the year

The identity is illustrated in the figure below and represents three approaches to measuring the same thing.

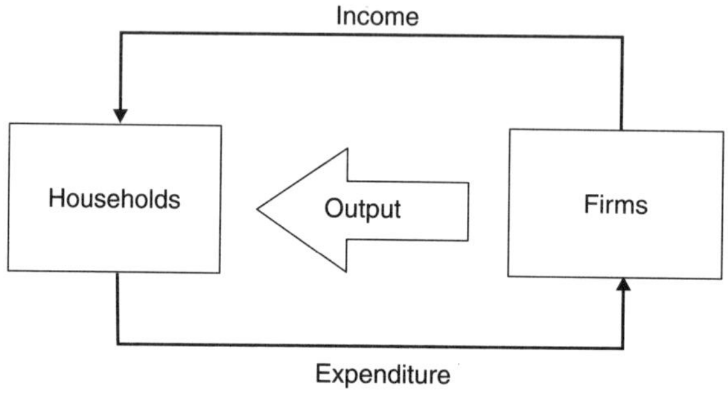

Figure 7.1: National income accounting identity

Official national income accounts show each approach to the measurement of economic activity (ie the output account, the income account and the expenditure account) as a separate account.

UK national income is in excess of £1,000bn per year (ie over £ trillion).

Uses of national income accounting measures

(a) To assess the state of the economy for purposes of constructing economic policy

(b) To monitor the impact of government economic policies

(c) To enable government and business to compare the progress and prospects of different economies

(d) To establish the material standard of living in an economy.

We looked at National Income in Chapter 1. It would be useful at this stage to look again at Chapter 1 and re-read the sub-section called 'Key measures of national economic output'.

1.2 Key measures of national economic output

Definition

> **National income** is the sum of all incomes which arise as a result of economic activity, that is from the production of goods and services.

> **Activity 2** **(5 minutes)**
>
> Which of the following will cause a rise in national income?
>
> A An increase in capital consumption (depreciation)
> B A rise in imports
> C A rise in subsidies
> D A rise in indirect taxes

1.3 The circular flow of income in the economy

There is a **circular flow of income** in an economy, which means that expenditure, output and income will all have the same total value.

Income and expenditure flows

Firms must pay households for the factors of production, and households must pay firms for goods. The income of firms is the sales revenue from the sales of goods and services.

This creates a **circular flow** of income and expenditure, as illustrated in Figure 7.2. This is a basic **closed economy**, without foreign trade.

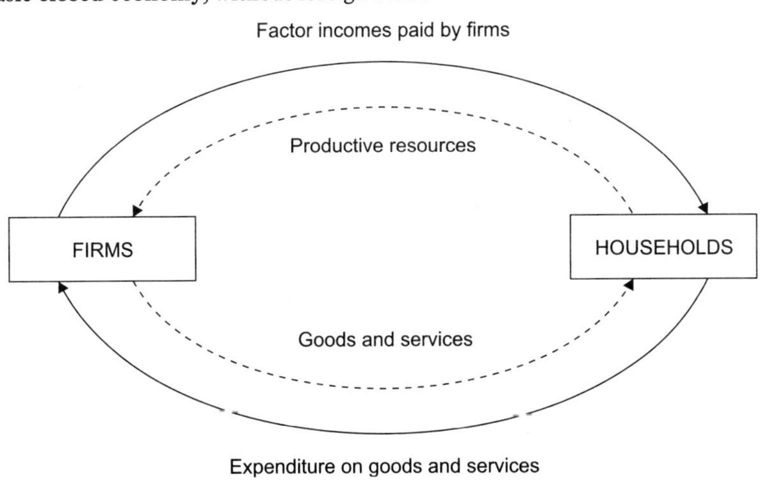

Figure 7.2: Circular flow of income

Households earn **income** because they have provided the factors of production which enable firms to provide goods and services. The income earned is used as **expenditure** on these goods and services that are made.

(a) The **total sales value** of goods produced should equal the **total expenditure** on goods, assuming that all goods that are produced are also sold.

(b) The amount of **expenditure** should also equal the **total income** of households, because it is households that consume the goods and they must have income to afford to pay for them.

The government and the circular flow of income

The government has several functions within the national economy, and so plays several different roles in the circular flow of income.

(a) It acts as the **producer** of certain goods and services instead of privately-owned firms, and the production of public administration services, education and health services, the police force, armed forces, fire services and public transport are all aspects of output. The government in this respect acts, like firms, as a producer and must also pay wages to its employees.

(b) It acts as the **purchaser** of final goods and services and adds to total consumption expenditure. National and local government obtain funds from the firms or households of the economy in the form of taxation and then use these funds to buy goods and services from other firms.

(c) It **invests** by purchasing capital goods, for example building roads, schools and hospitals.

(d) It makes **transfer payments** from one section of economy to another, for example by taxing working households and paying pensions, and by paying unemployment benefits and social security benefits.

Withdrawals and injections into the circular flow of income

Our simplified diagram of the circular flow of income needs to be amended to allow for two things.

- **Withdrawals** from the circular flow of income
- **Injections** into the circular flow of income

Definitions

> **Withdrawals**: movements of funds out of the cycle of income and expenditure between firms and households.
>
> **Injections**: movements of funds in the other direction.

Withdrawals from the circular flow of income

(a) **Savings (S).** Households do not spend all of their income. They save some, and these savings out of income are withdrawals from the circular flow of income.

(b) **Taxation (T).** Households must pay some of their income to the government, as taxation. Taxes cannot be spent by households.

(c) **Imports (M).** When we consider national income, we are interested in the economic wealth that a particular country is earning.

   (i) Spending on imports is expenditure, but on goods made by firms in other countries.

   (ii) The payments for imports go to firms in other countries, for output created in other countries.

   (iii) Spending on imports therefore withdraws funds out of a country's circular flow of income.

Be aware that **saving** is different from **investment**; saving simply means withdrawing money from circulation. Think of it as cash kept in a money box rather than being put into a bank to earn interest.

Injections into the circular flow of income

(a) **Investment (I).** Investment in capital goods is a form of spending on output, which is additional to expenditure by households. Just as savings are a withdrawal of funds, investment is an injection of funds into the circular flow of income, adding to the total economic wealth that is being created by the country.

(b) **Government spending (G).** Government spending is also an injection into the circular flow of income. In most mixed economies, total spending by the government on goods and services represents a large proportion of total national expenditure. The funds to spend come from either taxation income or government borrowing.

(c) **Exports (X).** Firms produce goods and services for export. Exports earn income from abroad, and therefore provide an injection into a country's circular flow of income.

The open economy

Figure 7.3 shows the circular flow of income, taking account of withdrawals and injections. This is an **open economy,** since it participates in foreign trade.

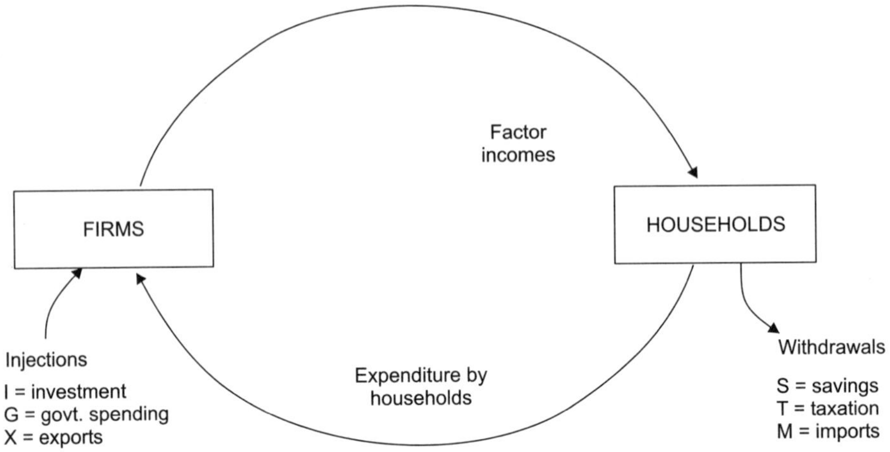

Figure 7.3: Circular flow of income showing withdrawals and injections

1.4 The three approaches to national income accounting

There are three main approaches.

(a) **The expenditure approach**. The economic wealth created in a period can be measured by the amount of expenditure on the goods and services that are produced by the nation's economy.

(i) The expenditures will be incurred by consumers, the government and foreign buyers of exports. Expenditures on **imports** represent wealth created by other countries, and so the value of expenditure on imports must be deducted from the total expenditure figure.

(ii) Expenditures by firms are **excluded,** to avoid double-counting. Firms buy goods and services which become costs of the goods or services that they produce and sell themselves. If we included expenditure by firms, we would be double-counting the value of the wealth created by the suppliers of raw materials and components and the providers of services to other firms.

(b) **The income approach**. This approach measures the income of individuals from employment and from self-employment, the profits of firms and public corporations and rent on property. (Interest earnings will be included within the profits of companies or the income of individuals.)

(c) **The value added or output approach**. This approach is to measure the value added by all activities which produce goods and services, that is their net output in the period.

All three approaches will in theory result in the same total amount for economic wealth created in the period, which we call **national income.** In practice, statistical discrepancies arise which cause differences between the figures.

Activity 3 **(10 minutes)**

We stated above that, in the expenditure approach to measuring national income, expenditures by firms are excluded to avoid double counting.

Think carefully about this and ensure that you understand exactly what is meant. Jot down an explanation.

It will be useful to look at some simplified examples which illustrate the three approaches to measuring national income.

EXAMPLE: NATIONAL INCOME

Suppose that a small national economy consists of one firm. During a certain period of time, the firm undertakes certain transactions.

- It imports raw materials from abroad, costing £4,000
- It hires labour, who are paid wages of £9,000
- It sells all its output for £20,000 and so makes a profit of £7,000
- It pays its post-tax profits of £4,000 to shareholders as dividends.

The country's government taxes the labour force £2,000 and the company £3,000.

The firm's sales of £20,000 are to three types of customer.

(a) Domestic consumers spend £11,000. This £11,000 is the post-tax wages earned by the labour force (£7,000) plus the £4,000 in dividends earned by the company's shareholders.

(b) The government spends the £5,000 it has raised in taxes.

(c) Foreign buyers spend £4,000.

Required

Calculate the gross domestic product.

Solution

As we have seen, there are three ways of calculating national income.

(a) **The expenditure approach**

	£
Consumers' expenditure	11,000
Government expenditure	5,000
	16,000
Add exports	4,000
	20,000
Subtract imports	(4,000)
GDP	16,000

(b) **The income approach**

	£
Income from employment (here pre-tax wages)	9,000
Gross (pre-tax) profit of the firm	7,000
GDP	16,000

The income is measured before deducting tax.

(c) **The value added or output approach**

	£
Output of firm at sales value	20,000
Less cost (sales value) of goods or services purchased from outside firms	(4,000)
GDP	16,000

The cost of goods and services purchased from outside firms – here just the imported materials of £4,000 – has to be subtracted so as either to avoid the double-counting of output, or to remove the value of output produced by firms in other countries.

The expenditure approach to measuring national income

Probably the most widely used measure of national income is the measurement of total spending or expenditure.

The table below shows figures for the UK.

UK national income (sample year): expenditure approach

	£bn
At current market prices	
Households' expenditure	663
Non-profit institutions' consumption	26
General government consumption	209
Gross domestic fixed capital formation	165
Value of increase/(decrease) in stocks and work-in-progress	(1)
Total domestic expenditure	1,062
Exports of goods and services	269
Imports of goods and services	(288)
Statistical discrepancy	0
Gross domestic product (GDP) at current market prices	1,043
Taxes on expenditure (indirect taxes) *less* subsidies	(118)
Gross value added at basic prices (GDP at factor cost)	925
Net property income from abroad	17
Gross national product (GNP) at current factor cost	932

The expenditure approach

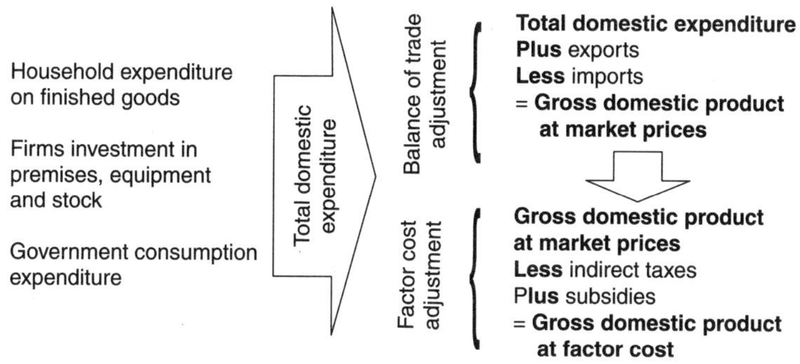

Features of expenditure approach

(a) Accounts broken down by purchaser

(b) Inserts estimated expenditure on non-traded outputs (eg imputed rent) to balance with output approach

(c) Adjusted for **balance of trade** and for **market to factor cost.**

The income approach to measuring national income

The second method of calculating national income is the income method. Since money spent by an individual or firm must become income to another, except for a residual error the results of the two methods are the same.

The income based approach covers several separate items of income.

(a) **Income from employment** (ie wages and salaries before deducting tax and including employers' national insurance contributions)

(b) **Pre-tax profits of companies**

(c) **Pre-tax profits of public corporations** (including nationalised industries)

(d) The **pre-tax 'surplus'** of other government enterprises

Interest earned by individuals and companies on any investments they hold is included in the first two figures.

These income components do not include two elements.

(a) Income from government pensions or social security payments are **transfer payments.**

(b) Any value for work done by individuals for no monetary reward, such as housework done by housewives or do-it-yourself home improvements are activities for which no money value can be given, and so are not economic activities.

Transfer payments are payments such as state pensions and benefits that are made by government, where the recipient does not make any contribution to output in return. They are payments which involve the transfer of wealth, rather than a reward for creating new economic wealth.

Transfer payments do not lead directly to any increase in marketable output of goods and are therefore excluded from the income figures.

The income approach

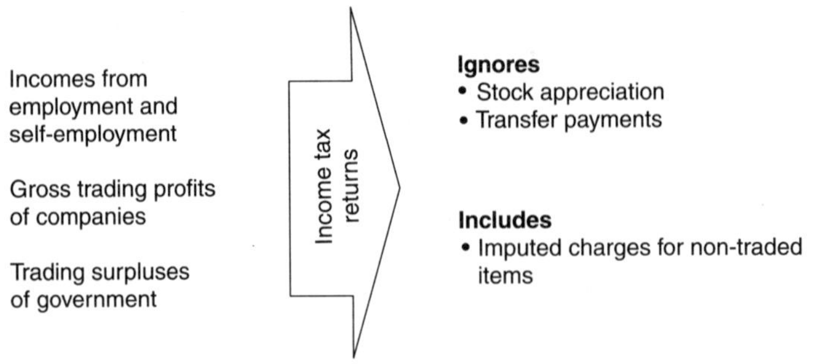

Features of income approach

(a) Accounts broken down by source of income

(b) Counts all incomes **gross** of tax (ie pre-tax)

(c) Ignores transfer payments (**payments for no productive efforts** eg welfare benefits grants) to avoid double counting (same income to wage earner + claimant)

(d) Adjusted for imputed values (eg rent from owner-occupied houses)

Activity 4 **(20 minutes)**

Which of the following is or are transfer payments?

(a) Salaries paid to Members of Parliament

(b) Incapacity benefit

The output or value added method of measuring national income

The third method of calculating national income is the value added or output method.

Since the goods and services we spend our money on must have been produced by some industry or another it is not surprising to find the amount we have all spent is the same as the total value of the output goods and services produced. This total value of output can be calculated by adding up the 'values added' at the various stages of the production and distribution process.

This seeks to measure value of **final products**: ie products of services that are not subsequently used as inputs to other production processes.

It avoids **double counting** by using a value added approach.

Output approach: value added

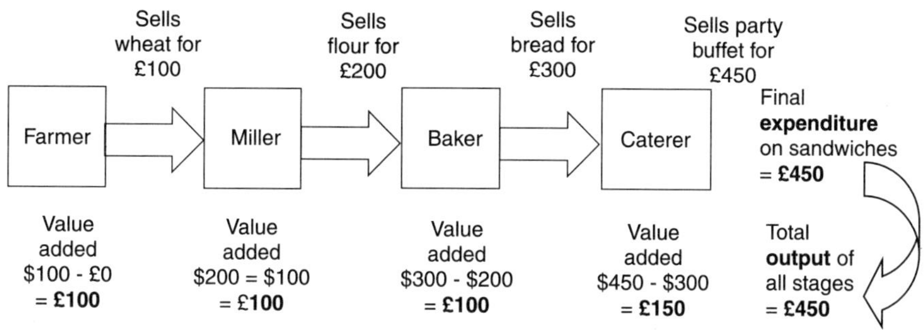

Features of output approach

(a) Accounts broken down by industrial sector

(b) Uses estimates for non-traded outputs (eg services of owner-occupied housing have an imputed rent added in)

(c) No **statistical discrepancy** adjustment. the remaining two accounts made to balance to the output account by having balancing figures inserted.

Adjustments to all approaches

Final adjustments – all approaches

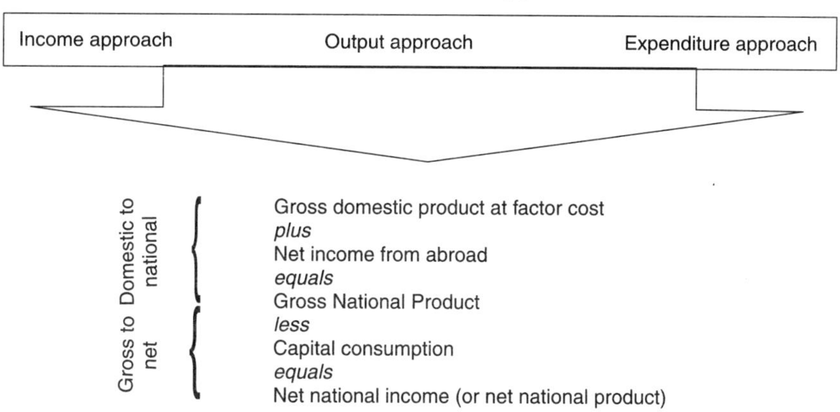

Net income from abroad

Difference between incomes earned by UK nationals from assets overseas and income going overseas due to foreign ownership of assets in the UK.

Capital consumption

Imputed charge for depreciation of nation's capital stock and infrastructure during the year.

2 AGGREGATE DEMAND AND SUPPLY ANALYSIS

2.1 The Keynesian approach

The origin of Keynesianism

Keynesian economics originated with *John Maynard Keynes*, a British economist whose book *The General Theory of Employment, Interest And Money* (1936), revolutionised macroeconomic analysis.

Pre-Keynesian economists had tried to explain unemployment as a temporary phenomenon. They believed that if there is a surplus of labour available (unemployment) then the forces of demand and supply, through the wages (price) mechanism, would restore equilibrium by bringing down wage levels, thus stimulating demand for labour. Any unemployment would only last as long as the labour market was adjusting to new equilibrium conditions. The pre-Keynesian theory was challenged during the 1930s. If pre-Keynesian theory was right, wages should have fallen and full employment should have been restored. However, this did not happen, and the depression continued for a long time.

It is instructive to note that it was during this economic situation that *Keynes* put forward his new theory. Its fundamental advance on earlier theory was to explain how **equilibrium could exist in the macroeconomy, but there could still be persistent unemployment and slow growth**.

The term **full employment national income** is used to describe the total national income that a country must earn in order to achieve full employment. By **full employment** we mean that the country's economic resources are fully employed. However, as far as labour is concerned, full employment does not mean that everyone has a job all the time. There will always be some **normal** or **transitional** unemployment as people lose their job or give up one job for another, and so **full** employment might mean, say, that 3 to 5% of the total working population is unemployed at any time.

Keynes also tried to explain the causes of **trade cycles** which are the continuous cycles of alternating economic boom and slump. Why does an economy not grow at a steady rate, or remain stable, instead of suffering the harmful effects of trade cycles?

Aggregate demand and aggregate supply

Keynes' basic idea was that demand and supply analysis could be applied to macroeconomic activity as well as microeconomic activity.

Definitions

> **Aggregate demand** (AD) means the total demand in the economy for goods and services.
>
> **Aggregate supply** (AS) means the total supply of goods and services in the economy.

Aggregate Supply depends on physical production conditions – the availability and cost of factors of production and technical know-how. *Keynes* was concerned with short-run measures to affect the economy, and he also wrote in a period of high unemployment when there was obviously no constraint on the availability of factors of production. His analysis therefore concentrated on the **demand side**. Supply side economics (discussed in the following chapter) describes the views of economists who do not subscribe to the Keynesian approach to dealing with current problems of national income and employment, and prefer instead to concentrate on the **supply side** – in other words, production factors.

Aggregate demand and national income

For Keynesian analysis to have practical value for the management of a national economy, it is necessary to establish how aggregate demand can be shifted.

To understand shifts in AD, we need to turn our attention to expenditure in the economy. A formula for the GNP (= total national expenditure) which was described in the previous chapter is:

$$E = C + I + G + (X - M)$$

where E is the total national expenditure (GNP)

C is the total domestic consumption (money spent on consumer goods)

I is the total industrial investment (money spent by private sector firms and the public sector on capital items) *

G is the total government spending (government 'current' or 'consumption' spending)

X is the total exports (including income from property abroad)

M is the total imports (including money paid as income to residents in other countries for property they hold in the country)

* Alternatively, government investment spending on capital items can be included in G leaving I to represent investment by firms only.

Demand management policies involve the manipulation of E (eg achieving economic growth) by influencing C, I, G or net exports.

If we ignore capital consumption, we can equate E (GNP) with national income. This is what we shall do in our analysis of the Keynesian model.

Withdrawals and injections

In the previous chapter on national income, the different approaches to calculating national income – the expenditure, income and value added approaches – were explained in terms of the circular flow of income around the economy.

For a national economy, there are certain withdrawals from and injections into this circular flow of income. Withdrawals divert funds out of the circular flow and injections add funds into it.

(a) **Withdrawals** from the circular flow of income (W) consist of imports (M), taxation (T) and savings (S).

(b) **Injections** into the circular flow of income (J) consist of exports (X), government spending (G), and investment spending by firms (I).

Keynes argued that for an equilibrium to be reached in the national income, not only must AD = AS, but also total **planned** withdrawals from the circular flow of funds **must be equal to total planned injections.** Thus, for equilibrium:

$W = J$, and so $M + T + S = X + G + I$

In the long term W will always equal J.

(a) The difference between the value of imports M and the value of exports X is the **balance of payments deficit** (or **surplus**). Even in the short term, this difference must be balanced by borrowing (or lending abroad), as we shall see in a later chapter.

(b) The difference between government spending and taxation can only be made up by government borrowing. Loans are eventually repaid.

(c) In the long run, savings will also equal investments, even though the people who save and the firms who invest are not the same. We shall look more closely at savings and investment later.

However, although W and J will be equal retrospectively and in the long run, it does not follow that **planned** J and **planned** W will equal each other **in the short-run,** since injections and withdrawals are made by different people.

This frustration of plans in the short run causes national income to change over time. The imbalance between J and W creates factors which can make the level of national income change. *Keynes* argued that the imbalance between planned withdrawals and planned injections explained **trade cycles** – the fluctuations in national income which give rise to booms and slumps – which prevent an economy from settling down at an equilibrium level.

2.2 Aggregate demand analysis: consumption, savings and investment

Consumption and savings (C and S)

Let us now go into a bit more detail on Keynesian analysis, and concentrate particularly on consumption, savings and investment. To simplify our analysis, we shall ignore government spending, taxation, imports and exports for the time being. By ignoring imports and exports, we are concentrating on a **closed economy** which is not in any way dependent on foreign trade.

If we ignore G, T, X, and M, we can look at a circular flow of income in which households divide all their income between two uses: consumption and saving.

Provided that national income is in equilibrium, we will have:

$Y = C + S$

where Y = national income
C = consumption
S = saving

This should seem logical to you. Income can only be either spent or saved. Since we have a closed economy, consumption must be of goods produced by the economy itself.

Savings

There are two ways of saving. One is to hold the income as money (banknotes and coin, or in a current bank account). The other way is to put money into some form of interest-bearing investment. In the long-run, there is no reason for people to hold banknotes or keep money in a current bank account, unless they intend to spend it fairly soon. If this is so, income that is not spent will be saved and income that is saved will, eventually, be invested. (The people who put their money into interest-bearing savings are not making any investment themselves in capital goods, but the institutions with whom they save will use the deposits to lend to investors and so indirectly there will be a real increase in investment when people save money in this way.)

Activity 5 **(20 minutes)**

What do you think are the main factors influencing the amount that people will save?

We can therefore conclude that in **conditions of equilibrium** for national income:

$Y = C + S$

and, $Y = C + I$

and so, $I = S$

In the short-run, however, savings and investment might not be equal and so there might not be equilibrium.

The propensities to consume and save

Even when a household has zero income, it will still spend. This spending will be financed by earlier **savings** (and, in the real world, by **welfare receipts**). There is thus a constant, basic level of consumption. This is called **autonomous** consumption. When the household receives an income, some will be spent and some will be saved. The **proportion** which is spent is called the **marginal propensity to consume** (MPC) while the **proportion** which is saved is equal to the **marginal propensity to save** (MPS).

In our analysis (ignoring G, T, X and M) saving and consumption are the only two uses for income, MPC + MPS = 1.

Therefore, we may say that a household's expenditure in a given period is made up of two elements.

(a) A fixed amount (a) which is the autonomous consumption.
(b) A further **constant** percentage of its income (b% of Y) representing the MPC.

Similarly, a national economy as a whole will spend a fixed amount £a, plus a constant percentage (b%) of national income Y.

We can then state a consumption function as $C = a + bY$.

Given a consumption function $C = a + bY$:

(a) The marginal propensity to consume is b, where b is the proportion of each extra £1 earned that is spent on consumption.

(b) The average propensity to consume will be the ratio of consumption to income:

$$\frac{C}{Y} = \frac{a+bY}{Y}$$

For example, suppose an individual household has fixed spending of £100 per month, plus extra spending equal to 80% of its monthly income.

(a) When its monthly income is £800, its consumption will be:

£100 + 80% of £800 = £740

(b) When its monthly income is £1,000 its consumption will be:

£100 + 80% of £1,000 = £900

The household's marginal propensity to consume is 80%.

Changes in the marginal propensity to consume and the marginal propensity to save will involve a change of preference by households between current consumption and saving for future benefits. A cause of such a change might be a change in interest rates, which makes the investment of savings more or less attractive than before.

Marginal propensity to withdraw

In a model that includes savings (S), taxes (T) and imports (M), the marginal propensity to withdraw (MPW) is given by:

MPW = MPS + MPT + MPM

The MPW is the proportion of national income that is withdrawn from the circular flow of income.

Investment (I)

The total volume of desired investment in the economy depends on factors similar to those influencing 'micro-level' investment decisions by firms.

- The rate of interest on capital
- The marginal efficiency of capital invested
- Expectations about the future and business confidence
- The strength of consumer demand for goods

A further determinant of MPC is the **attractiveness of savings.** If interest rates are high, households will wish to save more of their income to benefit from the higher rates of interest. The more they save, the less they consume. Conversely some goods are so expensive that they tend to be bought on credit; if interest rates are high there is less incentive to borrow and thus a lower tendency to purchase high-cost goods.

Given $C = a + bY$, the value of b may also be affected by the value of a. If the cost of essential commodities rises in relation to all other commodities, the value of a will rise. This means that a greater proportion of household consumption becomes fixed and there is less available for variable consumption bY. Thus a rise in a causes a fall in b.

We can show the consumption function in a graph, which shows the relationship between consumption, savings and (disposable) income.

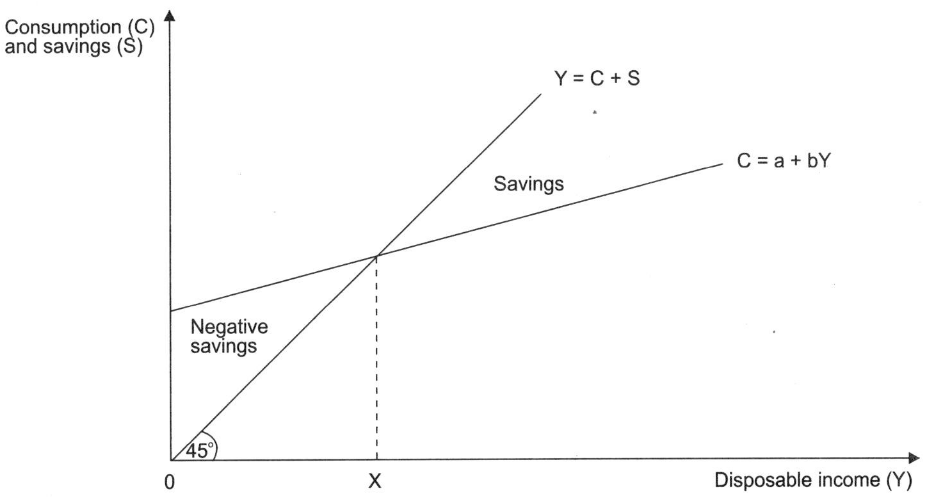

Figure 7.4: Income, consumption and savings (closed economy)

As we have seen, in a closed economy with no government sector, income must equal the sum of consumption and savings. Consumption will always be a minimum amount, and at lower levels of national income (below X in Figure 7.4) consumption will exceed national income. This means that households will be using up savings to buy goods.

The demand for funds to invest by firms and the willingness of investors to lend their savings for investment (the supply of funds) should adjust to one another through the price mechanism of the interest rate.

(a) **Higher interest rates** should make firms less willing to invest, because the marginal efficiency of capital will have to be higher to justify the higher interest cost. However, firms cannot always cut their investment plans quickly and at short notice.

Higher interest rates should have two other effects.

(i) They will tempt individuals to consume less of their income and save more, with a view to investing it.

(ii) They will also tempt individuals to invest more of their savings – that is, to hold less cash and more interest-bearing investments.

(b) **Lower interest rates** should have the opposite effect.

An investment involves the acquisition of more buildings, machinery, plant and equipment or stocks of goods and so on. The importance of the interest rate for investment should therefore be apparent in the marginal efficiency of capital. Firms should go on adding to their capital provided that the marginal efficiency of capital exceeds the interest rate, which is its marginal cost.

2.3 The multiplier

The **multiplier** involves the **process of circulation of income** in the national economy, whereby an injection of a certain size leads to a much larger increase in national income. The firms or households receiving the injection use at least part of the money to increase their own consumption. This provides money for other firms and households to repeat the process and so on.

The level of national income might increase or decrease for a number of reasons; for example, there might be an increase in productivity or an increase in the country's exports. *Keynes* showed that if there is an **initial** change in expenditure due to an increase in exports, or government spending or investment or consumer spending, a new equilibrium national income level will be reached.

The eventual total increase in national income will be greater in size than the initial increase in expenditure. This is because of the continuing circulation of the funds concerned.

Definition

> The ratio of the **total** increase in national income to an initial increase is called the **multiplier**.

$$\text{Multiplier} = \frac{\text{Total increase in national income}}{\text{Initial increase in national income}}$$

The multiplier can be defined as a measure of the effect on total national income of a unit change in a component of aggregate demand: I, G or X.

Multiplier values can therefore be measured specifically for each of these separately.

$$\text{Investment multiplier} = \frac{\text{Eventual change in national income}}{\text{Initial change in investment spending}}$$

$$\text{Government spending multiplier} = \frac{\text{Eventual change in national income}}{\text{Initial change in government spending}}$$

$$\text{Export multiplier} = \frac{\text{Eventual change in national income}}{\text{Initial change in exports}}$$

EXAMPLE: NUMERICAL ILLUSTRATION OF THE MULTIPLIER

A numerical illustration of the multiplier might help to explain it more clearly. In this example, we shall again ignore taxes, government spending, exports and imports, and assume a simple closed economy in which all income is either spent on consumption (C) or saved (S). Let us suppose that in this closed economy, marginal propensity to consume (MPC) is 90% or 0.9. Then, out of any addition to household income, 90% is consumed and 10% saved.

(a) If income goes up by £200, £180 would be spent on consumption, and £20 saved.

(b) The £180 spent on consumption increases the income of other people, who spend 90% (£162) and save £18.

(c) The £162 spent on consumption in turn becomes additional income to others, so that a snowball effect on consumption (and income and output) occurs, as follows.

			Increase in expenditure £	*Increase in savings* £
Stage	1	Income rises	200.00	
	2	90% is consumed	180.00	20.00
	3	A further 90% is consumed	162.00	18.00
	4	"	145.80	16.20
	5	"	131.22	14.58
		etc	.....	.....
		Total increase in income	2,000.00	200.00

In this example, an initial increase in income of £200 results in a final increase in national income of £2,000. The multiplier is 10.

The marginal propensity to save

The multiplier is the reciprocal of the marginal propensity to save. Since MPC = 0.9, MPS = 0.1.

$$\text{Multiplier} = \frac{1}{\text{MPS}} \text{ or } \frac{1}{1-\text{MPC}}$$

$$\text{Increase in national income} = \frac{\text{Initial increase in expenditure}}{\text{MPS}} = \frac{£200}{0.1} = £2{,}000$$

Note that at the new equilibrium, savings of £200 equal the initial increase in expenditure of £200 but national income has risen £2,000.

If the marginal propensity to consume were 80%, the marginal propensity to save would be 20% and the multiplier would only be 5. Because people save more of their extra income, the total increase in national income through extra consumption will be less.

The multiplier in the national economy

The multiplier in a national economy works in the same way. **An initial increase in expenditure will have a snowball effect**, leading to further and further expenditures in the economy. Since total expenditure in the economy is one way of measuring national income, it follows that an initial increase in expenditure will cause an even larger increase in national income. The increase in national income will be a multiplier of the initial increase in spending, with the size of the multiple depending on factors which include the marginal propensity to save.

If you find this hard to visualise, think of an increase in government spending on the construction of roads. The government would spend money paying firms of road contractors, who in turn will purchase raw materials from suppliers, and sub-contract other work. All these firms employ workers who will receive wages that they can spend on goods and services of other firms. The new roads in turn might stimulate new economic activity, for example amongst road hauliers, housebuilders and estate agents.

Depending on the size of the multiplier, an increase in investment would therefore have repercussions throughout the economy, increasing the size of the national income by a multiple of the size of the original increase in investment.

If, for example, the national income were £10,000 million and the average and the marginal propensity to consume were both 75%, in equilibrium, ignoring G, T, X and M:

Y = £10,000 million
C = £7,500 million
I = S = £2,500 million

Since MPC = 75%, MPS = 25%, and the multiplier is 4.

An increase in investment of £1,000 million would upset the equilibrium, which would not be restored until the multiplier had taken effect, and national income increased by 4 × £1,000 million = £4,000 million, with:

Y = £14,000 million
C = £10,500 million (75%)
I = S = £3,500 million (25%)

A downward multiplier or **demultiplier** effect also exists. A reduction in investment will have repercussions throughout the economy, so that a small disinvestment (reduction in expenditure/output) will result in a multiplied reduction in national income

The importance of the multiplier

The importance of the multiplier is that an increase in one of the components of aggregate demand will increase national income by more than the initial increase itself. Therefore if the government takes any action to increase expenditure (for example by raising government current expenditure, or lowering interest rates to raise investment) it will set off a general expansionary process, and the eventual rise in national income will exceed the initial increase in aggregate demand.

This can have important implications for a government when it is planning for growth in national income. By an initial increase in expenditure, a government can 'engineer' an even greater increase in national income, (provided that the country's industries can increase their output capacity), depending on the size of the multiplier.

The multiplier in an open economy

So far we have been considering a simplified economy in which income is either saved or spent on domestic production. The real world is more complex and we must now consider the effect of taxation and imports. Like savings, these are **withdrawals from the circular flow** and they therefore affect the multiplier. Thus, in an open economy, the value of the multiplier depends on three things.

(a) The marginal propensity to save (MPS)

(b) The marginal propensity to import, because imports reduce national income, and if households spend much of their extra income on imports, the snowball increase in total national income will be restricted because imports are a withdrawal out of the circular flow of income. One of the reasons for a low multiplier in the UK is the high marginal propensity to import.

(c) Tax rates, because taxes reduce the ability of people to consume and so are likely to affect the marginal propensity to consume and the marginal propensity to save.

Whereas the multiplier in a closed economy is the reciprocal of the marginal propensity to save, the multiplier in an open economy, taking into account government spending and taxation, and imports and exports, will be less. This is because government taxation and spending on imports reduces the multiplier effect on a country's economy.

For an open economy:

$$\text{Multiplier} = \frac{1}{s+m+t}$$

where s is the marginal propensity to save

m is the marginal propensity to import

t is the marginal propensity to tax – ie the amount of any increase in income that will be paid in taxes.

The multiplier as defined in this way may still be represented as below.

$$\text{Multiplier} = \frac{1}{1-\text{MPC}}$$

since any increase in income is totally accounted for by savings, tax imports and consumption.

For example, if in a country the marginal propensity to save is 10%, the marginal propensity to import is 45% and the marginal propensity to tax is 25%, the size of the multiplier would be:

$$\frac{1}{0.1+0.45+0.25} = \frac{1}{0.80} = 1.25$$

2.4 The business cycle

What is the business cycle?

Business cycles or **trade cycles** are the continual sequence of rapid growth in national income, followed by a slow-down in growth and then a fall in national income. After this recession comes growth again, and when this has reached a peak, the cycle turns into recession once more.

Four main phases of the business cycle can be distinguished.

- Recession
- Depression
- Recovery
- Boom

Recession tends to occur quickly, while recovery is typically a slower process. Figure 7.5 below can be used to help explain how this is so.

Diagrammatic explanation

At point A in Figure 7.5, the economy is entering a recession. In the recession phase, consumer demand falls and many investment projects already undertaken begin to look unprofitable. Orders will be cut, stock levels will be reduced and business failures will occur as firms find themselves unable to sell their goods. Production and employment will fall. The general price level will begin to fall. Business and consumer confidence are diminished and investment remains low, while the economic outlook appears to be poor. Eventually, in the absence of any stimulus to aggregate demand, a period of full **depression** sets in and the economy will reach point B.

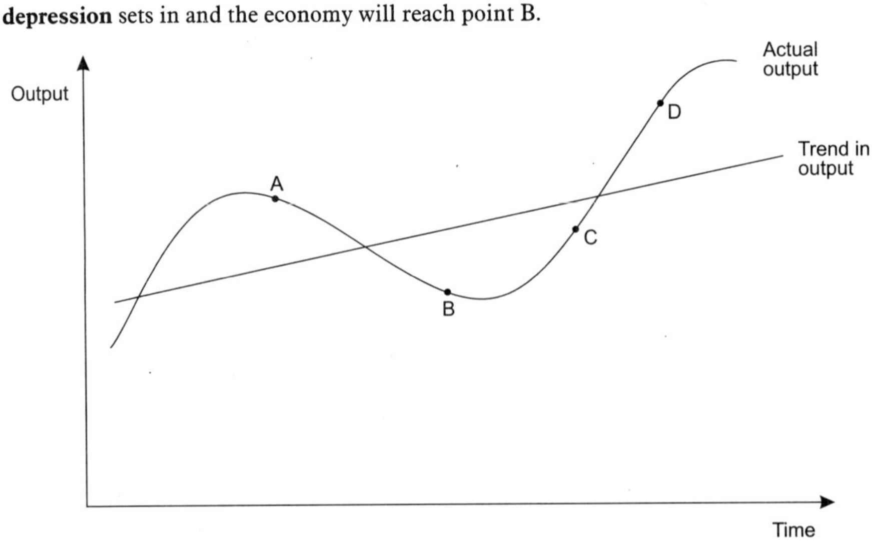

Figure 7.5: The business cycle

Analysis of the phases

Recession can begin relatively quickly because of the speed with which the effects of declining demand will be felt by businesses suffering a loss in sales revenue. The knock-on effects of destocking and cutting back on investment exacerbate the situation and add momentum to the recession. Recovery can be slow to begin because of the effect of recession on levels of confidence.

At point C the economy has reached the **recovery** phase of the cycle. Once begun, the phase of recovery is likely to quicken as confidence returns. Output, employment and income will all begin to rise. Rising production, sales and profit levels will lead to optimistic business expectations, and new investment will be more readily undertaken. The rising level of demand can be met through increased production by bringing existing capacity into use and by hiring unemployed labour. The average price level will remain constant or begin to rise slowly.

In the recovery phase, decisions to purchase new materials and machinery may lead to benefits in efficiency from new technology. This can enhance the relative rate of economic growth in the recovery phase once it is under way.

As recovery proceeds, the output level climbs above its trend path, reaching point D, in the **boom** phase of the cycle. During the boom, capacity and labour will become fully utilised. This may cause bottlenecks in some industries which are unable to meet increases in demand, for example because they have no spare capacity or they lack certain categories of skilled labour, or they face shortages of key material inputs. Further rises in demand will, therefore, tend to be met by increases in prices rather than by increases in production. In general, business will be profitable, with few firms facing losses. Expectations of the future may be very optimistic and the level of investment expenditure high.

It can be argued that wide fluctuations in levels of economic activity are damaging to the overall economic well-being of society. The inflation and speculation which accompanies boom periods may be inequitable in their impact on different sections of the population, while the bottom of the trade cycle may bring high unemployment. Governments generally seek to stabilise the economic system, trying to avoid the distortions of a widely fluctuating trade cycle.

We now move on to two key areas of macroeconomics – inflation and unemployment.

2.5 Inflation and its consequences

Inflation

Definition

> **Inflation** is the name given to an increase in price levels generally. It is also manifest in the decline in the purchasing power of money.

Historically, there have been very few periods when inflation has not been present. We discuss below why high rates of inflation are considered to be harmful. However, it is important to remember that **deflation** (falling prices) is normally associated with low rates of growth and even recession. It would seem that a healthy economy may require some inflation. This is recognised in the current UK inflation target of 2½%, and the European Central Bank's target of 2%. Certainly, if an economy is to grow, the money supply must expand, and the presence of a low level of inflation will ensure that growth is not hampered by a shortage of liquid funds.

Why is inflation a problem?

An economic policy objective which now has a central place in the policy approaches of the governments of many developed countries is that of stable prices. Why is a *high* rate of price inflation harmful and undesirable?

Redistribution of income and wealth

Inflation leads to a redistribution of income and wealth in ways which may be undesirable. Redistribution of wealth might take place from creditors to debtors. This is because debts lose 'real' value with inflation. For example, if you owed £1,000, and prices then doubled, you would still owe £1,000, but the **real value** of your debt would have been halved. In general, in times of inflation those with economic power tend to gain at the expense of the weak, particularly those on fixed incomes.

Balance of payments effects

If a country has a higher rate of inflation than its major trading partners, its exports will become relatively expensive and imports relatively cheap. As a result, the balance of trade will suffer, affecting employment in exporting industries and in industries producing import-substitutes. Eventually, the exchange rate will be affected.

Uncertainty of the value of money and prices

If the rate of inflation is imperfectly anticipated, no one has certain knowledge of the true rate of inflation. As a result, no one has certain knowledge of the value of money or of the real meaning of prices. If the rate of inflation becomes excessive, and there is 'hyperinflation', this problem becomes so exaggerated that money becomes worthless, so that people are unwilling to use it and are forced to resort to barter. In less extreme circumstances, the results are less dramatic, but the same problem exists. As prices convey less information, the process of resource allocation is less efficient and rational decision-making is almost impossible.

Resource costs of changing prices

A fourth reason to aim for stable prices is the resource cost of frequently changing prices. In times of high inflation substantial labour time is spent on planning and implementing price changes. Customers may also have to spend more time making price comparisons if they seek to buy from the lowest cost source.

Economic growth and investment

It is sometimes claimed that inflation is harmful to a country's economic growth and level of investment. A study by *Robert Barro* (*Bank of England Quarterly Bulletin*, May 1995) examined whether the evidence available supports this view. Barro found from data covering over 100 countries from 1960 to 1990 that, on average, an increase in inflation of ten percentage points per year reduced the growth rate of real GDP per capita by 0.2 to 0.3 percentage points per year, and lowered the ratio of investment to GDP by 0.4 to 0.6 percentage points. Although the adverse influence of inflation on economic growth and investment appears small, some causal effect would appear to exist, which could affect a country's standard of living fairly significantly over the long term.

Consumer price indices

We have already referred to the way in which inflation erodes the real value of money. In order to measure changes in the real value of money as a single figure, we need to group all goods and services into a single price index.

A consumer price index is based on a chosen 'basket' of items which consumers purchase. A weighting is decided for each item according to the average spending on the item by consumers.

Consumer price indices may be used for several purposes, for example as an indicator of inflationary pressures in the economy, as a benchmark for wage negotiations and to determine annual increases in government benefits payments. Countries commonly have more than one consumer price index because one composite index may be considered too wide a grouping for different purposes.

The RPI and the CPI

One important measure of the general rate of inflation in the UK used over many years has been the **Retail Prices Index (RPI)**. The RPI measures the percentage changes month by month in the average level of prices of the commodities and services, including housing costs, purchased by the great majority of households in the UK. The items of expenditure within the RPI are intended to be a representative list of items, current prices for which are collected at regular intervals.

In December 2003, it was confirmed that the standardised European measure, sometimes called the Harmonised Index of Consumer Prices (HICP) was now to be used as the basis for the UK's inflation target. The UK HICP is called the **Consumer Prices Index (CPI)**. The CPI excludes most housing costs.

The underlying rate of inflation

The term **underlying rate of inflation** is usually used to refer to the RPI adjusted to exclude mortgage costs and sometimes other elements as well (such as the local council tax). The effects of interest rate changes on mortgage costs help to make the RPI fluctuate more widely than the underlying rate of inflation.

RPIX is the underlying rate of inflation measured as the increase in the RPI excluding mortgage interest payments. Another measure, called **RPIY**, goes further and excludes the effects of VAT changes as well.

Causes of inflation

The following can cause inflation:

- Demand pull factors
- Cost push factors
- Import cost factors
- Expectations
- Excessive growth in the money supply

Demand pull inflation

Demand pull inflation occurs when the economy is buoyant and there is a high aggregate demand, in excess of the economy's ability to supply.

(a) Because aggregate demand exceeds supply, prices rise.

(b) Since supply needs to be raised to meet the higher demand, there will be an increase in demand for factors of production, and so factor rewards (wages, interest rates, and so on) will also rise.

(c) Since aggregate demand exceeds the output capability of the economy, it should follow that demand pull inflation can only exist when unemployment is low. A feature of inflation in the UK in the 1970s and early 1980s, however, was high inflation coupled with high unemployment.

Definition

> **Demand pull inflation** is inflation resulting from a persistent excess of aggregate demand over aggregate supply. Supply reaches a limit on capacity at the full employment level.

Traditionally Keynesian economists saw inflation as being caused by Demand pull factors. However, they now accept that Cost push factors are involved as well.

Cost push inflation

Cost push inflation occurs where the costs of factors of production rise regardless of whether or not they are in short supply. This appears to be particularly the case with wages.

Definition

> **Cost push inflation** is inflation resulting from an increase in the costs of production of goods and services, eg through escalating prices of imported raw materials or from wage increases.

Import cost factors

Import cost push inflation occurs when the cost of essential imports rise regardless of whether or not they are in short supply. This has occurred in the past with the oil price rises of the 1970s. Additionally, a fall in the value of a country's currency will have import Cost push effects since a weakening currency increases the price of imports.

Expectations and inflation

A further problem is that once the rate of inflation has begun to increase, a serious danger of **expectational inflation** will occur. This means, regardless of whether the factors that have caused inflation are still persistent or not, there will arise a generally held view of what inflation is likely to be, and so to protect future income, wages and prices will be raised now by the expected amount of future inflation. This can lead to the vicious circle known as the **wage-price spiral,** in which inflation becomes a relatively permanent feature because of people's expectations that it will occur.

Money supply growth

Monetarists have argued that inflation is caused by **increases in the supply of money**. There is a considerable debate as to whether increases in the money supply are a **cause** of inflation or whether increases in the money supply are a **symptom** of inflation. Monetarists have argued that since inflation is caused by an increase in the money supply, inflation can be brought under control by reducing the rate of growth of the money supply.

2.6 Unemployment

The rate of unemployment

The **rate of unemployment** in an economy can be calculated as:

$$\frac{\text{Number of unemployed}}{\text{Total workforce}} \times 100\%$$

The number of unemployed at any time is measured by government statistics. If the flow of workers through unemployment is constant then the size of the unemployed labour force will also be constant.

Flows into unemployment are:

(a) Members of the working labour force **becoming** unemployed

- Redundancies
- Lay-offs
- Voluntary quitting from a job

(b) People **out** of the labour force **joining** the unemployed

- School leavers without a job
- Others (for example, carers) rejoining the workforce but having no job yet

Flows out of unemployment are:

- Unemployed people finding jobs
- Laid-off workers being re-employed
- Unemployed people stopping the search for work

Consequences of unemployment

Unemployment results in the following problems.

(a) **Loss of output**. If labour is unemployed, the economy is not producing as much output as it could. Thus, total national income is less than it could be.

(b) **Loss of human capital**. If there is unemployment, the unemployed labour will gradually lose its skills, because skills can only be maintained by working.

(c) **Increasing inequalities in the distribution of income**. Unemployed people earn less than employed people, and so when unemployment is increasing, the poor get poorer.

(d) **Social costs**. Unemployment brings social problems of personal suffering and distress, and possibly also increases in crime such as theft and vandalism.

(e) **Increased burden of welfare payments**. This can have a major impact on government fiscal policy.

Causes of unemployment

Unemployment may be classified into several categories depending on the underlying causes.

Category	Comments
Real wage unemployment	This type of unemployment is caused when the supply of labour exceeds the demand for labour, but real wages do not fall for the labour market to clear. This type of unemployment is normally caused by strong trade unions which resist a fall in their wages. Another cause of this type of unemployment is the minimum wage rate, when it is set above the market clearing level.
Frictional	It is inevitable that some unemployment is caused not so much because there are not enough jobs to go round, but because of the *friction* in the labour market (difficulty in matching quickly workers with jobs), caused perhaps by a lack of knowledge about job opportunities. In general, it takes time to match prospective employees with employers, and individuals will be unemployed during the search period for a new job. Frictional unemployment is temporary, lasting for the period of transition from one job to the next.
Seasonal	This occurs in certain industries, for example building, tourism and farming, where the demand for labour fluctuates in seasonal patterns throughout the year.
Structural	This occurs where long-term changes occur in the conditions of an industry. A feature of structural unemployment is high regional un-employment in the location of the industry affected.

Category	Comments
Technological	This is a form of structural unemployment, which occurs when new technologies are introduced. (a) Old skills are no longer required. (b) There is likely to be a labour saving aspect, with machines doing the job that people used to do. With automation, employment levels in an industry can fall sharply, even when the industry's total output is increasing.
Cyclical or demand-deficient	It has been the experience of the past that domestic and foreign trade go through cycles of boom, decline, recession, recovery, then boom again, and so on. (a) During recovery and boom years, the demand for output and jobs is high, and unemployment is low. (b) During decline and recession years, the demand for output and jobs falls, and unemployment rises to a high level. Cyclical unemployment can be long-term, and a government might try to reduce it by doing what it can to minimise a recession or to encourage faster economic growth.

Seasonal employment and frictional unemployment will be short-term. Structural unemployment, technological unemployment, and cyclical unemployment are all longer term, and more serious.

Government employment policies

Job creation and reducing unemployment should often mean the same thing, but it is possible to create more jobs without reducing unemployment.

(a) This can happen when there is a greater number of people entering the jobs market than there are new jobs being created. For example, if 500,000 new jobs are created during the course of one year, but 750,000 extra school leavers are looking for jobs, there will be an increase in unemployment of 250,000.

(b) It is also possible to reduce the official unemployment figures without creating jobs. For example, individuals who enrol for a government financed training scheme are taken off the unemployment register, even though they do not have full-time jobs.

A government can try several options to create jobs or reduce unemployment.

(a) **Spending more money directly on jobs** (for example hiring more civil servants)

(b) **Encouraging growth** in the private sector of the economy. When aggregate demand is growing, firms will probably want to increase output to meet demand, and so will hire more labour.

(c) **Encouraging training in job skills**. There might be a high level of unemployment amongst unskilled workers, and at the same time a shortage of skilled workers. A government can help to finance training schemes, in order to provide a 'pool' of workers who have the skills that firms need and will pay for.

(d) **Offering grant assistance to employers** in key regional areas

(e) **Encouraging labour mobility** by offering individuals financial assistance with relocation expenses, and improving the flow of information on vacancies

Other policies may be directed at **reducing real wages to market clearing levels**.

(a) Abolishing **closed shop** agreements, which restrict certain jobs to trade union members

(b) Abolishing **minimum wage regulations**, where such regulations exist

Activity 6 **(5 minutes)**

Match the terms (a), (b) and (c) below with definitions A, B and C.

(a) Structural unemployment
(b) Cyclical unemployment
(c) Frictional unemployment

A Unemployment arising from a difficulty in matching unemployed workers with available jobs

B Unemployment occurring in the downswing of an economy in between two booms

C Unemployment arising from a long-term decline in a particular industry

2.7 Unemployment and inflation

The Phillips curve

In 1958 *A W Phillips* found a statistical relationship between unemployment and the rate of money wage inflation which implied that, in general, **the rate of inflation falls unemployment rose and** *vice versa*. A curve, known as a **Phillips curve**, can be drawn linking inflation and unemployment (Figure 7.6).

Definition

Phillips curve: a graphical illustration of the historic inverse relationship between the rate of wage inflation and the rate of unemployment.

Note the following two points about the Phillips curve.

(a) The curve crosses the horizontal axis at a positive value for the unemployment rate. This means that zero inflation will be associated with some unemployment; it is not possible to achieve zero inflation and zero unemployment at the same time.

(b) The shape of the curve means that the lower the level of unemployment, the higher the **rate of increase** in inflation.

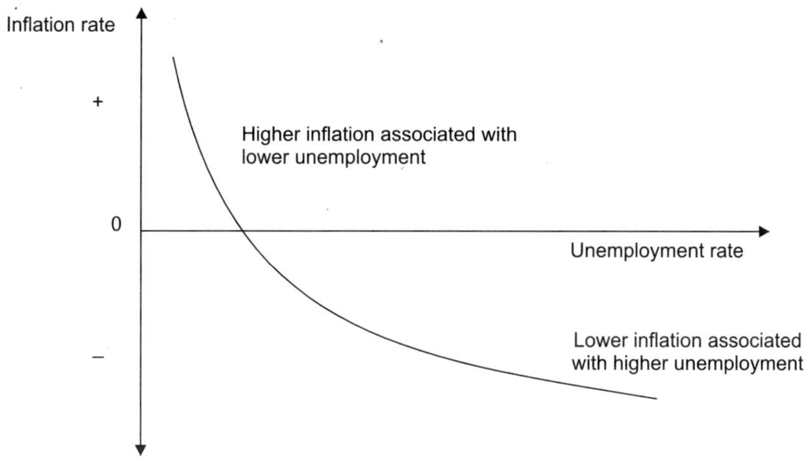

Figure 7.6: Phillips curve

The existence of a relationship between inflation and unemployment of the type indicated by the Phillips curve suggests that the government should be able to use demand management policies to take the economy to acceptable levels of inflation and unemployment.

This re-emphasises the argument of Keynesian economists that in order to achieve full employment, some inflation is unavoidable. If achieving full employment is an economic policy objective, a government must therefore be prepared to accept a certain level of inflation as a necessary evil.

However, the Phillips curve relationship between inflation and unemployment broke down at the end of the 1960s when Britain began to experience **rising inflation at the same time as rising unemployment.**

FOR DISCUSSION

Inflation rather than unemployment is the greatest threat to the UK economy. What do you think?

---

3 FISCAL, MONETARY AND SUPPLY SIDE POLICIES

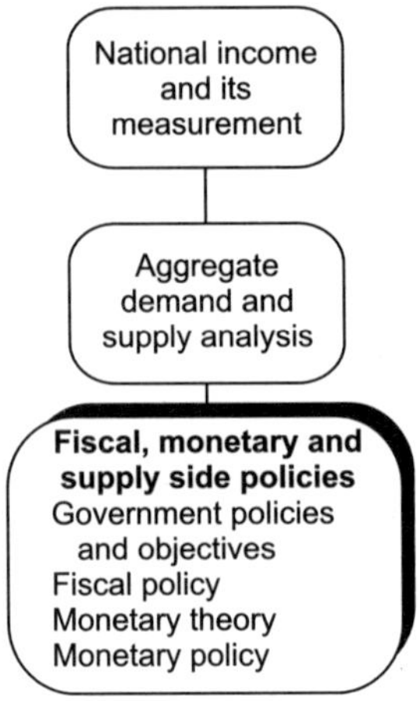

3.1 Government policies and objectives

Macroeconomic policy objectives relate to economic growth, inflation, unemployment and the balance of payments.

Economic policy objectives

All modern governments are expected to manage their national economies to some extent. Electorates generally suppose that government action can support or hinder the growth of prosperity and look to them for serviceable macroeconomic policies. There are four main objective of economic policy, though debate continues about their relative priority.

(a) **To achieve economic growth**, and growth in national income per head of the population. Growth implies an increase in national income in real terms. Increases caused by price inflation are not real increases at all.

(b) **To control price inflation** (to achieve stable prices). This has become a central objective of UK economic policy in recent years.

(c) **To achieve full employment**. Full employment does not mean that everyone who wants a job has one all the time, but it does mean that unemployment levels are low, and involuntary unemployment is short-term.

(d) **To achieve a balance between exports and imports** (on the country's balance of payments accounts) over a period of years. The wealth of a country relative to others, a country's creditworthiness as a borrower, and the goodwill between countries in international relations might all depend on the achievement of an external balance over time.

Definitions

> **Monetary policy**: government policy on the money supply, the monetary system, interest rates, exchange rates and the availability of credit.
>
> **Fiscal policy**: government policy on taxation, public borrowing and public spending.
>
> Monetary and fiscal policy attempt to attain the macroeconomic policy objectives by influencing aggregate demand.
>
> **Supply side** policies on the other hand attempt to the attain the macroeconomic policy objectives by shifting the aggregate supply curve.

3.2 Fiscal policy

Fiscal policy and the Budget

A feature of fiscal policy is that a government must **plan** what it wants to spend, and so how much it needs to raise in income or by borrowing. It needs to make a plan in order to establish how much taxation there should be, what form the taxes should take and so which sectors of the economy (firms or households, high income earners or low income earners) the money should come from. This formal planning of fiscal policy is usually done once a year and is set out in **the Budget**.

The two components of the budget which the government determines and through which it exercises its fiscal policy are:

(a) **Expenditure**. The government, at a national and local level, spends money to provide goods and services, such as a health service, public education, a police force, roads, public buildings and so on, and to pay its administrative work force. It may also, perhaps, provide finance to encourage investment by private industry, for example by means of grants.

(b) **Revenues**. Expenditure must be financed, and the government must have income. Most government income comes from **taxation,** albeit some income is obtained from **direct charges** to users of government services such as National Health Service charges.

A third element of the fiscal policy is:

(c) **Borrowing**. To the extent that a government's expenditure exceeds its income it must borrow to make up the difference. The amount that the government must borrow each year is now known as the **Public Sector Net Cash Requirement (PSNCR)** in the UK Its former name was **Public Sector Borrowing Requirement (PSBR).** Where the government borrows from has an impact on the effectiveness of fiscal policy.

Definition

> The **public sector net cash requirement (PSNCR)** is the annual excess of spending over income for the entire sector – not just the central government.

Functions of taxation

Taxation has several functions.

(a) **To raise revenues for the government** as well as for local authorities and similar public bodies (eg the European Union).

(b) **To discourage certain activities regarded as undesirable**. The imposition of Development Land Tax in the United Kingdom in the mid-70s (since abolished) was partially in response to growth in property speculation.

(c) **To cause certain products to be priced to take into account their social costs**. For example, smoking entails certain social costs, including especially the cost of hospital care for those suffering from smoking-related diseases, and the government sees fit to make the price of tobacco reflect these social costs.

(d) **To redistribute income and wealth**. Higher rates of tax on higher incomes will serve to redistribute income. UK inheritance tax goes some way towards redistributing wealth.

(e) **To protect industries from foreign competition.** If the government levies a duty on all imported goods much of the duty will be passed on to the consumer in the form of higher prices, making imported goods more expensive. This has the effect of transferring a certain amount of demand from imported goods to domestically produced goods.

(f) **To provide a stabilising effect on national income**. Taxation reduces the effect of the multiplier, and so can be used to dampen upswings in a trade cycle – ie higher taxation when the economy shows signs of a boom will slow down the growth of money GNP and so take some inflationary pressures out of the economy.

Qualities of a good tax

Adam Smith in his *Wealth of Nations* ascribed **four features to a good tax system**.

(a) **Equity**. Persons should pay according to their ability.

(b) **Certainty**. The tax should be well-defined and easily understood by all concerned.

(c) **Convenience**. The payment of tax should ideally be related to how and when people receive and spend their income (eg PAYE is deducted when wages are paid, and VAT is charged when goods are bought).

(d) **Economy**. The cost of collection should be small relative to the yield (eg by this criterion, the car road tax is an inefficient tax).

Further features of a good tax can be identified.

- **Flexibility**. It should be adjustable so that rates may be altered up or down.
- **Efficiency**. It should not harm initiative, but evasion should be difficult.
- It should attain its purpose **without distorting economic behaviour**.

Note the following distinctions.

(a) A **regressive tax** takes a higher **proportion** of a poor person's salary than of a rich person's. Television licences and road tax are examples of regressive taxes since they are the same for all people. High income earners, even though individual charges can vary from one local authority to another, and in spite of some rebates for the least well-off groups.

(b) A **proportional tax** takes the **same proportion** of income in tax from all levels of income. Schedule E income tax with a basic of tax at 23% is proportional tax, but only within a limited range of income.

(c) A **progressive tax** takes a **higher proportion** of income in tax as income rises. Income tax as a whole is progressive, since the first part of an individual's income is tax-free due to personal allowances and the rate of tax increases in steps from 20p in £1 to 40p in £1 as taxable income rises.

Direct and indirect taxes

A government must decide how it intends to raise tax revenues, from **direct or indirect taxes**, and in what proportions tax revenues will be raised from each source.

A **direct tax** is paid direct by a person to the Revenue authority. Examples of direct taxes in the UK are income tax, corporation tax, capital gains tax and inheritance tax. A direct tax can be levied on income and profits, or on wealth. Direct taxes tend to be progressive or proportional taxes. They are also usually unavoidable, which means that they must be paid by everyone.

An **indirect tax** is collected by the Revenue authority from an intermediary (a supplier) who then attempts to pass on the tax to consumers in the price of goods they sell. Indirect taxes are of two types.

Definitions

A **specific tax** is charged as a *fixed sum* per unit sold.

An **ad valorem tax** is charged as a *fixed percentage* of the price of the good.

Activity 7 **(5 minutes)**

The burden of an indirect tax must either be borne by the producer or passed on by the producer to consumers. If a producer feels able to pass on the whole of the burden, what can you deduce about the elasticity of demand for his product?

Fiscal policy and unemployment

Fiscal policy can be used to reduce unemployment and provide jobs.

(a) More government spending on capital projects would create jobs in the construction industries.

(b) Government-funded training schemes are a means of spending by government to improve training, so as to make people more qualified for jobs in private industry.

(c) A government might tax companies on the basis of the numbers and pay levels of people they employ (as with employers' national insurance contributions). Lower employment taxes would possibly make employers more willing to take on extra numbers of employees.

If government raises taxes and spending by the same amount, so that the budget remains in balance, there will be an **increase in aggregate monetary demand**. This is because tax payers would have saved some of the money they pay in increased tax and the government spends all of it within the economy. This effect is called the **balanced budget multiplier**.

Government spending, however, might create inflationary pressures, and inflation tends to create more unemployment. Fiscal policy must therefore be used with care, even to create new jobs.

FOR DISCUSSION

'The rich should pay a larger percentage of their income in tax than the poor'. What are the arguments for and against this statement?

3.3 Monetary theory

The classical quantity theory of money

The **classical quantity theory of money**, goes back many years. It is associated with *Irving Fisher's* book *The Purchasing Power of Money*, which was published in 1911. The classical quantity theory is based on the view that money is used only as a **medium of exchange** and people require it only in order to settle transactions in good and services.

If the number of transactions in the economy is fixed, and independent of the amount of the money supply, then the total money value of transactions will be PT, where:

P is the price level of goods and services bought and sold
T is the number or quantity of transactions

The amount of money needed to pay for these transactions will depend on the **velocity of circulation**. Money changes hands. A person receiving money can use it to make his own purchases. For example, if A pays B £2 for transaction X, B can use the £2 to pay C for transaction Y and C can use the same £2 to pay D for transaction Z. If the three transactions X, Y, and Z all occur within a given period of time then the money value of the transactions is:

£2 price level × 3 transactions = £6.

The total amount of money is the same £2 in circulation for all three transactions but this money has exchanged hands three times. The velocity of circulation is 3 and MV = 6, where M is the money supply and V is the velocity of circulation.

The quantity theory of money is summarised by this identity, known as the **Fisher equation.**

MV ≡ PT

MV **must** be equivalent to PT because they are two different ways of measuring the same transactions. In practice, the velocity of circulation V is calculated as the balancing figure in the equation below.

$$V = \frac{PT}{M}$$

Activity 8 **(10 minutes)**

Which of the following definitions correctly describes the velocity of circulation?

A The money stock in a given time period divided by the level of prices

B The number of times in a given period that a unit of money is used to purchase final output

C The total value of transactions in a given time period divided by the average price level

Definition

The **quantity theory of money** is the theory which holds that changes in the level of prices are caused predominantly by changes in the supply of money. This derives from the Fisher equation, MV = PT, assuming that the velocity of circulation V and the number of transactions T are stable.

The quantity theory of money makes three further **assumptions**.

(a) **V has a roughly constant value**. The velocity of circulation of money remains the same at all times, or at least only changes very slowly over time.

(b) **T is either given or it is independent of the amount of money, M**. The reason why T should be a given total was that the supporters of the quantity theory argued that full employment of resources is the norm and if all resources are fully utilised, the volume of transactions T must be a constant value.

(c) **The amount of M is determined by other factors and is independent of V, T or (most significantly) P**. The money supply could be controlled by government authorities, including the central bank.

Given these assumptions, the quantity theory of money becomes a theory of **price levels** because, since MV = PT, then:

$$P = \frac{V}{T}M$$

If V and T are roughly constant values, P will vary directly with increases or decreases in the amount of M: changes in the money supply M cause prices P to change. In other words, inflation is **directly related to** the money supply, and a 10% increase in the money supply, say, would result in 10% inflation.

There is a logic behind the algebra of the classical quantity theory and it relates to the basic assumption that money is used only for transactions relating to goods and services. If this is true, it follows that an excess of money will lead to increased attempts to spend it. Similarly, a shortage of money will have the effect of reducing demand. If the economy is utilising its productive resources to the full (that is, if there is full employment) it will not be possible to increase output. Any increase in demand will therefore cause prices to rise by the action of market forces. Similarly, any reduction in demand will cause prices to fall.

This theory is very satisfactory in explaining past experience of price rises and falls over long periods, as during the nineteenth century. In the first half of the nineteenth century there was large scale economic expansion, but the money supply was based on the gold standard and expanded only slowly: prices generally fell. In the second half of the century there were extensive increases in the supply of gold as a result of mining in Australia and America. The growth of economic activity, and hence output, did not match the growth in the gold supply and prices rose.

Important conclusions from the quantity theory of money equation.

(a) If the velocity of circulation of money, V, is more or less constant, then any **growth in the money supply**, M, over and above the potential in the economy to increase T, will cause **inflation**.

(b) If **the number of transaction or the output in the economy, T, is** growing and if the velocity of circulation, V, is constant, then a **matching growth in the money supply,** M, is needed to avoid deflation.

(c) Government's monetary policy should be to allow some growth in the money supply **if the economy is growing**, but not to let the growth in the money supply get out of hand.

The extent to which these conclusions are valid depends largely on whether the velocity of circulation of money is roughly constant or not. For example, if the money supply increases by 10%, and real growth in the economy (the increase in the volume of transactions) is 3%, we could predict that inflation will be about 7% – but only if the velocity of circulation is constant.

The quantity theory of money relates the money supply directly to the general level of prices. It has no close connection to the classical theory of interest rates. This was simply a supply and demand equilibrium price model for liquid funds. The rate of interest is effectively the price of borrowing and the reward of lending. This model was discussed in the chapter on markets for factors of production.

3.4 Monetary policy

Objectives of monetary policy

Monetary policy can be used as a means towards achieving ultimate economic objectives for inflation, the balance of trade, full employment and real economic growth. To achieve these **ultimate objectives**, the authorities will set **intermediate objectives** for monetary policy.

In the UK, the ultimate objective of monetary policy in recent years has been principally to reduce the rate of inflation to a sustainable low level. The intermediate objectives of monetary policy have related to the level of interest rates, growth in the money supply, the exchange rate for sterling, the expansion of credit and the growth of national income.

The money supply as a target of monetary policy

To monetarist economists, the **money supply** is an obvious intermediate target of economic policy. This is because they claim that an increase in the money supply will raise prices and incomes and this in turn will raise the demand for money to spend.

When such a policy is first introduced, the short-term effect would be unpredictable for three reasons.

(a) The effect on interest rates might be erratic.

(b) There might be a time lag before anything can be done. For example, it takes time to cut government spending and hence to use reduction in government borrowing as an instrument of monetary policy to control the growth in M_0 or M_4.

(c) There might be a time lag before control of the money supply alters expectations about inflation and wage demands.

Growth in the money supply, if it is a monetary policy target, should therefore be a **medium-term target**. When the UK government set targets for the growth of the money supply as a main feature of its economic policy strategy from 1980, it was consequently prepared to wait for some years to see any benefits from its policies and therefore set out its policy targets in a **medium-term** financial strategy.

There are other problems with using growth in the money supply as an intermediate policy target.

(a) There will be difficulty in selecting a suitable monetary aggregate, whose growth rate will either affect or reflect changes in economic conditions. For example, if the aim of controlling the money supply is to control inflation, but if M_4 increases by 20% per annum when the rate of inflation is just 5% per annum, targets for M_4 growth would be an unsuitable monetary policy objective.

(b) It is debatable whether controlling the growth in the money supply will result in control over the rate of inflation. In the UK, the fall in the velocity of circulation of the broad money supply aggregates through the 1980s has meant that the broad money supply has risen at a much faster rate than inflation.

Interest rates as a target for monetary policy

The authorities might decide that **interest rates** – the price of money – should be a target of monetary policy. This would be appropriate if it is considered that there is a direct relationship between interest rates and the level of expenditure in the economy, or between interest rates and the rate of inflation.

A rise in interest rates will raise the price of borrowing in the internal economy for both companies and individuals. If companies see the rise as relatively permanent, rates of return on investments will become less attractive and **investment plans may be curtailed**. Corporate profits will fall as a result of higher interest payments. Companies will reduce stock levels as the cost of having money tied up in stocks rises. Individuals should be expected to reduce or postpone consumption in order to reduce borrowings, and should become less willing to borrow for house purchase.

Although it is generally accepted that there is likely to be a connection between interest rates and investment (by companies) and consumer expenditure, **the connection is not a stable and predictable one**, and interest rate changes are only likely to affect the level of expenditure after a **considerable time lag**.

Other effects of raising interest rates

(a) High interest rates will keep the value of sterling higher than it would otherwise be. This will keep the cost of exports high, and so discourage the purchase of exports. This may be necessary to protect the balance of payments and to prevent 'import-cost-push' inflation. UK manufacturers have complained bitterly about this effect in recent years and BMW cited it as one of the reasons for disposing of Rover.

(b) High interest rates will attract foreign investors into sterling investments, and so provide capital inflows which help to finance the large UK balance of payments deficit.

An important reason for pursuing an interest rate policy is that the authorities are able to influence interest rates much more effectively and rapidly than they can influence other policy targets, such as the money supply or the volume of credit. As we have already seen, in 1997 the new Labour Government of the UK placed responsibility for interest rate decisions with the Bank of England, which sets rates with the objective of meeting the government's inflation target.

The exchange rate as a target of monetary policy

Why the exchange rate is a target

(a) If the exchange rate falls, exports become cheaper to overseas buyers and so more competitive in export markets. Imports will become more expensive and so less competitive against goods produced by manufacturers at home. A fall in the exchange rate might therefore be good for a domestic economy, by giving a **stimulus to exports** and **reducing demand for imports**.

(b) An increase in the exchange rate will have the opposite effect, with dearer exports and cheaper imports. If the exchange rate rises and imports become cheaper, there should be a reduction in the rate of domestic inflation. A fall in the exchange rate, on the other hand, tends to increase the cost of imports and adds to the rate of domestic inflation.

When a country's economy is heavily dependent on overseas trade, as the UK economy is, it might be appropriate for government policy to establish a target exchange value for the domestic currency. However, the exchange rate is dependent on both the domestic rate of inflation and the level of interest rates. Targets for the exchange rate cannot be achieved unless the rate of inflation at home is first brought under control.

Growth in money national income as a target of monetary policy

The authorities might set targets for the level of national income in the economy. For example, the policy might be for the growth in the national income (or GNP or GDP) to be X% per annum for Y years. However, it takes time to collect information about national income whereas targets of monetary policy should be items for which statistical data can be collected regularly and easily.

For this reason, although a target growth rate in national income itself is, in theory, probably the most suitable target of monetary policy, it is the least practical because the authorities would always be working with out-of-date information.

Instruments of monetary policy

There are a number of **techniques** or **instruments** which are available to the authorities to achieve their targets for monetary policies.

- Changing the level and/or structure of **interest rates** through **open market operations**
- **Reserve requirements**
- **Direct controls**, which might be either quantitative or qualitative
- **Intervention to influence the exchange rate**

Control over the level and structure of interest rates

When a government uses interest rates as an instrument of policy, it can try to influence either the general level of interest rates or the term structure of interest rates. It could do this by influencing either short-term interest rates or long-term interest rates. In the UK since 1997, the Bank of England has had responsibility for setting short-term interest rates. Long-term rates could possibly be influenced by increasing or reducing the PSBR.

Reserve requirements on banks as a means of controlling the money supply

As another technique for controlling money supply growth, the government might impose **reserve requirements** on banks. A reserve requirement might be a compulsory minimum cash reserve ratio (ie ratio of cash to total assets) or a minimum liquid asset ratio.

You will recall that any initial increase in bank deposits or building society deposits will result in a much greater eventual increase in deposits, because of the credit multiplier.

Ignoring leakages, the formula for the credit multiplier is:

$$D = \frac{C}{r}$$

where C is the initial increase in deposits
r is the liquid assets ratio or reserve assets ratio
D is the eventual total increase in deposits

If the authorities wished to control the rate of increase in bank lending and building society lending, they could impose minimum reserve requirements – ie a minimum value for r. **The bigger the value or r, the lower size of the credit multiplier would be.**

There are drawbacks to reserve requirements as a monetary policy instrument.

(a) Unless the same requirements apply to all financial institutions in the country, some institutions will simply take business from others. For example, reserve requirements on UK banks but not on building societies would give the building societies a competitive advantage over the banks, without having any effect on the control of total credit/money supply growth.

(b) Similarly, restrictions on domestic financial institutions which do not apply to foreign banks would put the domestic financial institutions at a competitive disadvantage in international markets. This is one reason why international co-operation on the capital adequacy of banks (the Basle agreement) is an important step towards better regulation of financial markets.

Direct controls as a technique of monetary control

Another way of controlling the growth of the money supply is to impose direct controls on bank lending. Direct controls may be either quantitative or qualitative.

(a) **Quantitative controls** might be imposed on either bank lending (assets), for example a 'lending ceiling' limiting annual lending growth, or bank deposits (liabilities). The purpose of quantitative controls might be seen as a means of keeping bank lending in check without having to resort to higher interest rates.

(b) **Qualitative controls** might be used to alter the type of lending by banks. For example, the government (via the Bank) can ask the banks to limit their lending to the personal sector, and lend more to industry, or to lend less to a particular type of firm (such as, for example, property companies) and more to manufacturing businesses.

Quantitative controls

Controls might be temporary, in which case, in time, interest rates would still tend to rise if the money supply growth is to be kept under control. However, the advantage of a temporary scheme of direct quantitative controls is that it gives the authorities time to implement longer term policy. Quantitative controls are therefore a way of bridging the time-lag before these other policies take effect.

Quantitative controls might be more permanent. If they are, they will probably be unsuccessful because there will be financial institutions that manage to escape the control regulations, and so thrive at the expense of controlled institutions.

Direct controls on banks, for example, might succeed in reducing bank deposits but they will not succeed in controlling the level of demand and expenditure in the economy if lending is re-directed into other non-controlled financial instruments of non-controlled financial institutions. For example, large companies might use their own bank deposits to set up a scheme of lending themselves.

Direct controls are therefore rarely effective in dealing with the source rather than the symptom of the problem. Direct controls tend to divert financial flows into other, often less efficient, channels, rather than to stop the financial flows altogether, ie 'leakages' are inevitable.

Qualitative controls

Qualitative controls might be **mandatory** or they might be applied through **moral suasion**. Mandatory directives of a qualitative nature are unlikely in practice, because they are difficult to enforce without the co-operation of banks and other financial institutions. Moral suasion, on the other hand, might be used frequently. This is a process whereby the Central Bank appeals to the banks to do one or more things.

- To restrain lending
- To give priority to certain types of lending such as finance for exports or for investment
- Refuse other types of lending such as loans to private individuals

Moral suasion might therefore be a temporary form of control. As just one example, in 1989, the governor of the Bank of England 'advised' the banks to be wary of lending in such large amounts to property companies, thereby trying to influence banks' lending decisions without giving them directives or instructions.

Exchange rate control as an instrument of monetary policy

The exchange rate and changes in the exchange rate, have implications for the balance of payments, inflation and economic growth. The government might therefore seek to achieve a target exchange rate for its currency. More will be said about exchange rates later.

3.4 Supply side policy

The supply side approach

The Keynesian policy of demand management relies upon the proposition that the level of aggregate demand determines the level of national income and prices, since demand creates supply. The **supply side approach** advocated by monetarists, on the other hand, focuses policy upon the **conditions of aggregate supply**, taking the view that the availability, quality and cost of resources are the long-term determinants of national income and prices. Supply side economists argue that by putting resources to work, an economy will automatically generate the additional incomes necessary to purchase the higher outputs.

Definition

> **Supply side economics** is an approach to economic policymaking which advocates measures to improve the supply of goods and services (eg through deregulation) rather than measures to affect aggregate demand.

Supply side economics is characterised by the following propositions.

(a) The predominant long-term influences upon output, prices, and employment are the conditions of aggregate supply.

(b) Left to itself, the **free market** will automatically generate the highest level of national income and employment available to the economy.

(c) **Inflexibility in the labour market** through the existence of trade unions and other restrictive practices retain wages at uncompetitively high levels. This creates unemployment and restricts aggregate supply.

(d) The rates of **direct taxation** have a major influence upon aggregate supply through their effects upon the **incentive** to work.

(e) There is only a **limited role for government** in the economic system. Demand management can only influence output and employment 'artificially' in the short run, whilst in the long run creating inflation and hampering growth. Similarly state owned industries are likely to be uncompetitive and accordingly restrict aggregate supply.

Supply side economic policies

Supply side economists advise **against government intervention** in the economy at both the microeconomic and macroeconomic levels. **Microeconomic intervention** by government is disliked by supply side economists for a number of reasons.

(a) **Price regulation** distorts the signalling function essential for markets to reach optimal equilibrium.

(b) **Wage regulation** distorts the labour market's ability to ensure full employment.

(c) **Public ownership** blunts the incentive effects of the profit motive and leads to inefficiency.

(d) **Government grants and subsidies** encourage inefficient and 'lame duck' industries.

(e) **Public provision of services** may not encourage efficiency and can limit the discipline of consumer choice.

(f) **Employment legislation** such as employment protection limits market flexibility through discouraging recruitment and encouraging over-manning.

Macroeconomic intervention by government is regarded by supply side economists as harmful for several reasons.

(a) **Demand management** will be inflationary in the long run.

(b) High taxes will act as a **disincentive**.

(c) The possibility of **politically motivated policy changes** will create damaging uncertainty in the economy. This will discourage long-term investment.

Although most would accept the need for **expansion of the money stock** by government to accommodate increases in aggregate demand, some supply-siders have denied even this role to the government.

The main supply side policies are:

(a) **Reduction in government expenditure** and greater involvement of the private sector in the provision of services.

(b) **Reduction in taxes** in order to increase incentives.

(c) **Increasing flexibility** in the labour market by curbing the power of trade unions.

(d) **Increasing competition** through deregulation and privatisation of utilities.

(e) **Abolition of exchange controls** and allowing the free movement of capital.

Chapter roundup

- National income accounting is the system through which economic activity on a national scale is measured.
- There are three key measures of national economic output.
  - National income
  - Gross national product (GNP)
  - Gross domestic product (GDP)
- There is a circular flow of income in an economy, which means that expenditure, output and income will all have the same total value.
- There are withdrawals from the circular flow of income (savings, taxation, import expenditure) and injections into the circular flow (investment, government spending, export income).
- Our basic model of circular flow means that Output = Expenditure = Income. GDP can therefore be measured by focusing on output, income or expenditure.
- The Keynesian model provides a way of explaining how national income is determined, and how national income equilibrium is reached.
- Consumption expenditure depends on income. It might be possible for a government to take measures to boost aggregate demand in the economy, although some price inflation will probably result. When there is inflation in the economy, measures could be taken to suppress aggregate demand.

Chapter roundup (continued)

- Changes in national income begin with a small change in expenditure, leading to an even larger eventual change in national income, due to the multiplier effect.
- Aggregate supply determines the way aggregate demand influences inflation and unemployment.
- Equilibrium national income is determined using aggregate supply and aggregate demand analysis.
- High rates of inflation are harmful to an economy. Inflation redistributes income and wealth. Uncertainty about the value of money makes business planning more difficult. Constantly changing prices impose extra costs.
- Demand pull inflation arises from an excess of aggregate demand over the productive capacity of the economy.
- Cost push inflation arises from increases in the costs of production.
- There appears to be a connection between the rate of inflation and unemployment. The Phillips curve has been used to show that when there is zero inflation, there will be some unemployment.
- Macroeconomic policy objectives relate to economic growth, inflation, unemployment and the balance of payments.
- Fiscal policy provides a method of managing aggregate demand in the economy.
- Direct taxes have the quality of being progressive or proportional. Income tax is usually progressive, with high rates of tax charged on higher bands of taxable income. Indirect taxes can be regressive, when the taxes are placed on essential commodities or commodities consumed by poorer people in greater quantities.
- A government must decide how it intends to raise tax revenues, from direct or indirect taxes, and in what proportions tax revenues will be raised from each source.
- If the government kept its own spending at the same level, but reduced levels of taxation, it would also stimulate demand in the economy because firms and households would have more of their own money after tax for consumption or saving/investing.
- Monetary theory deals with the way changes in monetary variables affect the aggregate demand in the economy and its ultimate impact on prices and output. There are three theories of how the changes in the money supply are transmitted to the real economy: the quantity theory, the Keynesian theory, and the monetarist theory.
- Monetary policy uses money supply, interest rates or credit controls to influence aggregate demand.
- Supply side policies provide a method of managing aggregate supply in the economy.

Quick quiz

1 Which of the following are withdrawals from the circular flow of income?

A Exports
B Savings
C Investment
D Government spending

2 Define the income approach to measuring income.

3 What is the gross domestic product?

4 For an equilibrium national income level to be reached, withdrawals from and injections into the circular flow of income must be equal. Why are they not always in balance?

5 What are the marginal propensity to consume and the marginal propensity to save?

6 How might a government try to influence the volume of investment by firms?

7 Injections into the economy are:

A Consumption and Investment
B Investment and Government Expenditure
C Investment, Government Expenditure and Export Demand
D Consumption, Investment, Government Expenditure and Export Demand

8 What is the difference between fiscal policy and monetary policy?

9 Distinguish between direct taxation and indirect taxation.

10 What are the two main types of inflation?

Answers to quick quiz

1 B only. The rest are injections into the circular flow of income.

2 National income is the aggregate of individuals income from employment and self-employment, the profits of entities and rent on property.

3 The total value of income/production within the UK without any deduction for capital consumption or depreciation.

4 The withdrawals and injections are not made by the same people.

5 When a household receives an increase in income, some will be spent and some will be saved. The proportion which is spent is the marginal propensity to consume, while the proportion which is saved is the marginal propensity to save.

6 Lower interest rates, investment grants and tax incentives may encourage investment. Governments can also stimulate demand by tax cuts or lower interest rates and improve business confidence by business friendly and growth enhancing policies like deregulation and controlling inflation. Policies to encourage technological development may also lead to increased investment.

7 C

8 A government's fiscal policy is concerned with taxation, borrowing and spending; and their effects upon the economy. Monetary policy is concerned with money, the money supply, interest rates, inflation and the exchange rate.

9 Direct taxes are levied on income while indirect taxes are levied on expenditure. Indirect taxes are regressive. Direct taxes can be progressive.

10 Demand pull and Cost push

Answers to activities

1 Capital – Interest
Enterprise – Profit
Land – Rent
Labour – Wages

2 D A rise in indirect taxes

3 Firms buy goods and services which become costs of the goods or services that they produce and sell themselves.

If we included expenditure by firms, we would be double-counting the value of the wealth created by the suppliers of raw materials and components and the providers of services to other firms.

4 (a) MPs' salaries are *not* transfer payments. MPs are like any other employees – they just happen to be employed by the Government.

(b) This falls within the category of social security payments, which are transfer payments.

5 The amount that people save will depend on:

(a) How much income they are getting, and how much of this they want to spend on consumption

(b) How much income they want to save for precautionary reasons, for the future

(c) Interest rates. If the interest rate goes up we would expect people to consume less of their income, and to be willing to save and invest more.

6 The pairings are (a) C, (b) B and (c) A.

7 Demand for the product must presumably be inelastic, at least in the opinion of the producer. Otherwise he would fear to pass on the tax burden by increasing his prices as this would lead to a fall in demand.

8 According to the quantity theory, $V = \frac{PT}{M}$. This is described by B, which is therefore the correct answer.

Answer A implies that $V = \frac{M}{P}$, and answer C implies that $V = \frac{PT}{P}$, both of which are incorrect.

Chapter 8 :
INTERNATIONAL TRADE

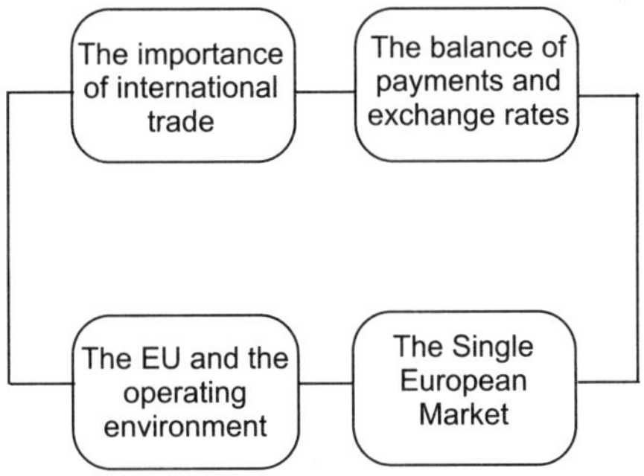

Introduction

This chapter begins with an introduction to the international economic environment. We focus first on foreign trade and see how countries can mutually benefit from trade based on differences in their comparative or opportunity costs of producing goods and services. We then look at the balance of payments and exchange rates and examine the UK's trade with the EU and other countries.

Raising finance to fund growth can be a critical issue and rapid growth, which is over-reliant on loan capital, can prove very risky. The merits of organic growth and growth by acquisition are discussed in this chapter.

The second part of the chapter concentrates on the EU and the UK's membership and the economies of Europe.

Your objectives

In this chapter you will learn about:

(a) The importance of international trade
(b) Trading blocs throughout the world
(c) The Balance of Payments and the Exchange Rate
(d) The UK membership of the EU
(e) The importance of the EU in world trade
(f) How the single market works for business

1 THE IMPORTANCE OF INTERNATIONAL TRADE

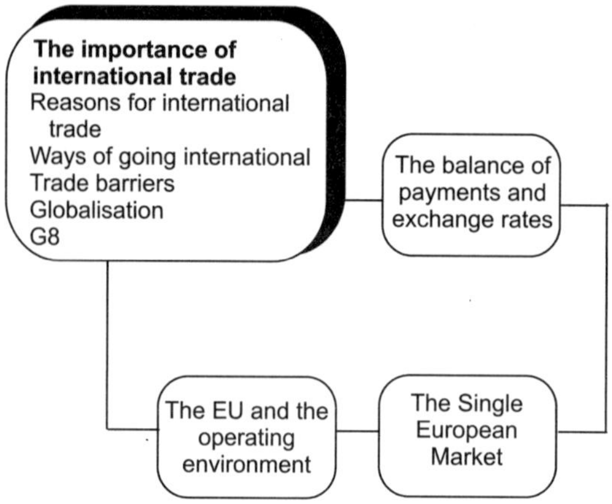

1.1 Reasons for international trade

International trade is the exchange of goods and services between countries. An **import** is the UK purchase of a good or service made overseas. An **export** is the sale of a UK-made good or service overseas.

Without international trade we would all be much poorer. There would be some items like tea, coffee, cotton clothes, avocados, foreign holidays and uranium that we would have to do without. There would be other items like spacecraft and wine that we could produce but very inefficiently.

The reasons for international trade are really only an extension of the reason for trade within a nation. Rather than people trying to be self-sufficient and do everything themselves, it makes sense to specialise.

For an individual company, exporting to overseas markets can be attractive for a number of reasons.

(a) Overseas markets represent new market segments.

(b) Saturation of its domestic market can force an organisation to seek overseas markets.

(c) As part of its portfolio management, an organisation may wish to reduce its dependence upon one geographical market.

(d) The nature of a firm's product may require an organisation to become active in an overseas market.

(e) Commercial buyers of products operating in a number of overseas countries may require their suppliers to be able to cater for their needs across national boundaries.

(f) Some goods and services are highly specialised and the domestic market is too small to allow economies of scale to be exploited.

(g) Economies of scale also result from extending the use of brands in overseas markets.

From the perspective of national economies, a number of reasons can be identified for the increasing importance of international trade:

(a) Goods and services are traded to exploit the concept of comparative cost advantage.

(b) The removal of many restrictions on international trade.

(c) Increasing household disposable incomes results in greater consumption of many categories of luxuries, such as overseas travel, which can only be provided by overseas suppliers.

(d) Cultural convergence that has resulted from improved communications.

The benefits of international trade are often quite clear. When a country, perhaps because of its climate, is unable to produce certain goods at home (or can do so only at a very high cost) it will have to import them from abroad and offer other goods which it produces cheaply in exchange. Britain, for instance, could produce bananas and pineapples, but only at a prohibitively high opportunity cost by growing them in hot houses. Similarly, countries like Japan with little or no natural endowment of resources such as oil, coal and other mineral deposits must buy their requirements from overseas. Nevertheless, the basis for trade is less obvious when, say, the USA, which can produce most goods more efficiently than the rest of the world, imports vast amounts of goods like cars, cameras, TVs and other electronic products from countries such as Japan, Taiwan and South Korea.

Definitions

Absolute advantage – a country has an absolute advantage in the production of a good if it can produce more of the good with a fixed amount of resources than can any other country (ie when the country uses fewer resources to produce a product than the other country).

Comparative advantage is the advantage in the production of a product enjoyed by one country over another when that product can be produced at a lower opportunity cost.

The **opportunity cost** of a product is the alternative products that must be sacrificed to facilitate its production.

The theory of comparative cost advantage states that the world economy will benefit if all countries:

(a) Concentrate on producing what they are good at and export the surplus

(b) Import from other countries those goods that other countries are better able to produce than themselves.

This may best be explained and illustrated with a simple numerical example. This example assumes for simplicity only two nations, each of which can only produce two goods, no transportation costs and no economies/diseconomies of scale. Each nation has the same endowment of resources but their aptitude in producing the two goods (which we will call cars and wheat) differs. If at present, each applies half of its resources to each good, let us suppose that the following pattern of production results.

	Cars Number	*Wheat* Units
Nation A	100	50
Nation B	20	80
Total	120	130

If we examine the relative or comparative cost of each good in each nation we find in:

A each car produced involves an opportunity cost of ½ a unit of wheat; each unit of wheat involves foregoing 2 cars

B each car involves foregoing 4 units of wheat; each unit of wheat involves foregoing ¼ of a car

Clearly, the opportunity cost of car manufacture is least in Nation A, while Nation B enjoys a comparative advantage in wheat growing. If we now persuade the governments of each nation to switch their production capacity to specialising in the good where their advantage is greatest (and remembering the assumption of no scale economies) we find:

	Cars Number	*Wheat* Units
Nation A	200	0
Nation B	0	160
Total	200	160

Clearly, total world production has increased by 80 cars and 30 units of wheat, and trade is possible within the exchange limits of 1 car for 4 units of wheat (B's opportunity cost) and one unit of wheat for 2 cars (A's opportunity cost). For example, B could offer 60 units of surplus wheat for 20 cars (an exchange rate of 3:1) and still be better off by 20 units of wheat, while A would then have 180 cars and 60 units of wheat, resulting in both nations being better off than without specialisation. However, transport costs in practice will eat into these gains, while diminishing returns may prevent the production gains from being so significant.

This neat theorem may also apply (with modification) even where one nation is more efficient in producing all goods. If the production arrangement prior to specialisation is:

	Cars Number	*Wheat* Units
Nation A	100 (200)	50 (0)
Nation B	20 (0)	40 (80)
Total	120 (200)	90 (80)

specialisation will result in A producing 200 cars as before and B producing 80 units of wheat so that while the output of cars has risen by 80 the joint output of wheat has fallen by 10 units. If we have further information about how the two nations value these goods, eg, if we know that they attach a greater value to 80 more cars than to 10 more units of wheat, then this reallocation of resources and output may be deemed acceptable. However, if our aim is to increase the output of some goods without reducing any others, then a more limited specialisation may generate the desired effect.

Overall, we may state that any rearrangement of the pattern of world production that increases the output of all goods or of one good with other outputs unchanged must have a beneficial impact on total welfare.

Activity 1 **(5 minutes)**

Suppose Germany can produce one ton of sausage with 100 units of resources and a case of wine with 50 units of resources, while France can produce one ton of sausage with 600 units of resources and a case of wine with 100 units of resources.

Which of the following statements describes the comparative advantage of France or Germany?

A France has a comparative advantage in exporting wine
B France has a comparative advantage in exporting sausage
C Germany has a comparative advantage in exporting wine
D None of the above

1.2 Ways of going international

A new foreign market represents both a potential opportunity and a risk to an organisation. A company's market entry strategy should aim to balance these two elements.

An assessment of risk is required in deciding whether an organisation should enter a foreign market on its own or in association with another organisation. The former maximises the strategic and operational control that the organisation has over its overseas operations, but it exposes it to the greatest risk where the overseas market is relatively poorly understood.

There are a number of entry strategies that a firm can adopt in order to develop international markets and these are described below.

(a) **Exporting** – it is often possible for a company to gain a feel for a foreign market by exporting to it from its home base. Exporting is likely to be the less satisfactory option for manufacturers who produce high-volume, low-value products for which transport costs could put them at a competitive disadvantage in overseas markets.

Negotiations for the sale of goods can be conducted through local agencies working on a commission basis or through local distributors who purchase the goods from the exporter and then sell them on to the local users. In both cases some degree of exclusivity is normally given in exchange for the local organisations agreeing to certain conditions such as not representing competitors, carrying out a certain amount of local marketing or undertaking the local servicing of products. Alternatively the company may set up a local sales office or form a foreign sales subsidiary to sell, or sell and service, its goods.

(b) **Global e-commerce** – the development of the Internet has offered new opportunities for organisations to enter foreign markets. The service sector has been at the leading edge of developments in electronic commerce, helped by the absence of a tangible content that must be physically delivered.

(c) **Licensing/franchising** – rather than setting up its own operations in an overseas market, a company can license a local company to manufacture and sell a product in the local market. The resources provided include technical know-how, managerial skills and/or patent and trade mark rights and in exchange the licensor receives from the licensee a percentage of the licensed goods sold and/or a lump sum down payment.

A particularly contained form of licensing is **franchising** where the franchiser provides foreign franchisees with a complete package of materials and services, including equipment, products, product ingredients, trademark and trade name rights, managerial advice and a standardised operating system.

Fast food chains such as Kentucky Fried Chicken and McDonald's are good examples of franchising operations. As with licensing, the franchising route offers easy access to international markets.

(e) **Management contracting** – rather than setting up its own operations overseas, a company with a proven track record in a product area may pursue the option of running other companies' businesses for them.

(f) **Overseas production** – which can be achieved by **direct investment** in manufacturing facilities in a foreign country, either totally or partially through a **joint venture** when two or more firms come together to operate in a way that is of value to all concerned. Strategic alliances are agreements between two or more organisations where each partner seeks to add to its competencies by combining its resources with those of a partner. Such activities are becoming more attractive as the rate of environmental change accelerates. Alternatively, the company may set up an overseas **manufacturing subsidiary,** which may be wholly owned or may have some form of local equity participation. In some countries local participation is mandatory – Zambia insists that its state holding companies own at least 51% of any foreign company's subsidiaries.

Direct investment in a foreign subsidiary gives an organisation maximum control over its foreign operations, but can expose it to a high level of risk on account of the poor understanding that it may have of the overseas market. Companies can either set up the overseas subsidiary from scratch or merge with or acquire an existing operation. **Greenfield** development ie, setting up from scratch, is often employed by companies handling products which are highly technical in design or method of manufacture as well as by those desiring direct involvement in the development of new markets and wishing to dispense with intermediate agents. It is also the only method available when breaking into new ground or when there are no suitable companies willing to be acquired or involved in other ways.

Although the final cost may be greater its spread over time is more favourable and realistic. Moreover, it minimises disruption and avoids the behavioural problems associated with acquisitions and mergers.

(g) **Acquisitions and mergers** are preferred to 'Greenfield development' when:

(i) Time is of the essence

(ii) The cost of upgrading internal competencies is greater than acquisition costs

(iii) There is no knowledge/resources on which internal development could be based

(iv) An additional firm operating in the market may create a situation of over supply

Problems associated with acquisitions and mergers involve finding the right firm which is agreeable to a deal, negotiating a fair price and integrating activities in the post acquisition phase.

Having analysed an overseas market and decided to enter it, an organisation must make decisions that will allow it to successfully enter and develop that market. Decisions focus on the extent to which the organisation should adapt its products to the needs of the local market, as opposed to the development of a uniform product that is globally applicable in all of its markets.

Sometimes, products can be exported to a foreign market with little need for adaptation to local needs. Improved communications and greater opportunities for travel have helped create much more uniform worldwide demand for products.

A promotional programme that has worked at home may fail miserably in a foreign market. Usually, this is a result of the target country's differing cultural values, although legislation can additionally call for a reformulation of promotion.

There is usually no reason to assume that the pricing policies adopted in the domestic market will prove to be equally effective in an overseas market. Furthermore, it may be of no great importance to customers that comparability between different markets is maintained.

It is also crucial to consider more operational issues of how a company is going to get its products through to the final consumer.

(a) Consumers' attitudes towards intermediaries may differ significantly in overseas markets.

(b) Differences in the social, economic and technological environments of a market can be manifested in the existence of different patterns of intermediaries.

(c) What is a legal method of distributing goods and services in the domestic market may be against the law of an overseas country.

Adaptation to local regulations governing employment is particularly important for labour intensive service industries.

For relatively straightforward goods and services, a large proportion of staff would be recruited locally, leaving just senior management posts filled by expatriates.

Activity 2 **(10 minutes)**

A large UK manufacturer of confectionery wishes to expand into European markets. However, the UK style of chocolate is not widely appreciated in Europe. What mode of entry would you suggest for the manufacturer?

1.3 Trade barriers

Unfortunately, the principles of comparative cost advantage may sound fine in theory, but it can be difficult to achieve the benefits in practice. In reality, the global ideals described above can become obscured by narrower national interests.

Despite a plethora of international agreements to facilitate trade between nations, minor, and sometimes major, trade disputes occur between nations.

Why do countries impose restrictions on trade? The answer is very simple; the primary reason is to protect domestic workers from competition from abroad. The basis for the decision is mainly political although there is some economic basis for protectionism.

Protection

Definition

> **Protection** is the practice of shielding a sector of the economy from foreign competition.

Protection of domestic industries against foreign competition is often explained by increasing imports displacing domestic production and creating structural unemployment in import-competing industries.

At times of recession and heavy general unemployment, governments may try to stimulate demand for domestic output by import controls to divert spending away from foreign output.

The case for protection

(a) Protection saves jobs.

(b) Some countries engage in unfair trade practices. Foreign firms may receive subsidies or other government benefits. They may be **dumping** (selling goods abroad at below cost price to capture a market).

(c) Cheap foreign labour makes competition unfair.

(d) Protection safeguards national security and strategic industries. To protect the manufacture of essential goods.

(e) Protection discourages dependency.

(f) Protection safeguards infant industries. If **sunrise firms** producing new-technology goods (eg computers) are to survive against established foreign producers then temporary tariffs or quotas may be needed.

(g) Reducing imports improves the balance of trade.

(h) Protection safeguards declining industries from creating further structural unemployment.

Disadvantages of protectionism

(a) Prevents countries enjoying the full benefits of international specialisation and trade.

(b) Invites retaliation from foreign governments.

(c) Protects inefficient home industries from foreign competition. Consumers pay more for inferior produce.

Protection methods

Protection methods include tariffs, quotas, exchange controls, export subsidies and administrative practices that discriminate against imports through customs delays or setting specifications met by domestic, but not foreign, producers.

Tariffs (import duties) are surcharges on the price of imports. The effect of the tariff is to:

(a) Raise the price of the import
(b) Reduce the demand for imports
(c) Encourage demand for home-produced substitutes
(d) Raise revenue for the government

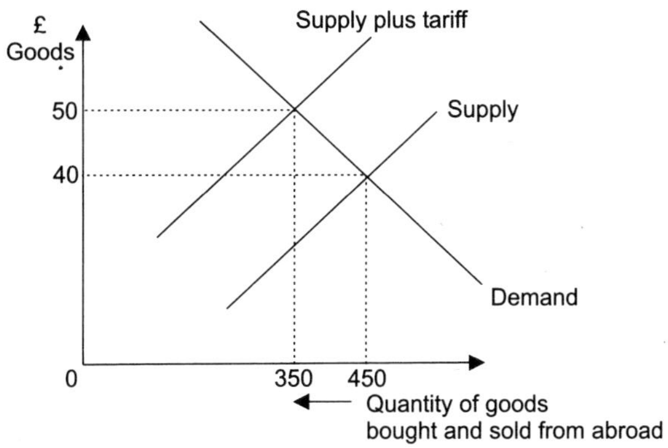

Figure 8.1: Impact of a tariff

Quotas restrict the actual quantity of an import allowed into a country. Note that a quota:

(a) Raises the price of imports
(b) Reduces the volume of imports
(c) Encourages demand for domestically made substitutes

Exchange controls (currency restrictions) prevent domestic residents from acquiring sufficient foreign currency to pay for imports.

Export subsidies are government payments made to domestic firms to encourage exports. Closely related to subsidies is dumping. A firm or industry sells products on the world market at prices below the cost of production.

Activity 3 **(20 minutes)**

In the USA the steel industry was complaining that foreign steel producers were 'dumping' cheap steel onto the US market rendering US steel producers uncompetitive. President George W. Bush took the decision to impose a tariff on steel imports into the US amounting to 30%; his decision pleased the steel producers but angered the steel users, who therefore faced a choice; continue buying from foreign suppliers and pay a higher price or buy from the US producers. On the face of it the second option looked to be the best but US steel producers took advantage of the protection they had been afforded to raise their prices.

(a) How do you think the steel users reacted to this?
(b) Explain how the tariff works

International agreements

There have been many attempts to develop international agreements for the free movement of trade. At their simplest, international trade agreements comprise bilateral agreements between two countries to open up trade between the two.

The **Organisation for Economic Co-operation and Development (OECD)** works by trying to co-ordinate the economic policies of members, to co-ordinate programmes of economic aid and by providing specialised services, especially information.

The World Bank acts as an adviser to governments in the provision of international finance.

The **International Monetary Fund (IMF)** is essentially a world forum for international negotiations on governments' fiscal policies. Established in 1944 at Bretton Woods, the main aim of the IMF is to stabilise exchange rates and to lend money to countries needing foreign currency. Over 140 member countries pay a sum of their own currency into a pool. The amount paid in depends on the size of their economy. Each country can then borrow foreign currency from the pool according to their contribution to settle temporary balance-of-payments problems. Countries can draw up to 25 per cent of their quota before the IMF begins to set conditions on the loan. In 1967 the IMF created a new international currency called **special drawing rights** (SDRs) that governments use to settle debts with other countries.

The World Trade Organisation (WTO) was set up in 1995 and succeeded the General Agreement on Tariffs and Trade (GATT). The aim of the WTO is to help trade flow smoothly, freely, fairly and predictably. It:

(a) Administrates trade agreements
(b) Acts as a forum for trade negotiations
(c) Settles trade disputes
(d) Reviews national trade policies
(e) Assists developing countries in trade policy issues

It has proceeded to reduce tariffs and quotas through several negotiating 'rounds' and has also tried to redress the distortion to world trade and the unfair competitive advantage given to subsidised exporters of agricultural products.

A wide range of other agreements and institutions affect international trading companies. An example in this category is the agreement to set up a European Bank for Reconstruction and Development. On a regional scale groups of countries or trade blocs have also been trying to lower trade barriers between them and stimulate regional trade.

The world's two most powerful economies, the United States, and the European Union, have each wanted to forge links to neighbouring countries and deny access to rivals. Other major trading countries, like the fast growing exporters on the Pacific Rim and the big agricultural exporting nations, have also sought to create looser trade groupings to foster their interests.

The formation of free trade zones and trade blocs is one of the major issues facing the world trading system – whether it will lead to increased protectionism, or whether the trade blocs will promote trade liberalisation. There are a number of types of trade blocs.

(a) **Free Trade Areas**. Sovereign countries belonging to the free trade area trade freely amongst them but have individual trade barriers with countries outside the free trade area. All members have most favoured nation status, which means that they are all treated equally. Examples include North American Free Trade Area (NAFTA) between the USA, Canada and Mexico; Asia Pacific Economic Cooperation (APEC) and the Common Market for Eastern and Southern Africa (COMESA)

(b) **Customs Unions**. The countries are no longer fully sovereign over trade policy. There will be some degree of unification of custom or trade policies. They will have a common external tariff (CET), which is applied to all countries outside the customs union. The countries will be represented at trade negotiations with organisations such as the World Trade Organisation by supra-national organisations eg the European Union.

(c) **Common Market**. This trading bloc is a customs union, which has in addition the free movement of factors of production such as labour and capital between the member countries without restriction. Mercosur is an example of a common market comprising of a number of South American nations.

(d) **Economic Union**. This is a common market where the level of integration is more developed. The member states may adopt common economic policies eg the Common Agricultural Policy (CAP) of the European Union. They may have a fixed exchange rate regime such as the ERM of the EMU. Indeed, they may have integrated further and have a single common currency. This will involve common monetary policy. The ultimate act of integration is likely to be some form of political integration where the national sovereignty is replaced by some form of over-arching political authority.

The **European Union (EU)** is an economic and political union of 27 member states. Committed to regional integration, the EU was established by the Treaty of Maastricht in 1993 upon the foundations of the European Communities. With over 500 million citizens, the EU combined generated an estimated 21% (US$14.8 trillion) of the gross world product in 2009.

The EU has developed a single market through a standardised system of laws which apply in all member states, and ensures the free movement of people, goods, services, and capital. It maintains common policies on trade, agriculture, fisheries and regional development. Sixteen member states have adopted a common currency, the euro, constituting the Eurozone.

The United States has linked with Canada and Mexico to form a free trade zone, the **North American Free Trade Agreement (NAFTA)**. Many observers consider NAFTA to be the same sort of economic and political union as the European Union (EU). The EU, like NAFTA, is an economic union that fosters greater trade and cooperation between a large handful of the countries of Europe. EU members, however, have a common currency, while NAFTA members do not. Also, the EU has a political element and its own government, neither of which NAFTA has.

The **Cairns group** of agricultural exporting nations was formed in 1986 to lobby at the last round of world trade talks in order to free up trade in agricultural products. It is named after the town in Australia where the first meeting took place. Highly efficient agricultural producers, including those in both developed and developing countries, want to ensure that their products are not excluded from markets in Europe and Asia. The Cairns Group is composed of Argentina, Australia, Bolivia, Brazil, Canada, Chile, Colombia, Costa Rica, Guatemala, Indonesia, Malaysia, New Zealand, Pakistan, Paraguay, Peru, the Philippines, South Africa, Thailand, and Uruguay.

The **Asia-Pacific Economic Cooperation forum** is a loose grouping of the countries bordering the Pacific Ocean who have pledged to facilitate free trade. Its 21 members range from China and Russia to the United States, Japan and Australia, and account for 45% of world trade. Progress on free trade initiatives was seriously dented by the Asian crisis, which hurt the economies of the fast-growing newly industrialised countries like South Korea and Indonesia.

The **European Economic Area (EEA)** was created by the signing of a treaty in Oporto in May 1992. It allows Iceland, Liechtenstein and Norway to participate in the EU's single market without a conventional EU membership. In exchange, they are obliged to adopt all EU legislation related to the single market, except those pieces of legislation that relate to agriculture and fisheries.

The purpose of the treaty is to allow the free movement of goods, persons, services and capital throughout the EEA. If a country wishes to join the EU, it must first become a member of the EEA. Areas of EU policy that lie outside of the EEA are relations with other countries (trading and development), fiscal policy, economic and monetary union (EMU) and the common agricultural policy (CAP).

1.4 Globalisation

Globalisation may be defined as the interdependence of different national economies. It reflects the tendency of markets to become global rather than national and for it to be difficult to view any national economy as a stand-alone entity.

Factors driving globalisation

- Improved communications, for example the speed of access to the internet
- Reduction of transport costs
- Political realignments, for example the collapse of the soviet block
- Growth of global industries and institutions
- Break down of some trade barriers by free trade organisations and treaties

Global institutions

A number of Institutions are central to the process of globalisation including the World Bank (WB), International Monetary Fund (IMF) and the European Central Bank. WB and IMF were both established after the Second World War and are based in Washington DC. WB has developed from its original function to provide finance and other aid in the form of commercial loans to developing countries to become much more involved in controlling the economic policy of those countries. Similarly the IMF has moved from a concern with supervision of the fixed rate exchange rate regime established after the war to becoming much more involved in the economic policy decisions of a number of countries with regard to government budgets, monetary policy, overall borrowing and trade. The IMF acts as a central bank to individual countries when in need of emergency funding to avoid a collapse of their currency and to ensure the smooth running of international trade. Recent examples where the IMF has provided emergency loans to countries in difficulties include Russia, Argentina and Turkey.

Impacts of globalisation

Globalisation used to be the unquestioned model for economic growth and stability but there are now many critics of the phenomena.

For globalisation

(a) Emergence of new growth markets, for example in the less developed countries

(b) Enhanced competitiveness as more producers and customers make up the global marketplace

(c) Growth of previously poor economies, such as China

(d) Cross-national business alliance and mergers

(e) International support for poorer nations and assistance provided in development of their economies

(f) World economic equalisation

Criticisms of globalisation

(a) The main institutions of globalisation follow the collective will of the G8 countries and are more concerned therefore in aiding the economic wealth of these countries. The G8 is examined in the next section.

(b) IMF, WB and ECB along with powerful multinational organisations dictate economic policy in countries but do not include real representation of these countries within their organisations. This lack of accountability has been called 'global governance without global government' (Joseph Stiglitz, *Globalisation and its Discontents*)

(c) World poverty is still an issue and many fear that the policies adopted by WB, IMF and others, for example in restricting subsidy in Africa and opening up their markets for Western imports that are produced under subsidy, actually makes some nations poorer.

(d) There is no enduring political and economic stability in the world and the collapse of one part of the economy, for example in South America, could have disastrous knock on effects for the rest of the world.

(e) Not all countries are included in global activity Instead there is an increasing tendency for groups of counties, usually located in the same region to become involved in each others economies, for example the countries in the Eurozone.

1.5 The Group of Eight (G8)

G8, or the Group of Eight, is an informal body whose members meet annually to tackle global challenges through discussion and action. The G8 comprises eight of the world's leading nations (France, Germany, Italy, Japan, UK, US, Canada and Russia).

The leaders of these countries meet face-to-face at an annual summit. The G8's roots lie in the oil crisis and global economic recession of the early 1970s. Though G8 was set up as a forum for economic and trade matters, political issues often creep onto the agenda.

G8 members can agree on policies and can set objectives, but compliance with these is voluntary. The G8 has clout in other world bodies because of the economic and political muscle of its members.

Critics of the G8 have accused the body of representing the interests of an elite group of industrialised nations, to the detriment of the needs of the wider world. Important countries with fast-growing economies and large populations (eg China and India) are not represented. There are no African or Latin American members.

The G8's positive stance on globalisation has provoked a vigorous response from opponents, and riots have sometimes overshadowed summit agendas, for example in Toronto, Canada in June 2010.

2 THE BALANCE OF PAYMENTS AND EXCHANGE RATES

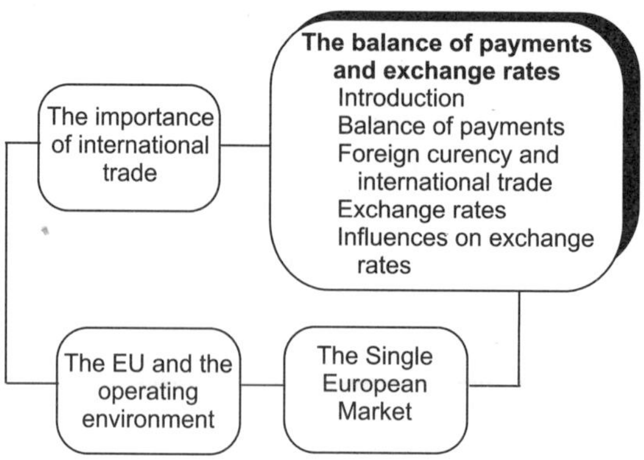

2.1 Introduction

We have so far ignored the fact that foreign trade, like domestic trade, is carried out through the intermediary of money. Unfortunately, money denominated in the currency of one country cannot normally be used directly to settle the debts in another country. If I want to buy goods in India I have to exchange my pounds for rupees. International trade means buying and selling foreign currency against the domestic currency and gives rise to international payments problems not encountered in domestic economies. In the long run, if a country wants to import goods or services or wants to invest overseas it must receive enough foreign exchange from exports or from inflows of investment to cover its payments abroad. In the short run it may have reserves of foreign exchange or it may borrow to finance its payments deficit – an excess of payments over receipts. But when the reserve and credit facilities run out the country must take steps to remove the deficit.

2.2 The balance of payments

The **balance of payments accounts** consist of a current account with visibles and invisibles sections and transactions in capital (external assets and liabilities including official financing). The sum of the balances on these accounts must be zero, although in practice there is a balancing figure for measurement errors.

The nature of the balance of payments

Under the current method of presentation of the UK balance of payments statistics, **current account** transactions are sub-divided into four parts.

- Trade in goods
- Trade in services
- Income
- Transfers

Before 1996, the term **visibles** was used in official statistics for trade in goods and the term **invisibles** was used for the rest. These terms have now been dropped in order to give more emphasis to the balances for trade in goods and services, although you may still find them mentioned.

Income is divided into two parts.

- Income from employment of UK residents by overseas firms
- Income from capital investment overseas

Transfers are also divided into two parts:

- Public sector payments to and receipts from overseas bodies such as the EU. Typically these are interest payments

- Non-government sector payments to and receipts from bodies such as the EU

The **capital account** balance is made up of public sector flows of **capital** into and out of the country, such as government loans to other countries.

The balance on the **financial account** is made up of flows of capital to and from the non-government sector, such as direct investment in overseas facilities; portfolio investment (in shares, bonds and so on); and speculative flows of currency. Movements on government foreign currency reserves are also included under this heading.

Net errors and omissions

A balancing item appears in the balance of payments accounts because of errors and omissions in collecting statistics for the accounts (for example, sampling errors for items such as foreign investment and tourist expenditure and omissions from the data gathered about exports or imports).

The sum of the balance of payments accounts must always be zero (ignoring statistical errors in collecting the figures). This is for the same reason that a balance sheet must always balance: for every debit there must be a credit.

The UK balance of payments accounts

A UK balance of payment account at a particular point in time is summarised below.

UK balance of payments accounts

	£bn
Current account	
Trade in goods	(26,767)
Trade in services	11,538
Income	8,332
Transfers	(4,084)
Current balance	(10,981)
Capital account	776
Financial account	5,853
Net errors and omissions	4,352
	0

Given that the balance of payments in principle sums to zero, you may wonder what is meant by a surplus or deficit on the balance of payments. When journalists or economists speak of the balance of payments they are usually referring to the deficit or surplus on the **current account**, or possibly to the surplus or deficit on trade in goods only (this is also known as the **balance of trade**).

2.3 Foreign currency and international trade

With international trade, there is often a need for foreign currency for at least one of the parties to the transaction.

(a) If a UK exporter sells goods to a US buyer, and charges the buyer £20,000, the US buyer must somehow obtain the sterling in order to pay the UK supplier. The US buyer will do this by using some of his US dollars to buy the £20,000 sterling, probably from a bank in the USA.

(b) If a UK importer buys goods from Germany, he might be invoiced in euros, say €100,000. He must obtain this foreign currency to pay his debt, and he will do so by purchasing the euros from a UK bank in exchange for sterling.

(c) If a UK investor wishes to invest in US capital bonds, he would have to pay for them in US dollars, and so he would have to sell sterling to obtain the dollars.

Thus **capital outflows**, such as investing overseas, not just payments for imports, cause a demand to sell the domestic currency and buy foreign currencies. On the other hand, exports and capital inflows to a country cause a demand to buy the domestic currency in exchange for foreign currencies.

Exporters might want to sell foreign currency earnings to a bank in exchange for domestic currency, and importers may want to buy foreign currency from a bank in order to pay a foreign supplier.

Exchange rates and the UK balance of payments

As in any other market, the market for foreign exchange is a market in which buyers and suppliers come into contact, and 'prices' (exchange rates) are set by supply and demand. Exchange rates change continually. Significant movements in the exchange rate for a country's currency can have important implications for the country's balance of payments.

Equilibrium in the balance of payments

A balance of payments is in equilibrium if, over a period of years, the exchange rate remains stable and autonomous credits and debits are equal in value (the annual trade in goods and services is in overall balance). However, equilibrium will not exist if these things require the government to introduce measures which create unemployment or higher prices, sacrifice economic growth or impose trade barriers (eg import tariffs and import quotas).

Surplus or deficit in the current account

A surplus or deficit on the balance of payments usually means a **surplus or deficit on the current account.**

A problem arises for a country's balance of payments when the country has a deficit on current account year after year, although there can be problems too for a country which enjoys a continual current account **surplus.**

The problems of a **deficit** on the current account are probably the more obvious. When a country is continually in deficit, it is importing more goods and services that it is exporting. This leads to two possible consequences.

(a) It may borrow more and more from abroad, to build up external liabilities which match the deficit on current account, for example encouraging foreign investors to lend more by purchasing the government's gilt-edged securities.

(b) It may sell more and more of its assets. This has been happening recently in the USA, for example, where a large deficit on the US current account has resulted in large purchases of shares in US companies by foreign firms.

Even so, the demand to buy the country's currency in the foreign exchange markets will be weaker than the supply of the country's currency for sale. As a consequence, there will be pressure on the exchange rate to depreciate in value.

If a country has a **surplus** on current account year after year, it might invest the surplus abroad or add it to official reserves. The balance of payments position would be strong. There is the problem, however, that if one country which is a major trading nation (such as Japan) has a continuous surplus on its balance of payments current account, other countries must be in continual deficit. These other countries can run down their official reserves, perhaps to nothing, and borrow as much as they can to meet the payments overseas, but eventually, they will run out of money entirely and be unable even to pay their debts. Political pressure might therefore build up within the importing countries to impose tariffs or import quotas.

How can a government rectify a current account deficit?

The government of a country with a balance of payments deficit will usually be expected to take measures to reduce or eliminate the deficit. A deficit on current account may be rectified by one or more of the following measures.

(a) A depreciation of the currency (called **devaluation** when deliberately instigated by the government, for example by changing the value of the currency within a controlled exchange rate system).

(b) Direct measures to restrict imports, such as tariffs or import quotas or exchange control regulations.

(c) Domestic deflation to reduce aggregate demand in the domestic economy.

The first two are **expenditure switching** policies, which transfer resources and expenditure away from imports and towards domestic products while the last is an **expenditure reducing** policy.

2.4 Exchange rates

Definition

> An **exchange rate** is the ratio at which two currencies are traded. The price of one currency in terms of another.

For any pair of countries there is a range of exchange rates that can lead automatically to both countries realising the gains from specialisation and comparative advantage.

Exchange rates determine the terms of trade.

Currencies are just like any other commodity that is traded in a market. If the demand for a currency is great relative to its supply, then its 'price' (or exchange rate) will rise. The opposite will happen if there is excess supply of that currency.

For the UK, the dollar exchange rate means the number of dollars ($) one pound (£) can buy. The exchange rate is determined by the supply and demand for **sterling** (pounds).

Americans want to exchange dollars for pounds to buy British goods and services and/or lend or invest in the UK. Britons want to exchange pounds for dollars for the same reasons.

Changes in the supply of, or demand for, a currency can come about for a number of reasons.

(a) Changes in demand for a nation's currency can result from a significant change in exports from that country.

(b) An increase in imports by UK firms from Japan would have an opposite effect.

(c) Demand for foreign currencies can arise from transactions involving the purchase of assets overseas.

(d) Demand for a currency at any given time is influenced by individuals' confidence about future price levels for a currency.

Fluctuations in exchange rates can cause considerable uncertainty.

A fall in the value of sterling (**depreciation**) means one pound now buys fewer dollars. Sterling depreciates if Americans demand fewer pounds (shown in figure 10.2 below) or if UK citizens offer more pounds. UK exports become cheaper and UK imports become dearer. Hence, a sterling depreciation improves the balance of payments.

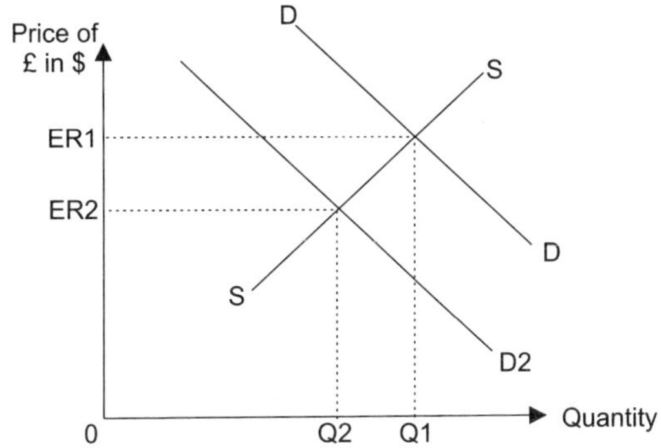

Figure 8.2: Effect on Sterling if Americans demand fewer pounds

A rise in the value of sterling (**appreciation**) means one pound now buys more dollars. UK exports become dearer and UK imports become cheaper. Hence a sterling appreciation worsens the balance of payments.

The launch of the Euro in 1999 as a common currency for EU member states overcomes problems of fluctuating exchange rates between traders in countries that have adopted the Euro.

Opinion has been divided about the effects of the Euro on UK business organisations. Advocates of the Euro point to the greatly reduced transaction costs involved in trading with other EU countries and the greatly reduced risk of adverse currency movements.

Activity 4 **(5 minutes)**

Suppose the exchange rate for yen in terms, of dollars, were to decrease, because Japanese investors no longer want to invest in American securities. This would:

A Make it harder for America to export
B Make it easier for America to import
C Make it easier for America to export
D Reduce the Japanese standard of living

Fixed exchange rates

An alternative to market-based fluctuating exchange rates is a fixed exchange rate system. Here, countries agree to maintain the value of each other's currency, or at least to keep fluctuations within a very narrow range. Where necessary, governments take action to maintain the agreed rates of exchange.

2.5 Influences on exchange rates

Factors influencing the exchange rate for a currency

In this section we cover the major factors that influence movements on the foreign exchange markets, other than government intervention.

(a) **Total income and expenditure** (demand) in the domestic economy determines the demand for goods. This includes imported goods and demand for goods produced in the country which would otherwise be exported if demand for them did not exist in the home markets.

(b) **Output capacity and the level of employment** in the domestic economy might influence the balance of payments, because if the domestic economy has full employment already, it will be unable to increase its volume of production for exports.

(c) The **growth in the money supply** influences interest rates and domestic inflation.

Inflation and the exchange rate

If the rate of inflation is higher in one country than in another country, the value of its currency will tend to weaken against the other country's currency.

Purchasing power parity theory

Purchasing power parity theory attempts to explain changes in the exchange rate exclusively by the rate of inflation in different countries. The theory predicts that the exchange value of a foreign currency depends on the relative purchasing power of each currency in its own country.

As a simple example, suppose that there is only one commodity, which costs £110 in the UK and €165 Euros in France. The purchasing power parity exchange rate would be £1

= €1.5. If, as a result of inflation, the cost of the commodity in the UK rises to £120, purchasing power parity theory would predict that the exchange rate would adjust to:

$$1.5 \times \frac{110}{120} \times £1 = €1.375$$

If the exchange rate remained at £1 = €1.5, it would be cheaper in the UK to import more of the commodity from France for £110 rather than to produce it in the UK, As a result, the UK would have a balance of trade deficit in that commodity. This would only be corrected by an **alteration in the exchange rate**, with the pound weakening against the euro.

Purchasing power parity theory states that an exchange rate varies according to relative price changes, so that:

$$\text{'Old' exchange rate} \times \frac{\text{Price level in country A}}{\text{Price level in country B}} = \text{'New' exchange rate}$$

Assessment formula

The theory is not usually adequate in explaining movements in exchange rates **in the short-term**, mainly because it ignores payments between countries (ie demand and supply transactions) and the influence of supply and demand for currency on exchange rates.

The relevant formula is:

$$\text{Future rate US\$/£} = \text{Spot US\$/£} \times \frac{1 + \text{US inflation rate}}{1 + \text{UK inflation rate}}$$

However you may have to use other currencies in it. Note that 'Future rate' here means the spot exchange rate at a future date. This formula does not relate the forward rate quoted now to the spot rate discussed below.

EXAMPLE: PURCHASING POWER PARITY THEORY

Suppose that inflation is running at 8% in the US and 4% in the UK. The exchange rate between the two countries is 1.7600 $/£. What is the predicted rate in one year's time, using purchasing power parity?

Solution

Using purchasing power parity, Future rate US$/£ = 1.7600 × (1 + 0.08)/(1 + 0.04) = 1.8277

Interest rates and the exchange rate

It would seem logical to assume that if one country raises its interest rates, it will become more profitable to invest in that country, and so an increase in investment from overseas will push up the **spot exchange rate** because of the extra demand for the currency from overseas investors.

This may be true in the short-term, but the market adjusts **forward rates** for this. If this were not so, then investors holding the currency with the lower interest rates would switch to the other currency for (say) three months, ensuring that they would not lose on returning to the original currency by fixing the exchange rate in advance at the forward rate. If enough investors acted in this way (known as **arbitrage**), forces of supply and demand would lead to a change in the forward rate to prevent such risk-free profit-making.

Interest rate parity

The **interest rate parity** condition relates the forward and spot rates for two currencies to the interest rates prevailing in those two countries: we introduced this idea at paragraph 1.4 of this chapter.

$$\text{Forward rate US\$/£} = \text{Spot US\$/£} \times \frac{1 + \text{nominal US interest rate}}{1 + \text{nominal UK interest rate}}$$

EXAMPLE: INTEREST RATE PARITY

The current exchange rate between the US and UK is $/£ 1.7500. The current central bank lending rates in both countries are 6% in the US, 5% in the UK. What is the one-year forward exchange rate?

Solution

Here use of the formula is straightforward, as we are given the US and UK figures.

Forward rate US$/£ = 1.7500 × (1 + 0.06)/(1 + 0.05) = 1.7667

The balance of payments and the exchange rate

If exchange rates respond to **demand and supply for current account items**, then the balance of payments on the current account of all countries would tend towards equilibrium. This is not so, and **in practice other factors influence exchange rates more strongly**.

Demand for currency to invest in overseas capital investments and supply of currency from firms disinvesting in an overseas currency have more influence on the exchange rate, in the short term at least, than the demand and supply of goods and services.

If a country has a **persistent deficit in its balance of payments current account**, international confidence in that country's currency will eventually be eroded. In the long term, its exchange rate will fall as capital inflows are no longer sufficient to counterbalance the country's trade deficit.

Speculation and exchange rate fluctuations

Speculators in foreign exchange are investors who **buy or sell assets in a foreign currency**, in the **expectation of a rise or fall in the exchange rate**, from which they seek to make a profit. Speculation could be destabilising if it creates such a high volume of demand to buy or sell a particular currency that the exchange rate fluctuates to levels where it is overvalued or undervalued in terms of what hard economic facts suggest it should be.

If a currency does become undervalued by heavy speculative selling, investors can make a further profit by purchasing it at the undervalued price and selling it later when its price rises.

Speculation, when it is destabilising, could **damage a country's economy** because the uncertainty about exchange rates disrupts trade in goods and services.

3 THE SINGLE EUROPEAN MARKET

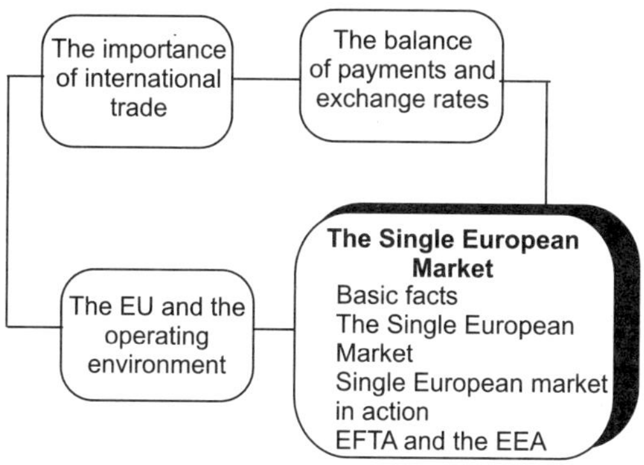

3.1 Basic facts

History

The idea of creating a single 'common market' goes back to the time when the European Economic Community (EEC) was set up in 1957. This is now referred to as the European Union. Before the EEC was set up, co-operation had commenced with the European Coal and Steel Community in 1955.

The original six member countries of the EEC (Belgium, France, Italy, Luxembourg, Netherlands and West Germany) had removed all restrictions on trade in coal, steel and iron ore between the six countries. The aim had been to gain economies of scale and allow more effective competition with the USA and other foreign producers.

The EEC extended this principle and aimed eventually to be a full common market with completely free trade between members in all products, and with completely free movement of labour, enterprise and capital. By uniting many of the countries of Western Europe, it was hoped too that the EEC could be an effective political and economic force in a world dominated by political giants such as the USA and the USSR, and by economic giants such as the USA (and later Japan)

All internal tariffs between the six members had been abolished and common external tariffs established by 1968. But this still only made the EEC a *customs union,* since a number of restrictions on internal trade remained (legal, administrative, fiscal, etc.). Nevertheless the aim was eventually to create a full common market.

In 1973 the UK, Denmark and Ireland joined; Greece joined in 1981, Spain and Portugal in 1986, and Sweden, Austria and Finland in 1995.

After successfully growing from six to fifteen members, the European Union has now undergone its biggest enlargement ever in terms of scope and diversity. Ten countries – Cyprus, the Czech Republic, Estonia, Hungary, Latvia, Lithuania, Malta, Poland, the Slovak Republic and Slovenia joined on 1 May 2004, (the 'accession countries'). Bulgaria and Romania joined in 2007, while Turkey is currently negotiating its membership.

In order to join the Union, they need to fulfill the economic and political conditions known as the 'Copenhagen criteria', according to which a prospective member must:

(a) Be a stable democracy, respecting human rights, the rule of law, and the protection of minorities

(b) Have a functioning market economy

(c) Adopt the common rules, standards and policies that make up the body of EU law.

The EU assists these countries in taking on EU laws, and provides a range of financial assistance to improve their infrastructure and economy.

European Council of Ministers

This consists of 25 foreign ministers, one from each country. It receives proposals from the Commission, and has the power to decide on all EU issues. Which ministers are represented on the Council depends on the purpose of the meeting. Thus finance ministers represent their country on economic issues, agricultural ministers on farm policy, etc.

The main source of power is still the member states (despite 'Brussels-bashing'), which participate in the Council of Ministers. However, government ministers can conveniently blame the EU when things go wrong

European Parliament

Constituencies in the member countries elect MEPs to serve in the European Parliament in Strasbourg. Its powers are rather limited in practice, but in theory both the Commission and the Council are answerable to it.

The European Court of Justice

This meets in Luxembourg and decides on areas of legal dispute arising from the Rome Treaty, whether between governments, institutions or individuals.

The European Commission

The European Commission is the executive of the EU. The main tasks of the Commission are to:

(a) Ensure that Community rules and the principles of the 'common market' are observed

(b) Make policy proposals to the Council of Ministers

(c) Enforce the implementation of legislation

(d) Administer Community expenditure

The European Commission has 27 members: one Commissioner appointed from each member state. The Commission's term of office is five years, like that of the European Parliament. What is more, the European Parliament is consulted before the member states appoint the President of the commission and the full Commission has to be approved by Parliament before being appointed by mutual agreement by the governments of the member states.

Article 17 of the Treaty on European Union identifies the Commission responsibilities: develop medium-term strategies; draft legislation and arbitrate in the legislative process; represent the EU in trade negotiations; make rules and regulations, for example in competition policy; draw up the budget of the European Union; and to scrutinize the implementation of the treaties and legislation.

3.2 The Single European Market

The EU consists of:

(a) The European Economic Community or EEC (the 'common' market or customs union)

(b) The European Coal and Steel Community (to control iron, steel and coal resources)

(c) The Atomic Energy Community or Euratom (to control the peaceful use of atomic energy)

In addition, there are two areas of intergovernmental cooperation in the fields of Common Foreign and Security Policy (CFSP) and Justice and Home Affairs (JHA).

The European Union has a common market, including a free trade area and a customs union.

(a) A **free trade** area exists when there is no restriction on the movement of goods and services between countries. Such freedom exists on trade within the EU, but there are restrictions on trade between the EU countries and other countries.

(b) The **customs union** of the EU:

  (i) Establishes a free trade area between member states

  (ii) Erects common external tariffs to charge on imports from non-member countries.

The EU thus promotes free trade among member states while acting as a protectionist bloc against the rest of the world.

FOR DISCUSSION

What does the internal market mean for the EU citizen? Prioritise the following according to your own values:

- Better value for money
- Greater choice of goods and services
- Improved job opportunities
- Trouble-free travel within the EU
- Unlimited cross-border shopping
- Right to work and live in another EU country

Import duties and levies in the EU

No customs duties are levied within the Union. All states levy VAT. All EU countries charge the same duty (which is a tax people have to pay to bring their goods into your country) on imports from elsewhere in the world. This has been very important in opening up national markets to firms in other EU countries. Governments in the past often protected their own industries by charging high duties, which had the effect of making, say, a foreign car too expensive to buy. Such protection led to customers paying higher prices than they needed to. Free competition is basic to good quality, wide variety of choice and value for money. When they face competition, firms have to make sure that they are efficient and are producing what customers want at a price they are prepared to pay.

This has been an issue for the car industry because differential pricing in member states has led to customers buying where it is cheapest and driving the car to their home state in order to save money.

FOR DISCUSSION

The single European market only benefits firms from the member states of the EU. Do you agree?

How the single market works for business

A **common market** encompasses the idea of a customs union but has a number of additional features. In addition to free trade among member countries there is also complete mobility of funds and labour. A British citizen has the freedom to work in any other country of the European Union, for example. A common market will also aim to achieve stronger links between member countries, for example by harmonising government economic policies and by establishing a closer political confederation.

The reduction of **frontier controls** on goods and people will affect businesses in a number of ways.

On goods:

(a) An end to customs documentation
(b) No need for traders to submit tax declarations

For people:

(a) Few limits on the amount of purchases that people can carry across borders, for private consumption.

(b) The Schengen agreement abolishes border controls between its member states.

(c) No passport checks on EU citizens travelling between member states.

(d) Co-operation between police and immigration authorities.

The internal market might have the following general effects.

(a) Firms learn to compete more effectively, and can benefit from economies of scale.

(b) Open trade policy makes EU firms match the world best.

(c) Stable exchange rates cement the internal market.

(d) Supporters hold that the Social Chapter, which enshrines basic workplace rights, will bring economic prosperity accompanied by better living and working conditions. Others consider it bad for business.

(e) Internal market rules embody a high level of environmental protection.

Elimination of trade restrictions covers the following areas.

(a) European regulations and standards mean that products approved in any one EU country can be freely marketed throughout the Union.

(b) There is a progressive opening up of government and other public body contracts to all EU contractors on an equal basis.

(c) There is more competition and efficiency in Europe-wide services in telecommunications and information technology by developing common standards for equipment.

(d) The road haulage market is being liberalised by eliminating bureaucratic 'red tape'. Shipping services between member countries are to be provided on equal terms. Competition on air routes should increase, resulting in lower fares.

(e) Banks and securities houses authorised in their home country should be free to provide banking and investment services anywhere in the EU. Insurers will have greater freedom to cover risks in other member countries. All restrictions on the movement of capital are being removed.

(f) Protection of ideas will become easier through harmonisation of national laws on patents, trade marks and copyright.

(g) Professional qualifications obtained in one country are generally acceptable in all other countries

Activity 5 **(15 minutes)**

Citizens of the European Union are entitled to work in any of the EU countries. In the past, individual countries made rules about residence or qualifications which, in effect, prevented people from other countries getting jobs. What opportunities exist for UK residents to find jobs in other EU countries? List some of the difficulties involved in going to work and live in another country.

Nearly 300 new laws had to pass through Parliament to complete the single European market. These cover standards for goods (for example food additives and hygiene) and measures to enable EU citizens to carry out their trade or profession anywhere in the EU by ensuring that their qualifications are recognised.

3.3 The Single European Market in action

Elimination of trade restrictions covers the following areas.

(a) Physical barriers (eg customs inspection) on good and services have been removed for most products. Companies have had to adjust to a new VAT regime as a consequence.

(b) Technical standards (eg for quality and safety) should be harmonised.

(c) Governments should not discriminate between EU companies in awarding public works contracts.

(d) Telecommunications should be subject to greater competition.

(e) It should be possible to provide financial services in any country.

(f) There should be free movement of capital within the community

(g) Professional qualifications awarded in one member state should be recognised in the others.

(h) The EU is taking a co-ordinated stand on matters related to consumer protection.

At the same time, you should not assume that there will be a completely 'level playing field'. There are many areas where harmonisation is a long way from being achieved. Here are some examples.

(a) **Company taxation.** Tax rates, which can affect the viability of investment plans, vary from country to country within the EU. A number of directives on *tax harmonisation* had to be dropped because it was not possible to reach agreement between all member states.

(b) **Indirect taxation (eg VAT).** While there have been moves to harmonisation, there are still differences between rates imposed by member states.

(c) **Differences in prosperity.** There are considerable differences in prosperity between the wealthiest EU economy (Germany), and the poorest (eg Greece). The UK comes somewhere in the middle.

(i) Grants are sometimes available to depressed regions, which might affect investment decisions.

(ii) Different marketing strategies are appropriate for different markets.

(d) **Differences in workforce skills**. Again, this can have a significant effect on investment decisions. The workforce in Germany is perhaps the most highly trained, but also the most highly paid, and so might be suitable for products of a high added value.

(e) **Infrastructure**. Some countries are better provided with road and rail than others. Where accessibility to a market is an important issue, infrastructure can mean significant variations in distribution costs.

Below are some examples of issues that affect our everyday lives.

Trading standards

Toys within the EU should nowadays have the letter CE (which stands for 'Communauté Européenne') on them to show that they meet the safety standards recognised by the EU.

The Food Law programme

The composition of certain food products, such as fruit juice, jam and coffee, has to be shown clearly on the packaging. All ingredients should be listed. Weights and measures are now harmonised across Europe. Goods have to be labelled and sold packaged in metric measures.

Transport

Laws have been introduced to make aviation, shipping and road transport more competitive. This should lead, among other things, to cheaper air fares.

However, the single market is not just about 'harmonisation' or making everything the same. Above all, it is about maximum choice, achieved by the greatest possible acceptance of each others' products and standards.

Agriculture

The **Common Agricultural Policy (CAP)** was designed to ensure a stable supply of food at reasonable prices while, at the same time, providing farmers with an adequate income. This was a major priority for the Community in the early post-war years when food shortages were a recent memory. However, the high price paid for food products under the CAP encouraged farmers to expand their production. By the 1970s this had led to large food surpluses – the 'wine lakes' and 'butter mountains'. The high prices paid to farmers for food have placed a considerable burden on the community budget which also has to subsidise sales of surplus food to countries outside the European Union. This has led to complaints from other agricultural trading nations such as Australia and New Zealand, which do not subsidise their agriculture and are suffering as a result.

To tackle this range of problems, the EU has begun to reform the CAP. The prices paid to farmers are being cut, for example by nearly 30% for wheat. This should bring food prices within the EU closer to the levels in the rest of the world, reduce costs to the EU budget and reduce prices in the shops. At the same time, farmers are being compensated for the loss of income (but this is less expensive in the long run than subsidising excess food production).

Further reforms are required, but an important step in the right direction has now been made. This is especially important as cutting agricultural subsidies is a key ingredient of the GATT agreement.

European Monetary System

The **European Monetary System (EMS)** was set up in 1979. Its purpose is to establish greater monetary stability in the European Union. The exchange rates between currencies can fluctuate considerably. For instance, the number of pounds needed to buy a hundred Deutschmarks changed a lot in the past. This resulted in extra costs for businesses which sold goods or services in more than one country. Exchange rate changes could turn a profit into a loss, or vice versa. Businesses either had to accept this risk or take special measures to reduce it.

At the heart of the EMS was the Exchange Rate Mechanism (ERM). Members of the ERM agreed to make sure that the value of their currencies did not change much in relation to each other. Within the system, a form of money called the European Currency Unit (ECU) was used as a measure of value and a means of making loans between member states. But the ERM did not work for the UK, which withdrew from it in 1992. The UK had pegged its exchange rate too high and the UK entered at the wrong time (just after German re-unification).

Consequences of membership of an exchange rate system

Exchange rate stability within an exchange rate regime may help dampen inflation by preventing a government from allowing the currency to drift downwards in value to compensate for price inflation. At the same time, it means that interest rate policy must be consistent with keeping the currency stable. If interest rates are too high, foreign investors will buy sterling, leading to capital inflows, much of which may be of short-term 'hot money', and there will be upward pressure on the currency. If interest rates are too low, there will conversely be downward pressure on the currency.

Other possible consequences of stabilisation within an exchange rate system are that there may be effects on people's expectations and on the perceived risk of exchange rate movements between member currencies. As well as allowing firms to plan and forecast with greater certainty, exchange rate stability ought to make a currency less risky to hold.

An important development is the Single European currency. This has been a controversial issue. We discuss this in more detail later.

The environment

Pollution respects no frontier, as Chernobyl, acid rain and damage to the ozone layer have all shown. It is crucial that international agreements are reached and acted on.

There is a long way to go on the whole question of protection of our natural environment and the Union has decided to establish the European Environment Agency to help it to develop policies in this area.

Activity 6 **(30 minutes)**

Find out what objectives were laid down for environment protection within Europe by the Maastricht Summit.

There are other international trade groups for comparison with the EU. One, EFTA, has become part of the EU. Others are developing for other parts of the world.

3.4 European Free Trade Area (EFTA) and the European Economic Area (EEA)

The **European Free Trade Area (EFTA)** was established in 1959, originally with seven member countries, including the UK. The UK, Denmark, Portugal, Austria, Finland and Sweden have since transferred to the EU. Today, only Iceland, Norway, Switzerland, and Liechtenstein remain members of EFTA (of which Norway and Switzerland are the only remaining founding members).

EFTA countries account for less than 6% of world export trade. There is free trade between EFTA member countries but there is no harmonisation of tariffs with non-EFTA countries.

Definition

European Economic Area (EEA): In 1993, EFTA forged a link with the EU to create a European Economic Area (EEA), so extending the benefits of the EU single market to the EFTA member countries (excluding Switzerland, which stayed out of the EEA).

4 THE EUROPEAN UNION AND THE OPERATING ENVIRONMENT

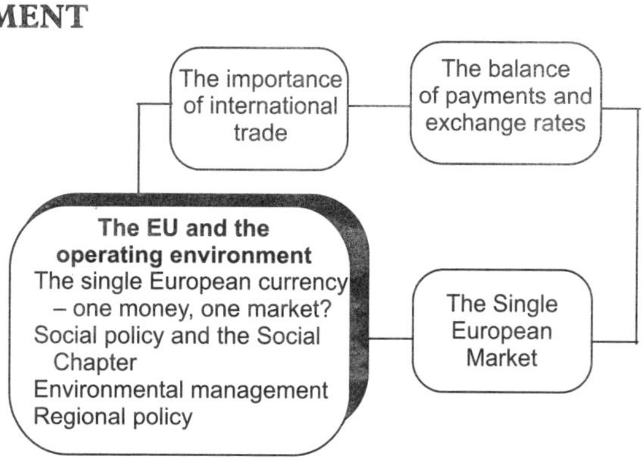

4.1 The Single European Currency – one money, one market?

European Economic and Monetary Union

One of the aims behind the European Monetary System has been European Economic and Monetary Union (EMU). This is a long-standing objective of the EU, reaffirmed in the Single European Act of 1985 and in the Maastricht agreement of 1991.

(a) **Monetary union** can be defined as a single currency area, which would require a monetary policy for the area as a whole.

(b) **Economic union** can be described as an unrestricted common market for trade, with some economic policy co-ordination between different regions in the union.

Although the whole package of measures included in European EMU is not paralleled anywhere else in the world, there have been many international monetary unions. For example, the UK and the Republic of Ireland were in currency union up to the 1970s. There are three main aspects to the European monetary union.

(a) A **common currency**. By this, we mean that instead of using the old deutschmarks in Germany and francs in France, a common currency (the 'euro') is used for normal everyday money transactions by everyone in the monetary union.

(b) A **European central bank**. The European Central Bank has the role of:

   (i) Issuing the common currency

   (ii) Conducting monetary policy on behalf of the central government authorities

   (iii) Acting as lender of last resort to all European banks

   (iv) Managing the exchange rate for the common currency

(c) A **centralised monetary policy** applies across all the countries within the union. This involves the surrender of control over aspects of economic policy and therefore surrender of some political sovereignty by the government of each member state to the central government body of the union.

The conditions set out at Maastricht were that no EU country could participate in EMU unless the following economic 'convergence criteria' were met.

(a) Consumer price inflation must, over the previous year, have been no more than 1.5 per cent higher than the average of the three best performing EU countries.

(b) Long-term interest rates must, over the previous year, have averaged no more than 2 per cent more than the average of three countries with the best consumer price inflation performance.

(c) A government's deficit should not exceed 5 per cent of GDP (gross domestic product) unless it has declined substantially or continuously or unless it is only temporarily above 3 per cent; additionally, the ratio of government debt to GDP should be no more than 60 per cent (unless it is approaching 60% at a satisfactory rate).

(d) The currency of the country should have remained within the normal bands of the ERM for a minimum of two years, without any devaluation.

For and against EMU

The arguments for and against EMU can be summarised as follows, with particular reference to the UK's position.

For	Against
Economic policy stability	*Loss of national control over economic policy*
EMU members are required to keep to strict economic criteria.	Under EMU, monetary policy is largely in the hands of the new European central bank.
Politicians in member countries are less able to pursue short-term economic policies, for example just before an election, to gain political advantage.	Individual countries' fiscal policies also need to stay in line with European policy criteria.
	The European economic policy framework puts great emphasis on price stability.
	Restrictive monetary policies can result in disproportionate unemployment and output effects.
Facilitation of trade	*The need to compensate for weaker economies*
Eliminates risk of currency fluctuations affecting trade and investment between EMU member countries.	For the UK, the possible benefits of being economically linked to stronger European economies are reduced and possibly even outweighed by the need to compensate for weaker economies.
Eliminates need to 'hedge' against such risks.	Stronger economies may be under pressure to 'bail out' member countries which borrow too much in order to hold the system together.
Lower interest rates	*Confusion in the transition to EMU*
Savings in foreign exchange transaction costs for companies, as well as tourists.	
Enhances ease of trade with non– EU countries.	
Removes risk of inflation and depreciating currencies, reducing interest rates	Introduction of a new currency and coinage can cause confusion to businesses and consumers.
Stabilises interest rates at a level closer to that of Germany, reducing interest costs for businesses and government.	Firms have used it as an opportunity to push through price rises.

For	**Against**
Preservation of the City's position	*Lower confidence arising from loss of national pride*
If the UK opts out of EMU, the City's position as one of the major European financial capitals will be threatened.	Sterling is a symbol of national cohesion.
In turn, the City's role as a leading global financial market would also be jeopardised	EMU puts its members on the road to a federal Europe, it is suggested, making the UK parliament into little more than a regional town hall within Europe, with no more power than local government. Such a move might dent national pride and diminish confidence.
Inward investment from the rest of the EU would also be likely to adversely affect economic performance	The proposal to have national variants of euro coins and notes is merely a cosmetic attempt to preserve national identities.

FOR DISCUSSION

Do you think a single currency benefits business?

What are the advantages and disadvantages for the UK, as a country, in accepting a single currency?

The extent of the EU's involvement in social issues is also a matter of dispute, as it is a source of regulation for business.

4.2 Social policy and the Social Chapter

Articles 117–128 of the Treaty of Rome, which dealt with social policy, promoted close co-operation between member states, particularly in matters relating to training, employment, working conditions, social security and collective bargaining. They also stated the need to observe the equal pay principle and make provision for the harmonisation of social security measures to accommodate migrant workers. In practice, during the 1980s there was little harmonisation of Community social policy. But in 1989 the European Commission presented a *Social Charter to* the EC heads of state. This spelt out a series of worker and social rights that should apply across the whole Community. These rights were grouped under twelve headings covering the following areas.

1. The right to freedom of movement, eg recognition of qualifications.
2. Employment and remuneration, eg fair remuneration, possible minimum wage.
3. Improvement of living and working conditions.
4. Right to social protection – social security.

5. Right to freedom of association and collective bargaining.
6. Right to vocational training.
7. Right of men and women to equal treatment.
8. Right of workers to information, consultation and participation.
9. Right to health protection and safety in the workplace.
10. Protection of children and adolescents.
11. Protection of elderly – pensions.
12. Protection of disabled people.

However, the Charter was only a recommendation and each element had to be approved separately by the Council.

Then in December 1991 the Maastricht Treaty was signed. This set out a timetable for economic and monetary union for the EC, but also included a 'Social Chapter', which attempted to move the Community forward in implementing the details of the social charter in areas such as maximum hours, minimum working conditions, health and safety protection, information and consultation of workers, and equal opportunities.

The UK Conservative government refused to sign this part of the Maastricht Treaty. It maintained that such measures would increase costs of production and make EU goods less competitive in world trade. Critics of the UK position argued that the refusal to adopt minimum working conditions (and also a minimum wage) would make the UK the 'sweatshop' of Europe. One of the first acts of the incoming Labour Government in 1997 was to sign up to the Social Chapter.

4.3 Environmental management

The EU has been active in raising environmental standards among its member states for many years, for example on lead in petrol and on water pollution levels. The Union wishes to encourage the manufacture of products that are less damaging to the environment.

A product may be awarded an eco-label if its manufacture does not use too much energy and raw material, or result in harmful emissions into the air, water and soil, or generate too much waste and noise. Clean, lowest-risk, sustainable technologies are to be used.

Waste is one of the main drawbacks for our environment. EU initiatives in this field are as follows.

(a) **List of hazardous waste**. The council has defined a list of different types of hazardous waste.

(b) **Waste packaging**. A new directive covers both new and used packaging. In five years the member states will have to recover between 50% and 65% of waste packaging and between 25% and 45% of it will have to be recycled, with a minimum of 15% for each type of packing material. In order to achieve this target they must set up a collection and recovery system. Each member state can manage its waste according to its own needs as long as it respects European requirements. At the end of ten years the directive will be reviewed and the targets altered.

(c) **Incineration of hazardous waste**. The EU established measurements and methods on how to avoid or reduce as much as possible the harmful effects of the burning of hazardous waste, such as the pollution of the air, the soil, the ground and surface water. Operating conditions and emission limit values were set for factories etc, as were strict conditions on waste water resulting from the purification of flue gases. For plants not specifically designed for that purpose, restrictive conditions under which the incineration of hazardous waste could take place were also set.

Activity 7 **(5 minutes)**

List three possible advantages to a firm of having an EU eco-label on its product.

Making EU industry fit for sustainable development

The Commission has decided to introduce a strategy to implement a system of monitoring and protecting the environment based on two closely related objectives.

(a) To support **sustainable development** in agriculture, energy and transport which will create jobs and improve competition in business while, at the same time, safeguard natural resources.

(b) Secondly, to establish a 'satellite' national accounting framework to track the development of valuable natural resources and the corresponding environmental statistics as accurately as possible, since Europe-wide statistics are needed.

To achieve these objectives, the Commission intends:

(a) To establish a joint European approach to reporting on the state of the physical environment

(b) To create a European system of environmental pressure indices

(c) To design a report combining economic performance with environmental degradation for each country

The aim is to come up with an idea of the cost of damage caused to the environment and the cost of the restoration work.

In order to provide accurate statistics, EUROSTAT will work with the assistance of the European Environment Agency and various other Commission services and other competent authorities. This new model will make it possible to identify the level of performance in each member state, both in economic terms and in terms of its impact on the environment. The results of this 'green' book-keeping will be available in two years and these statistics will then be used to redefine guidelines for policies such as those for transport, energy and agriculture.

Air-combating atmospheric pollution – CO_2 emissions

In the context of world-wide efforts to combat climate change, the EU committed itself to stabilising CO_2 emissions by the year 2000 at 1990 levels. But the Council failed – due to the opposition of the UK – to reach agreement on a European-wide 'carbon' tax on the use of fossil fuels, such as oil or coal, as proposed by the European Commission. Nevertheless, the Commission recommends further insistence on implementing the current European and national programmes and introducing the CO_2/energy tax which it has proposed.

To overcome the political deadlock, consideration is now being given to an action by the other member states. This would amount to a European Commission supervision of a CO_2 tax based on the harmonisation of excise duties in the member states.

4.4 Regional policy

Definition

> **Regional policy**: Set of measures aimed at influencing the geographic distribution of economic activity.

The reasons for the geographical disparities in incomes, living standards, (un)employment, etc include:

(a) **Depopulation of rural areas** due to increasing mechanisation of agriculture and the creation of surplus labour

(b) **Decline of traditional manufacturing sectors** (coal, mining, shipbuilding, steel, textiles) and of the regions that concentrated activity in them

(c) **Increasing reliance on services**, that must be located close to markets, so that there develops a vicious circle of small markets – less services – even smaller markets, etc.

A common thread in all the above is the decline in transportation costs and emergence of increasing returns to scale; the former means that proximity to markets is important, and the latter that bigger firms (serving bigger markets) become more productive/ efficient and therefore grow bigger.

Regional policy is an example of small-scale economic planning, with government as an enabler rather than a director. Regional policy can include:

(a) Providing tax incentives for investing in certain areas

(b) Relaxing town planning restrictions to make it easier for businesses to develop

(c) Awarding contracts to companies in one region rather than another (eg dividing operations between shipyards in different parts of the country).

(d) Developing new towns (eg Milton Keynes) to reduce population pressure in major conurbations. The UK Government has examined the issue of whether to encourage inner city developments in order to re-generate rundown areas. They have also considered whether to develop new 'rural towns' to encourage country dwellers to stay in their local area rather than migrate to existing towns and cities.

(e) Making infrastructural developments (eg roads, rail, airports)

The nature of the task facing EU authorities:

(a) How to identify the 'problem areas'; – there seems to be a consensus

(b) How to allocate responsibility for regional policies between EU level and national levels/governments

(c) How to engage in regional policy that would be compatible with the goal of completion of the internal market

(d) Where should the support be focused – attracting foreign investment, generating indigenous investment, or R&D, or augmenting the infrastructure?

(e) How to co-ordinate the regional effects of other policies (industrial, CAP, etc).

Chapter roundup

- The reasons for international trade are really only an extension of the reason for trade within a nation. Rather than people trying to be self-sufficient and do everything themselves, it makes sense to specialise.
- A new foreign market represents both a potential opportunity and a risk to an organisation. A company's market entry strategy should aim to balance these two elements.
- A country's balance of trade is the difference between the value of its exports and the value of its imports.
- The European Union comprises 15 member states, with a further enlargement planned. It is a free trade area, and a customs union with a common external tariff.
- The most powerful body is the Council of Ministers representing member states. The Commission does most of the work, in drafting legislation. Parliament has the power to amend legislation and approve the budget; it is also a forum for debate.
- The single market involves a certain amount of standardisation to ensure that consumers benefit from free trade. There is free movement of goods, services, people and capital.
- There are still significant differences between the member states, in terms of GDP per head and hours worked, to mention two examples.

Quick quiz

1 What is the difference between an absolute and a comparative advantage?

2 Give an example of an international franchising operation.

3 What is a Greenfield development?

4 What does a tariff do to the price of an import?

5 What effect does a quota have on the volume of imports?

6 What is an exchange rate?

7 Distinguish between a free trade area and a customs union.

8 What does the European Commission do?

9 List four examples of the Single European Market in action.

10 List as many as you can of the twelve sets of principles laid down in the Social Charter.

Answers to quick quiz

1 A country has an **absolute** advantage when it uses fewer resources to produce a product than the other country. A **comparative** advantage of a product enjoyed by one country over another is when that product can be produced at a lower opportunity cost.

2 McDonald's

3 Greenfield developments are organisations set up from scratch – when breaking into new ground or when there are no suitable companies willing to be acquired.

4 It raises the price.

5 It reduces the volume.

6 It is the price of one currency in terms of another.

7 **Free trade area**: restrictions on the movement of goods and services between countries. **Customs union**: establishes a free trade area between member states only.

8 It performs the 'executive' function of the government of the EU.

9 Examples include: trading standards, food law, transport, and agriculture.

10 As many as you can from the following.

- The right to freedom of movement, eg recognition of qualifications
- Employment and remuneration, eg fair remuneration, possible minimum wage
- Improvement of living and working conditions
- Right to social protection – social security
- Right to freedom of association and collective bargaining
- Right to vocational training
- Right of men and women to equal treatment

- Right of workers to information, consultation and participation
- Right to health protection and safety in the workplace
- Protection of children and adolescents
- Protection of elderly – pensions
- Protection of disabled people

Answers to activities

1 A France has a comparative advantage in exporting wine

2 The company would probably manufacture overseas, maybe buying an overseas company with existing expertise and available brands.

3 (a) In the USA, steel is a product that is used in a wide variety of different industries for many different purposes. The businesses react by trying to find a way round the problem. Some steel using businesses are rearranging their supply chain and rather than manufacturing component parts in the US they are transferring the work to Canada. The tariff does not affect steel imports landing in Canada and so getting a Canadian company to manufacture the component and then ship it to the US helps to keep costs low and avoids having to pay the tariff. The impact in manufacturing jobs in steel using businesses in the US though is evident; if the work is transferred to Canada there is no-longer a need for the workers in the US. An attempt to solve a problem in one sector by interfering in the market creates problems elsewhere. The question has to be what is the balance of the costs and benefits, not just in the short term but also in the long term, for all interested parties?

(b) Tariffs operate as a tax. The exporter pays the tax as the goods enter a country. In the example, steel exporters from, say the UK, would have to pay 30p in tax to the US government for every extra £1 of steel entering the US; this effectively raises the cost of production and so it raises its price to the buyer in the US to cover the cost of the tax. The supply curve shifts to the left by the amount of the tax leading to a rise in the price of steel in the US and a reduction in the amount bought and sold.

4 The answer is C it would make it easier for America to export – a dollar price would correspond to fewer yen. That *would* make it easier to export!

5 In theory you have the right to work in any EU country, so opportunities ought to be unlimited, but each country has its own rules and procedures (eg for tax and social security). Potential difficulties include unemployment problems across Europe – there may not be a job available, language issues – UK citizens are notorious for being the worst at learning languages, and lifestyle/cultural differences.

6 The Maastricht Summit laid down the following objectives for a EU environment policy:

(i) To preserve, protect and improve the quality of the environment

(ii) To protect human health

(iii) To make prudent and rational use of natural resources

7 Possible advantages could include enhanced reputation for environmental responsibility, ability to charge a premium (higher) price, opportunities for marketing, ability to supply goods to environmentally ethical companies.

Glossary

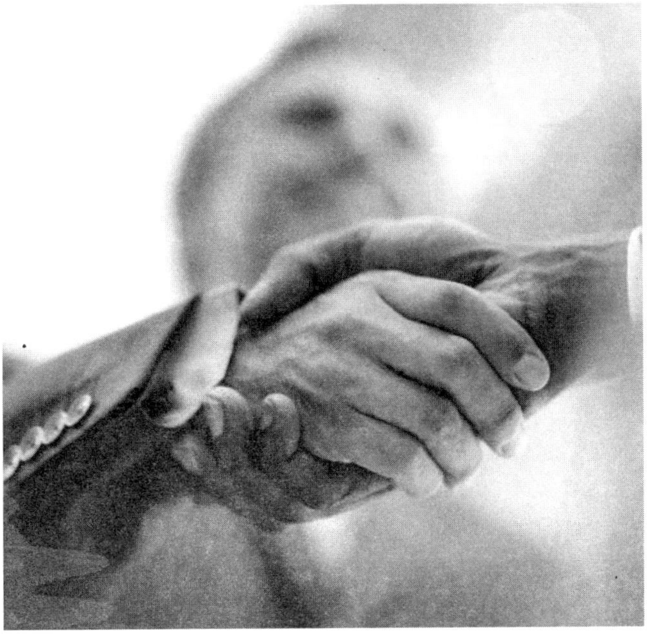

Absolute advantage – a country has an absolute advantage in the production of a good if it can produce more of the good with a fixed amount of resources than can any other country.

***Ad valorem* tax**. An **ad valorem tax** is charged as a *fixed percentage* of the price of the good.

Aggregate demand (AD) means the total demand in the economy for goods and services.

Aggregate supply (AS) means the total supply of goods and services in the economy.

Average cost (AC). Average cost for a given level of output is simply the total cost divided by the total quantity produced.

Bank multiplier. The **bank multiplier** or **credit multiplier** is the name given to banks' ability to create credit, and hence money, by maintaining their cash reserves at less than 100% of the value of their deposits.

Barriers to entry: factors which make it difficult for suppliers to enter a market.

Capital gearing ratio: measure of the proportion of a company's capital that is borrowed expressed as $\frac{\text{Prior charge capial}}{\text{Total capital}}$

Ceteris paribus is the assumption that all other things remain equal.

Command economy – sometimes referred to as state controlled. In this type of economy decisions are taken collectively, usually by central planning committees.

Comparative advantage is the advantage in the production of a product enjoyed by one country over another when that product can be produced at a lower opportunity cost.

Cost push inflation is inflation resulting from an increase in the costs of production of goods and services.

Current ratio: Formula used to ascertain whether a company has sufficient assets that should be converted into cash to meet its future commitments to pay off its current liabilities expressed as $\frac{\text{Current assets}}{\text{Current liabilities}}$

Demand for a good is the quantity of that good that potential purchasers would buy, or attempt to buy, if the price of the good were at a certain level.

Demand pull inflation is inflation resulting from a persistent excess of aggregate demand over aggregate supply.

Dividend cover: an indicator of how secure shareholders can expect to be in terms of their dividend being paid. It is expressed as $\frac{\text{Earnings per share}}{\text{Net dividend per ordinary share}}$

Economies of scale: factors which cause average cost to decline in the long run as output increases.

$$\textbf{EPS} = \frac{\text{Profit for the year available for ordinary shareholders}}{\text{Number of ordinary shares in issue}}$$

European Economic Area (EEA): In 1993, EFTA forged a link with the EU to create a European Economic Area (EEA) with a population of 380 million, so extending the benefits of the EU single market to the EFTA member countries (excluding Switzerland, which stayed out of the EEA).

Exchange rate. An **exchange rate** is the ratio at which two currencies are traded. The price of one currency in terms of another.

Externalities are effects of a transaction which extend beyond the parties to the transaction. The differences between the private and the social costs, or benefits, arising from an activity are externalities.

Fiscal policy: government policy on taxation, public borrowing and public spending.

Free market economy – sometimes called capitalism. In this type of economy most decisions are taken through the operation of the market mechanism.

Gross domestic product is the value of the goods and services produced by an economy in a given period.

Gross national income is GDP **plus** income accruing to domestic residents from investments abroad **less** income accruing to foreign residents from investments in the domestic economy.

Inflation is the name given to an increase in price levels generally.

Injections: movements of funds in the other direction.

Interest cover ratio shows whether a company is earning enough profit before interest and tax to pay its interest costs comfortably and have funds available for its shareholders. It is expressed as: $\frac{\text{Profit before interest and tax}}{\text{Interest charges}}$

Law of diminishing returns says that if one or more factors of production are fixed, but the input of another is increased, **the extra output generated by each extra unit of input will eventually begin to fall.**

Long-run. The **long-run** is a period sufficiently long to allow full flexibility in all the inputs used.

Macroeconomics is the study of the aggregated effects of the decisions of economic units. It looks at a complete national economy or the international economic system as a whole.

Marginal cost (MC). This is the addition to total cost of producing one more unit of output.

Market. A **market** is a situation in which potential buyers and potential sellers (*suppliers*) of a good or service come together for the purpose of exchange.

Market failure occurs when a free market mechanism fails to produce the most efficient allocation of resources.

Merit goods are considered to be worth providing in greater volume than would be purchased in a free market, because higher consumption is in the long-term public interest.

Microeconomics is the study of individual economic units; these are called **households** and **firms**.

Mixed economy: a type of economy where there is a balance between market forces and state intervention.

Monetary policy: government policy on the money supply, the monetary system, interest rates, exchange rates and the availability of credit.

Monopolistic competition is a market structure in which firms' products are comparable rather than homogeneous.

Monopoly. In a **monopoly**, there is only one firm, the sole producer of a good which has no closely competing substitutes.

Multiplier. The ratio of the **total** increase in national income to an initial increase is called the **multiplier**.

National income is the sum of all incomes which arise as a result of economic activity, that is from the production of goods and services.

National income accounting is the system through which activity and national scale is measured.

Oligopoly: a market structure where a few large suppliers dominate.

Open market operations: the Bank of England's dealings in the capital market. The bank uses open market operations to control interest rates.

Opportunity cost is the cost of an item measured in terms of the alternatives forgone.

Perfect competition: a theoretical market structure in which no supplier has an advantage over another.

Phillips curve: a graphical illustration of the historic inverse relationship between the rate of wage inflation and the rate of unemployment.

Price earnings ratio (P/E ratio): investment ratio which combines a measure of past performance with current price to reflect belief about the future. It is expressed as

$$\frac{\text{Share price}}{\text{Earnings per share}}.$$

Privatisation is the transfer by government of state owned activities to the private sector.

Product differentiation gives the products some market power by acting as a barrier to entry.

Productivity is a measure of the *efficiency* with which output has been produced.

Profit is equal to total revenue minus total cost of any level of output.

Protection is the practice of shielding a sector of the economy from foreign competition.

Public goods. Some goods, by their very nature, involve so much 'spill-over' of externalities that they are difficult to provide except as **public goods** whose production is organised by the government.

Public sector net cash requirement (PSNCR) is the annual excess of spending over income for the entire sector – not just the central government.

Quantity theory of money is the theory which holds that changes in the level of prices are caused predominantly by changes in the supply of money.

Quick ratio: used to ascertain company's Liquidity position, expressed as:

$$\frac{\text{Current assets less inventories (stocks)}}{\text{Current liabilities}}$$

Regional policy: Set of measures aimed at influencing the geographic distribution of economic activity.

Return on capital employed (ROCE):

$$\frac{\text{Profit on ordinary activities before interest and taxation}}{\text{Capital employed}}$$

Capital employed = Shareholders' funds plus 'creditors: amounts falling due after more than one year' plus any long-term provision for liabilities and charges (*or* total assets less current liabilities).

Scarcity is the excess of human wants over what can actually be produced.

Short-run. The **short-run** is a time period in which the amount of at least one input is fixed.

Specific tax. A **specific tax** is charged as a *fixed sum* per unit sold.

Supply is the quantity of a product that existing or would-be suppliers would want to produce at a given price.

Supply side economics is an approach to economic policymaking which advocates measures to improve the supply of goods and services rather than measures to affect aggregate demand.

The mixed economy. In this type of economy there is a balance between market forces and state intervention.

Total cost (TC). Total cost for a given level of output comprises total fixed cost (TFC) and total variable cost (TVC).

Withdrawals: movements of funds out of the cycle of income and expenditure between firms and households.

Index